Massachusetts Real Estate Principles and Practices   Ed. 4.2

J. Peter Regan
B.S.B.A., M.B.A., Notary Public, Broker
REALTOR®
Professor
North Shore Community College

Arthur J. Neuner
A.S., B.S., M.B.A., Broker, REALTOR®
Professor
North Shore Community College

North Shore Press, Inc., Melrose, Massachusetts

©1998 North Shore Press, Inc.
6 Eastman Place
Melrose, MA 02176
(781) 662-6757
Fax (781) 662-4214

Printed in the United States of America

Edition 4.2

10 9 8 7 6 5 4 3 2 1

Library of Congress Cataloging in Publication Data:

Regan, James Peter.

Massachusetts real estate principles and practices.

1. Real estate business - Law and legislation -
   Massachusetts - Examinations, questions, etc.

2. Real property - Massachusetts - Examinations,
   questions, etc I. Title.

KF2682.R43   346'.744'0437   77-15962

ISBN 0-9627396-1-8

Cover by John Fortunato, Beverly, Massachusetts

Acknowledgments

Edition 4.2 of Massachusetts Real Estate Principles and Practices is the result of the efforts of a number of individuals.

The authors would like to thank Charles Bergeron, Patricia DuBois and Walter King for their assistance in reviewing the manuscript.

A special thanks is extended to Angela Portosa and Stephen Ryan of the Massachusetts Association of Realtors® for their suggestions and review of the final draft and the most recent revisions.

And finally, a special acknowledgment to Frank MacIntosh for all of his guidance in the layout and printing of this text.

Table of Contents

Chapter 1 Property and Property Rights

Chapter 2 Estates

Chapter 3 Condos, Coops & Timeshare

Chapter 4 Leases

Chapter 5 Contracts/Purchase & Sale Agreement

Chapter 6 Transfer of Title/Deeds

Chapter 7 Financing and Mortgages

Chapter 8 Real Estate Brokerage

Chapter 9 Appraisal

Chapter 10 Massachusetts Consumer Protection / Environmental Laws & Regulations

Chapter 11 Fair Housing / ADA

Chapter 12 Massachusetts License Law

Chapter 13 Review of Basic Math

Chapter 14 Measurement

Chapter 15 Formulas

Chapter 16 Interest

Chapter 17 Profit and Loss

Chapter 18 Return on Investment

Chapter 19 Taxation

Chapter 20 Proration and Settlement

Chapter 21 Commissions

Chapter 22 Depreciation

Glossary G-1

Index I-1

What is a REALTOR®?

The term REALTOR® is a registered collective-membership mark which identifies a real estate professional who is a member of the NATIONAL ASSOCIATION OF REALTORS® and subscribes to its strict Code of Ethics.

The purpose of the Massachusetts Association of REALTORS® is to serve its members in concert with its local real estate boards and Boards of REALTORS®.

The Association provides and promotes services and programs designed to enhance members' ability and freedom to conduct their individual businesses successfully and professionally with integrity and competency. It seeks, through collective action, to promote the preservation and extension of real property rights.

By endorsing this publication, the Massachusetts Association of REALTORS® does not warrant the accuracy or reliability of the statements, representations or advice contained in this text. The reader should not rely upon MAR in using or citing information contained in this publication.

Code of Ethics and Standards of Practice

of the

NATIONAL ASSOCIATION OF REALTORS®

Effective January 1, 1995

Where the word REALTORS® is used in this Code and Preamble, it shall be deemed to include REALTOR-ASSOCIATE®s.

While the Code of Ethics establishes obligations that may be higher than those mandated by law, in any instance where the Code of Ethics and the law conflict, the obligations of the law must take precedence.

Preamble...

Under all is the land. Upon its wise utilization and widely allocated ownership depend the survival and growth of free institutions and of our civilization. REALTORS® should recognize that the interests of the nation and its citizens require the highest and best use of the land and the widest distribution of land ownership. They require the creation of adequate housing, the building of functioning cities, the development of productive industries and farms, and the preservation of a healthful environment.

Such interests impose obligations beyond those of ordinary commerce. They impose grave social responsibility and a patriotic duty to which REALTORS® should dedicate themselves, and for which they should be diligent in preparing themselves. REALTORS®, therefore, are zealous to maintain and improve the standards of their calling and share with their fellow REALTORS® a common responsibility for its integrity and honor.

In recognition and appreciation of their obligations to clients, customers, the public, and each other, REALTORS® continuously strive to become and remain informed on issues affecting real estate and, as knowledgeable professionals, they willingly share the fruit of their experience and study with others. They identify and take steps, through enforcement of this Code of Ethics and by assisting appropriate regulatory bodies, to eliminate practices which may damage the public or which might discredit or bring dishonor to the real estate profession.

Realizing that cooperation with other real estate professionals promotes the best interests of those who utilize their services, REALTORS® urge exclusive representation of clients; do not attempt to gain any unfair advantage over their competitors; and they refrain from making unsolicited comments about other practitioners. In instances where their opinion is sought, or where REALTORS® believe that comment is necessary, their opinion is offered in an objective, professional manner, uninfluenced by any personal motivation or potential advantage or gain.

NATIONAL ASSOCIATION OF REALTORS®

430 North Michigan Avenue
Chicago, Illinois 60611-4087

REALTOR®

The term REALTOR® has come to connote competency, fairness, and high integrity resulting from adherence to a lofty ideal of moral conduct in business relations. No inducement of profit and no instruction from clients ever can justify departure from this ideal.

In the interpretation of this obligation, REALTORS® can take no safer guide than that which has been handed down through the centuries, embodied in the Golden Rule, "Whatsoever ye would that others should do to you, do ye even so to them."

Accepting this standard as their own, REALTORS® pledge to observe its spirit in all of their activities and to conduct their business in accordance with the tenets set forth below.

Duties to Clients and Customers

Article 1

When representing a buyer, seller, landlord, tenant, or other client as an agent, REALTORS® pledge themselves to protect and promote the interests of their client. This obligation of absolute fidelity to the client's interests is primary, but it does not relieve REALTORS® of their obligation to treat all parties honestly. When serving a buyer, seller, landlord, tenant or other party in a non-agency capacity, REALTORS® remain obligated to treat all parties honestly. *(Amended 1/93)*

- **Standard of Practice 1-1**

  REALTORS®, when acting as principals in a real estate transaction, remain obligated by the duties imposed by the Code of Ethics. *(Amended 1/93)*

- **Standard of Practice 1-2**

  The duties the Code of Ethics imposes on agents/representatives are applicable to REALTORS® acting as agents, transaction brokers, facilitators, or in any other recognized capacity except for any duty specifically exempted by law or regulation. *(Adopted 1/95)*

- **Standard of Practice 1-3**

  REALTORS®, in attempting to secure a listing, shall not deliberately mislead the owner as to market value.

- **Standard of Practice 1-4**

  REALTORS®, when seeking to become a buyer/tenant representative, shall not mislead buyers or tenants as to savings or other benefits that might be realized through use of the REALTOR®'s services. *(Amended 1/93)*

- **Standard of Practice 1-5**

  REALTORS® may represent the seller/landlord and buyer/tenant in the same transaction only after full disclosure to and with informed consent of both parties. *(Adopted 1/93)*

- **Standard of Practice 1-6**

  REALTORS® shall submit offers and counter-offers objectively and as quickly as possible. *(Adopted 1/93, Amended 1/95)*

- **Standard of Practice 1-7**

  When acting as listing brokers, REALTORS® shall continue to submit to the seller/landlord all offers and counter-offers until closing or execution of a lease unless the seller/landlord has waived this obligation in writing. REALTORS® shall not be obligated to continue to market the property after an offer has been accepted by the seller/landlord. REALTORS® shall recommend that sellers/landlords obtain the advice of legal counsel prior to acceptance of a subsequent offer except where the acceptance is contingent on the termination of the pre-existing purchase contract or lease. *(Amended 1/93)*

• Standard of Practice 1-8

REALTORS® acting as agents of buyers/tenants shall submit to buyers/tenants all offers and counter-offers until acceptance but have no obligation to continue to show properties to their clients after an offer has been accepted unless otherwise agreed in writing. REALTORS® acting as agents of buyers/tenants shall recommend that buyers/tenants obtain the advice of legal counsel if there is a question as to whether a pre-existing contract has been terminated. *(Adopted 1/93)*

• Standard of Practice 1-9

The obligation of REALTORS® to preserve confidential information provided by their clients continues after the termination of the agency relationship. REALTORS® shall not knowingly, during or following the termination of a professional relationship with their client:
1) reveal confidential information of the client; or
2) use confidential information of the client to the disadvantage of the client; or
3) use confidential information of the client for the REALTOR®'s advantage or the advantage of a third party unless the client consents after full disclosure except where the REALTOR® is:
   a) required by court order; or
   b) it is the intention of the client to commit a crime and the information is necessary to prevent the crime; or
   c) necessary to defend the REALTOR® or the REALTOR®'s employees or associates against an accusation of wrongful conduct. *(Adopted 1/93, Amended 1/95)*

• Standard of Practice 1-10

REALTORS® shall, consistent with the terms and conditions of their property management agreement, competently manage the property of clients with due regard for the rights, responsibilities, benefits, safety and health of tenants and others lawfully on the premises. *(Adopted 1/95)*

• Standard of Practice 1-11

REALTORS® who are employed to maintain or manage a client's property shall exercise due diligence and make reasonable efforts to protect it against reasonably foreseeable contingencies and losses. *(Adopted 1/95)*

Article 2

REALTORS® shall avoid exaggeration, misrepresentation, or concealment of pertinent facts relating to the property or the transaction. REALTORS® shall not, however, be obligated to discover latent defects in the property, to advise on matters outside the scope of their real estate license, or to disclose facts which are confidential under the scope of agency duties owed to their clients. *(Amended 1/93)*

• Standard of Practice 2-1

REALTORS® shall be obligated to discover and disclose adverse factors reasonably apparent to someone with expertise in only those areas required by their real estate licensing authority.

Article 2 does not impose upon the REALTOR® the obligation of expertise in other professional or technical disciplines. *(Amended 11/86)*

• Standard of Practice 2-2

When entering into listing contracts, REALTORS® must advise sellers/landlords of:
1) the REALTOR®'s general company policies regarding cooperation with subagents, buyer/tenant agents, or both;
2) the fact that buyer/tenant agents, even if compensated by the listing broker, or by the seller/landlord will represent the interests of buyers/tenants; and
3) any potential for the listing broker to act as a disclosed dual agent, e.g. buyer/tenant agent. *(Adopted 1/93)*

• Standard of Practice 2-3

When entering into contracts to represent buyers/tenants, REALTORS® must advise potential clients of:
1) the REALTOR®'s general company policies regarding cooperation with other firms; and
2) any potential for the buyer/tenant representative to act as a disclosed dual agent, e.g. listing broker, subagent, landlord's agent, etc. *(Adopted 1/93)*

• Standard of Practice 2-4

REALTORS® shall not be parties to the naming of a false consideration in any document, unless it be the naming of an obviously nominal consideration.

• Standard of Practice 2-5

Factors defined as "non-material" by law or regulation or which are expressly referenced in law or regulation as not being subject to disclosure are considered not "perinent" for purposes of Article 2. *(Adopted 1/93)*

Article 3

REALTORS® shall cooperate with other brokers except when cooperation is not in the client's best interest. The obligation to cooperate does not include the obligation to share commissions, fees, or to otherwise compensate another broker. *(Amended 1/95)*

• Standard of Practice 3-1

REALTORS®, acting as exclusive agents of sellers/landlords, establish the terms and conditions of offers to cooperate. Unless expressly indicated in offers to cooperate, cooperating brokers may not assume that the offer of cooperation includes an offer of compensation. Terms of compensation, if any, shall be ascertained by cooperating brokers before beginning efforts to accept the offer of cooperation. *(Amended 1/94)*

• Standard of Practice 3-2

REALTORS® shall, with respect to offers of compensation to another REALTOR®, timely communicate any change of compensation for cooperative services to the other REALTOR® prior to the time such REALTOR® produces an offer to purchase/lease the property. *(Amended 1/94)*

• Standard of Practice 3-3

Standard of Practice 3-2 does not preclude the listing broker and cooperating broker from entering into an agreement to change cooperative compensation. *(Adopted 1/94)*

- ## Standard of Practice 3-4

  REALTORS®, acting as listing brokers, have an affirmative obligation to disclose the existence of dual or variable rate commission arrangements (i.e., listings where one amount of commission is payable if the listing broker's firm is the procuring cause of sale/lease and a different amount of commission is payable if the sale/lease results through the efforts of the seller/landlord or a cooperating broker). The listing broker shall, as soon as practical, disclose the existence of such arrangements to potential cooperating brokers and shall, in response to inquiries from cooperating brokers, disclose the differential that would result in a cooperative transaction or in a sale/lease that results through the efforts of the seller/landlord. If the cooperating broker is a buyer/tenant representative, the buyer/tenant representative must disclose such information to their client. *(Amended 1/94)*

- ## Standard of Practice 3-5

  It is the obligation of subagents to promptly disclose all pertinent facts to the principal's agent prior to as well as after a purchase or lease agreement is executed. *(Amended 1/93)*

- ## Standard of Practice 3-6

  REALTORS® shall disclose the existence of an accepted offer to any broker seeking cooperation. *(Adopted 5/86)*

- ## Standard of Practice 3-7

  When seeking information from another REALTOR® concerning property under a management or listing agreement, REALTORS® shall disclose their REALTOR® status and whether their interest is personal or on behalf of a client and, if on behalf of a client, their representational status. *(Amended 1/95)*

- ## Standard of Practice 3-8

  REALTORS® shall not misrepresent the availability of access to show or inspect a listed property. *(Amended 11/87)*

Article 4

REALTORS® shall not acquire an interest in or buy or present offers from themselves, any member of their immediate families, their firms or any member thereof, or any entities in which they have any ownership interest, any real property without making their true position known to the owner or the owner's agent. In selling property they own, or in which they have any interest, REALTORS® shall reveal their ownership or interest in writing to the purchaser or the purchaser's representative. *(Amended 1/91)*

- ## Standard of Practice 4-1

  For the protection of all parties, the disclosures required by Article 4 shall be in writing and provided by REALTORS® prior to the signing of any contract. *(Adopted 2/86)*

Article 5

REALTORS® shall not undertake to provide professional services concerning a property or its value where they have a present or contemplated interest unless such interest is specifically disclosed to all affected parties.

Article 6

When acting as agents, REALTORS® shall not accept any commission, rebate, or profit on expenditures made for their principal, without the principal's knowledge and consent. *(Amended 1/92)*

- ## Standard of Practice 6-1

  REALTORS® shall not recommend or suggest to a client or a customer the use of services of another organization or business entity in which they have a direct interest without disclosing such interest at the time of the recommendation or suggestion. *(Amended 5/88)*

- ## Standard of Practice 6-2

  When acting as agents or subagents, REALTORS® shall disclose to a client or customer if there is any financial benefit or fee the REALTOR® or the REALTOR®'s firm may receive as a direct result of having recommended real estate products or services (e.g., homeowner's insurance, warranty programs, mortgage financing, title insurance, etc.) other than real estate referral fees. *(Adopted 5/88)*

Article 7

In a transaction, REALTORS® shall not accept compensation from more than one party, even if permitted by law, without disclosure to all parties and the informed consent of the REALTOR®'s client or clients. *(Amended 1/93)*

Article 8

REALTORS® shall keep in a special account in an appropriate financial institution, separated from their own funds, monies coming into their possession in trust for other persons, such as escrows, trust funds, clients' monies, and other like items.

Article 9

REALTORS®, for the protection of all parties, shall assure whenever possible that agreements shall be in writing, and shall be in clear and understandable language expressing the specific terms, conditions, obligations and commitments of the parties. A copy of each agreement shall be furnished to each party upon their signing or initialing. *(Amended 1/95)*

- ## Standard of Practice 9-1

  For the protection of all parties, REALTORS® shall use reasonable care to ensure that documents pertaining to the purchase, sale, or lease of real estate are kept current through the use of written extensions or amendments. *(Amended 1/93)*

Duties to the Public

Article 10

REALTORS® shall not deny equal professional services to any person for reasons of race, color, religion, sex, handicap, familial status, or national origin. REALTORS® shall not be parties to any plan or agreement to discriminate against a person or persons on the basis of race, color, religion, sex, handicap, familial status, or national origin. *(Amended 1/90)*

- ## Standard of Practice 10-1

  REALTORS® shall not volunteer information regarding the racial, religious or ethnic composition of any neighborhood and shall not engage in any activity which may result in panic selling. REALTORS® shall not print, display or circulate any statement or advertisement with respect to the selling or renting of a property that indicates any preference, limitations or discrimination based on race, color, religion, sex, handicap, familial status or national origin. *(Adopted 1/94)*

Article 11

The services which REALTORS® provide to their clients and customers shall conform to the standards of practice and competence which are reasonably expected in the specific real estate disciplines in which they engage; specifically, residential real estate brokerage, real property management, commercial and industrial real estate brokerage, real estate appraisal, real estate counseling, real estate syndication, real estate auction, and international real estate.

REALTORS® shall not undertake to provide specialized professional services concerning a type of property or service that is outside their field of competence unless they engage the assistance of one who is competent on such types of property or service, or unless the facts are fully disclosed to the client. Any persons engaged to provide such assistance shall be so identified to the client and their contribution to the assignment should be set forth. *(Amended 1/95)*

• Standard of Practice 11-1

The obligations of the Code of Ethics shall be supplemented by and construed in a manner consistent with the Uniform Standards of Professional Appraisal Practice (USPAP) promulgated by the Appraisal Standards Board of the Appraisal Foundation. *(Adopted 1/95)*

• Standard of Practice 11-2

The obligations of the Code of Ethics in respect of real estate disciplines other than appraisal shall be interpreted and applied in accordance with the standards of competence and practice which clients and the public reasonably require to protect their rights and interests considering the complexity of the transaction, the availability of expert assistance, and, where the REALTOR® is an agent or subagent, the obligations of a fiduciary. *(Adopted 1/95)*

Article 12

REALTORS® shall be careful at all times to present a true picture in their advertising and representations to the public. REALTORS® shall also ensure that their professional status (e.g., broker, appraiser, property manager, etc.) or status as REALTORS® is clearly identifiable in any such advertising. *(Amended 1/93)*

• Standard of Practice 12-1

REALTORS® shall not offer a service described as "free of charge" when the rendering of a service is contingent on the obtaining of a benefit such as a listing or commission.

• Standard of Practice 12-2

REALTORS® shall not represent that their services are free or without cost if they expect to receive compensation from any source other than their client. *(Adopted 1/95)*

• Standard of Practice 12-3

The offering of premiums, prizes, merchandise discounts or other inducements to list, sell, purchase, or lease is not, in itself, unethical even if receipt of the benefit is contingent on listing, selling, purchasing, or leasing through the REALTOR® making the offer. However, REALTORS® must exercise care and candor in any such advertising or other public or private representations so that any party interested in receiving or otherwise benefiting from the REALTOR®'s offer will have clear, thorough, advance understanding of all the terms and conditions of the offer. The offering of any inducements to do business is subject to the limitations and restrictions of state law and the ethical obligations established by any applicable Standard of Practice. *(Amended 1/95)*

• Standard of Practice 12-4

REALTORS® shall not offer for sale/lease or advertise property without authority. When acting as listing brokers or as subagents, REALTORS® shall not quote a price different from that agreed upon with the seller/landlord. *(Amended 1/93)*

• Standard of Practice 12-5

REALTORS® shall not advertise nor permit any person employed by or affiliated with them to advertise listed property without disclosing the name of the firm. *(Adopted 11/86)*

• Standard of Practice 12-6

REALTORS®, when advertising unlisted real property for sale/ lease in which they have an ownership interest, shall disclose their status as both owners/landlords and as REALTORS® or real estate licensees. *(Amended 1/93)*

• Standard of Practice 12-7

Only REALTORS® as listing brokers, may claim to have "sold" the property, even when the sale resulted through the cooperative efforts of another broker. However, after transactions have closed, listing brokers may not prohibit successful cooperating brokers from advertising their "cooperation," "participation," or "assistance" in the transaction, or from making similar representations.

Only listing brokers are entitled to use the term "sold" on signs, in advertisements, and in other public representations. *(Amended 1/90)*

Article 13

REALTORS® shall not engage in activities that constitute the unauthorized practice of law and shall recommend that legal counsel be obtained when the interest of any party to the transaction requires it.

Article 14

If charged with unethical practice or asked to present evidence or to cooperate in any other way, in any disciplinary proceeding or investigation, REALTORS® shall place all pertinent facts before the proper tribunals of the Member Board or affiliated institute, society, or council in which membership is held and shall take no action to disrupt or obstruct such processes. *(Amended 1/90)*

• Standard of Practice 14-1

REALTORS® shall not be subject to disciplinary proceedings in more than one Board of REALTORS® or affiliated institute, society or council in which they hold membership with respect to alleged violations of the Code of Ethics relating to the same transaction or event. *(Amended 1/95)*

• Standard of Practice 14-2

REALTORS® shall not make any unauthorized disclosure or dissemination of the allegations, findings, or decision developed in connection with an ethics hearing or appeal or in connection with an arbitration hearing or procedural review. *(Amended 1/92)*

Standard of Practice 14-3

REALTORS® shall not obstruct the Board's investigative or disciplinary proceedings by instituting or threatening to institute actions for libel, slander or defamation against any party to a professional standards proceeding or their witnesses. *(Adopted 11/87)*

Standard of Practice 14-4

REALTORS® shall not intentionally impede the Board's investigative or disciplinary proceedings by filing multiple ethics complaints based on the same event or transaction. *(Adopted 11/88)*

Duties to REALTORS®

Article 15

REALTORS® shall not knowingly or recklessly make false or misleading statements about competitors, their businesses, or their business practices. *(Amended 1/92)*

Article 16

REALTORS® shall not engage in any practice or take any action inconsistent with the agency of other REALTORS®.

Standard of Practice 16-1

Article 16 is not intended to prohibit aggressive or innovative business practices which are otherwise ethical and does not prohibit disagreements with other REALTORS® involving commission, fees, compensation or other forms of payment or expenses. *(Adopted 1/93, Amended 1/95)*

Standard of Practice 16-2

Article 16 does not preclude REALTORS® from making general announcements to prospective clients describing their services and the terms of their availability even though some recipients may have entered into agency agreements with another REALTOR®. A general telephone canvass, general mailing or distribution addressed to all prospective clients in a given geographical area or in a given profession, business, club, or organization, or other classification or group is deemed "general" for purposes of this standard.

Article 16 is intended to recognize as unethical two basic types of solicitations:

First, telephone or personal solicitations of property owners who have been identified by a real estate sign, multiple listing compilation, or other information service as having exclusively listed their property with another REALTOR®; and

Second, mail or other forms of written solicitations of prospective clients whose properties are exclusively listed with another REALTOR® when such solicitations are not part of a general mailing but are directed specifically to property owners identified through compilations of current listings, "for sale" or "for rent" signs, or other sources of information required by Article 3 and Multiple Listing Service rules to be made available to other REALTORS® under offers of subagency or cooperation. *(Amended 1/93)*

Standard of Practice 16-3

Article 16 does not preclude REALTORS® from contacting the client of another broker for the purpose of offering to provide, or entering into a contract to provide, a different type of real estate service unrelated to the type of service currently being provided (e.g., property management as opposed to brokerage). However, information received through a Multiple Listing Service or any other offer of cooperation may not be used to target clients of other REALTORS® to whom such offers to provide services may be made. *(Amended 1/93)*

Standard of Practice 16-4

REALTORS® shall not solicit a listing which is currently listed exclusively with another broker. However, if the listing broker, when asked by the REALTOR®, refuses to disclose the expiration date and nature of such listing; i.e., an exclusive right to sell, an exclusive agency, open listing, or other form of contractual agreement between the listing broker and the client, the REALTOR® may contact the owner to secure such information and may discuss the terms upon which the REALTOR® might take a future listing or, alternatively, may take a listing to become effective upon expiration of any existing exclusive listing. *(Amended 1/94)*

Standard of Practice 16-5

REALTORS® shall not solicit buyer/tenant agency agreements from buyers/tenants who are subject to exclusive buyer/tenant agency agreements. However, if a buyer/tenant agent, when asked by a REALTOR®, refuses to disclose the expiration date of the exclusive buyer/tenant agency agreement, the REALTOR® may contact the buyer/tenant to secure such information and may discuss the terms upon which the REALTOR® might enter into a future buyer/tenant agency agreement or, alternatively, may enter into a buyer/tenant agency agreement to become effective upon the expiration of any existing exclusive buyer/tenant agency agreement. *(Adopted 1/94)*

Standard of Practice 16-6

When REALTORS® are contacted by the client of another REALTOR® regarding the creation of an agency relationship to provide the same type of service, and REALTORS® have not directly or indirectly initiated such discussions, they may discuss the terms upon which they might enter into a future agency agreement or, alternatively, may enter into an agency agreement which becomes effective upon expiration of any existing exclusive agreement. *(Amended 1/93)*

Standard of Practice 16-7

The fact that a client has retained a REALTOR® as an agent in one or more past transactions does not preclude other REALTORS® from seeking such former client's future business. *(Amended 1/93)*

Standard of Practice 16-8

The fact that an agency agreement has been entered into with a REALTOR® shall not preclude or inhibit any other REALTOR® from entering into a similar agreement after the expiration of the prior agreement. *(Amended 1/93)*

Standard of Practice 16-9

REALTORS®, prior to entering into an agency agreement, have an affirmative obligation to make reasonable efforts to determine whether the client is subject to a current, valid exclusive agreement to provide the same type of real estate service. *(Amended 1/93)*

Standard of Practice 16-10

REALTORS®, acting as agents of buyers or tenants, shall disclose that relationship to the seller/landlord's agent at first contact and shall provide written confirmation of that disclosure to the seller/landlord's agent not later than execution of a purchase agreement or lease. *(Amended 1/93)*

Standard of Practice 16-11

On unlisted property, REALTORS® acting as buyer/tenant agents shall disclose that relationship to the seller/landlord at first contact for that client and shall provide written confirmation of such disclosure to the seller/landlord not later than execution of any purchase or lease agreement.

REALTORS® shall make any request for anticipated compensation from the seller/landlord at first contact. *(Amended 1/93)*

Standard of Practice 16-12

REALTORS®, acting as agents of sellers/landlords or as subagents of listing brokers, shall disclose that relationship to buyers/tenants as soon as practicable and shall provide written confirmation of such disclosure to buyers/tenants not later than execution of any purchase or lease agreement. *(Amended 1/93)*

Standard of Practice 16-13

All dealings concerning property exclusively listed, or with buyer/tenants who are exclusively represented shall be carried on with the client's agent, and not with the client, except with the consent of the client's agent. *(Adopted 1/93)*

Standard of Practice 16-14

REALTORS® are free to enter into contractual relationships or to negotiate with sellers/landlords, buyers/tenants or others who are not represented by an exclusive agent but shall not knowingly obligate them to pay more than one commission except with their informed consent. *(Amended 1/94)*

Standard of Practice 16-15

In cooperative transactions REALTORS® shall compensate cooperating REALTORS® (principal brokers) and shall not compensate nor offer to compensate, directly or indirectly, any of the sales licensees employed by or affiliated with other REALTORS® without the prior express knowledge and consent of the cooperating broker.

Standard of Practice 16-16

REALTORS®, acting as subagents or buyer/tenant agents, shall not use the terms of an offer to purchase/lease to attempt to modify the listing broker's offer of compensation to subagents or buyer's agents nor make the submission of an executed offer to purchase/lease contingent on the listing broker's agreement to modify the offer of compensation. *(Amended 1/93)*

Standard of Practice 16-17

REALTORS® acting as subagents or as buyer/tenant agents, shall not attempt to extend a listing broker's offer of cooperation and/or compensation to other brokers without the consent of the listing broker. *(Amended 1/93)*

Standard of Practice 16-18

REALTORS® shall not use information obtained by them from the listing broker, through offers to cooperate received through Multiple Listing Services or other sources authorized by the listing broker, for the purpose of creating a referral prospect to a third broker, or for creating a buyer/tenant prospect unless such use is authorized by the listing broker. *(Amended 1/93)*

Standard of Practice 16-19

Signs giving notice of property for sale, rent, lease, or exchange shall not be placed on property without consent of the seller/landlord. *(Amended 1/93)*

Article 17

In the event of a contractual dispute between REALTORS® associated with different firms, arising out of their relationship as REALTORS®, the REALTORS® shall submit the dispute to arbitration in accordance with the regulations of their Board or Boards rather than litigate the matter.

In the event clients of REALTORS® wish to arbitrate contractual disputes arising out of real estate transactions, REALTORS® shall arbitrate those disputes in accordance with the regulations of their Board, provided the clients agree to be bound by the decision. *(Amended 1/94)*

Standard of Practice 17-1

The filing of litigation and refusal to withdraw from it by REALTORS® in an arbitrable matter constitutes a refusal to arbitrate. *(Adopted 2/86)*

Standard of Practice 17-2

Article 17 does not require REALTORS® to arbitrate in those circumstances when all parties to the dispute advise the Board in writing that they choose not to arbitrate before the Board. *(Amended 1/93)*

The Code of Ethics was adopted in 1913. Amended at the Annual Convention in 1924, 1928, 1950, 1951, 1952, 1955, 1956, 1961, 1962, 1974, 1982, 1986, 1987, 1989, 1990, 1991, 1992, 1993 and 1994.

EXPLANATORY NOTES

The reader should be aware of the following policies which have been approved by the Board of Directors of the National Association:

In filing a charge of an alleged violation of the Code of Ethics by a REALTOR®, the charge must read as an alleged violation of one or more Articles of the Code. Standards of Practice may be cited in support of the charge.

The Standards of Practice serve to clarify the ethical obligations imposed by the various Articles and supplement, and do not substitute for, the Case Interpretations in **Interpretations of the Code of Ethics.**

Modifications to existing Standards of Practice and additional new Standards of Practice are approved from time to time. Readers are cautioned to ensure that the most recent publications are utilized.

NATIONAL ASSOCIATION
OF REALTORS®
430 North Michigan Avenue
Chicago, Illinois 60611-4087

1 Property and Property Rights

The following terms and concepts will be covered in this chapter. They will also be found in the glossary at the back of the text.

Terms And Concepts

Air Rights
Ad Valorem Taxation
Board of Appeals
Building Code
Bundle of Rights
Chattel
Chattel Personal
Chattel Real
Corporeal
Emblements
Eminent Domain
Escheat
Fixture
Heterogeneity
Improvements
Incorporeal
Intangible
Intestate
Location
Long Term Investment

Mineral Rights
Non-Homogeneity
Personal Property
Personalty
Possession Rights
Property
Real Estate
Real Property
Realty
Scarcity
Situs
Subsurface Rights
Surface Rights
Tangible
Taxation
Trade Fixture
Variance
Zoning
Police Power

Property

The concept of property deals with the rights and interests an individual may have in something that is owned. There are two basic types of property that we need to identify and understand, **Real Property** and **Personal Property.**

Real Property

Real Property consists of the land plus whatever is affixed to the land and all the rights and benefits so attached. This also includes that which is below and above the surface of the land starting from a point in the center of the earth upward to infinity. But, this common law definition has been modified over the years to meet the needs of our twentieth century society. For instance, rights in the space above property called **Air Rights** will not be the same in different geographic areas. Because of legal air transport, courts have interpreted these rights to extend only to that point which may be "effectively used" while higher altitudes could be considered public airspace.

Two other classifications of rights are **Subsurface** and **Surface**. Subsurface rights, also known as **Mineral Rights**, include the landowners' interest in the property below the surface to access oil, gas, or other solid minerals. Surface rights, on the other hand, are the more common types of interest the home owner is concerned with and is the category within which a typical residential real estate salesperson works.

Surface Rights include improvements to benefit the use of the owner. **Improvements** on the land would include structures such as the house or a garage while improvements to the land are streets, sewer or landscaping.

Real property rights also can be broken down into two different types: **Corporeal** and **Incorporeal**. The **Tangible Rights** of property ownership such as improvement on and to the land are referred to as corporeal. Those other additional rights obtained when a person holds title to a piece of realty that are **Intangible** such as a "right of way" over an adjoining parcel of land are considered **Incorporeal**.

For our purpose and throughout the text, **Real Estate**, **Real Property** and **Realty** will be considered synonymous and therefore interchangeable. As a matter of practice in the real estate profession, real property may be referred to as property alone. So when we refer to a "piece of property", we are referring to a piece of real property and not personal property.

Personal Property

Personal Property is anything that is not real property. Just as a piece of real estate is known as realty, a piece of personal property is known as **Personalty**. Therefore, anything that is not attached to the land is personal property or personalty. An article of personal property is also known as a **Chattel**. For example, Mrs. Jones sells her property at 42 Main Street. Along with the land itself, she has sold the house because it is attached to the land, plus the furnace, plus plumbing fixtures, kitchen cabinets, doors, etc., all of which are attached to and part of the realty.

However, when Mrs. Jones moves, she may keep her couch, chairs, clothing, lawn mower, television, etc., because they are not attached and therefore are personalty or chattels.

An apartment lease is not part of the realty and is therefore personal property. A **Chattel Personal** can go forward with the seller such as furniture and a **Chattel Real** stays with the property such as a lease. One of the key factors in determining whether property is real or personal is portability. If an object can be picked up and removed without damage to the premises, then it is personal property. If the object cannot be removed without damage to the premises, as in the case of a bathtub, then it is considered part of the real property.

Emblements are growing crops that are produced annually through labor and industry and are considered personal property even prior to harvest. A tenant has the right to such crops resulting from the tenant's labor even if the harvest occurs after the tenancy ends. (Also known as **Fructus Industriales**).

Fixture

Property may change from real to personal or from personal to real. Trees that are growing and attached to the land are considered part of the real estate. Those same trees when cut down are considered portable, not part of the realty, and are therefore personalty. This is obviously of great importance when selling land that has timber or crops growing on it.

Personal property that becomes real property is known as a **Fixture**. Carpeting that is purchased in a store is personal property. Once that carpet has been installed as wall-to-wall and nailed in place, it becomes a part of the real estate and therefore realty itself.

As you can see, it becomes extremely important in a real estate transaction to make certain that the buyer and the seller understand and agree on what is expected to remain with the property and what is not. Many a real estate transaction has fallen through or resulted in hard feelings because the parties did not understand these concepts. It is the job of the real estate broker or salesperson to make sure that these areas are clear and that everyone is in agreement about what stays and what goes.

If the parties (i.e., buyer and seller) agree, an item that would normally remain as realty may be taken with the seller, for example a favorite rosebush given to the seller by a relative. Conversely, an item that would normally be taken by the seller may remain, for example a refrigerator or cellar workbench.

When the parties agree that an article of personal property will remain that item remains personalty and does not become realty merely because it remains with the house.

Fixture Determination

In determining whether or not an item is a fixture, we must consider three things:

1) **The intent of the parties**
2) **The method of annexation**
3) **The agreement of the parties**

Intent of The Parties

When the fixture was attached to the real property did the individual intend that the item remain? Ex: bathtub, kitchen sink, chandelier, heating system.

Method of Annexation

Was the fixture permanently attached or could it be easily removed without damage to the property?

Agreement of The Parties

Do the parties (buyer and seller) agree that the item in question is a fixture and will remain? Most items are clearly real property or personal property and there is no doubt if they stay or do not stay. However, if there is any chance of a misunderstanding, the prudent thing to do is to list any questionable item on the listing, in the offer and on the formal Purchase and Sale Agreement.

Some typical items of potential misunderstanding:
1) Kitchen chandelier that was a wedding present. Stay or go?
2) Oriental stair runner (nailed down) that matches an oriental living room rug (not nailed down). Stay or go?
3) A set of shelves in a den fixed to the wall with two screws. Stay or go?
4) Ten foot long work bench in basement, not attached but won't fit out the cellar door. Stay or go?
5) Four foot by five foot child's play house in yard. Stay or go?

In each of these cases ask the seller's intent, include on the listing and the purchase and sale agreement with both buyer and seller signing and you will have eliminated any misunderstanding.

Trade Fixture

A **trade fixture** is a fixture that is attached to the real estate by a tenant as a part of the tenant's trade or business. Trade fixtures do not automatically become part of the real estate. Because of the landlord - tenant relationship, the tenant may remove trade fixtures and take them with him. An example would be bowling alley equipment or display cases in a butcher shop. The tenant is responsible for any damage caused by the removal of the trade fixture. The trade fixture should be removed by the end of the lease or they may be considered abandoned and become the landlord's property.

Physical Characteristics of Real Property

Land has specific physical characteristics that make it different from other commodities that are bought or sold.

1) **Land is immobile**
2) **Land is indestructible**
3) **Land is unique**

Land is Immobile

A part of real property can be moved but the basic piece of real estate remains fixed in place. Although you may like the topography of a particular lot but not its location, try as you might you will not be able to move it to another area of town.

Land is Indestructible

A part of real property can be destroyed but the basic parcel of real estate remains where it is forever. No matter how much man moves the surface of the realty around it can't be destroyed.

Land is Unique

No two pieces of property are ever completely the same. Each parcel of land has its own qualities in areas such as improvements, rights, restrictions, zoning, shape, size, location, and on and on This makes each property unique and causes differences in values. It also makes it easy to identify each distinct piece of property through its property description. For this reason, a lawsuit can develop if a seller changes his or her mind before the property transfers and tries to substitute another parcel of land or back out of the transaction altogether. The buyer can not purchase a duplicate of the agreed upon property and the courts recognize this. This uniqueness is also known as its **Heterogeneity** or **Non-homogeneity**.

Economic Characteristics of Real Property

Land has a number of Economic Characteristics that affect value.

1) Scarcity
2) Improvements
3) Long-term Investment
4) Location (Situs)

Scarcity

The amount of available land is in general terms fixed and governed by the laws of supply and demand. This is particularly true of specific markets such as available office space in an urban area or limited available housing in a sub-division or certain part of town. As property becomes less available or scarce, its value goes up.

Improvements

The nature of the things one adds to the land affects value, including roads, utilities and structures such as a house or office building.

Long Term Investment

Because the life cycle of real estate has a long time line which can run for decades or sometimes even hundreds of years, investing in real estate is considered **Fixed** or permanent in nature. Even though it may take twenty or thirty years to recoup your investment, you know that the property will still be there when the debt has been liquidated. The stability of this type of investment does generate a caveat. Within the time it takes to pay off a mortgage, the character of the neighborhood or value could change due to zoning laws or other economic factors. This could be for the good, as in the case of a new school or bad, if the property nearby was zoned for a use different from residential.

Location

Economically, of all the factors that influence value, it is common knowledge that the **Location (or Situs)** of property is a prime factor that influences what it is worth. The reasons that cause certain neighborhoods to be more desirable are numerous and varied including: Proximity to transportation, schools, zoning, scenery, quality of land, community services, tax base and quality of construction, to name a few.

Property Rights

In defining property, we said we were dealing with the property rights of an individual. There are five major categories of rights that private ownership enjoys:

1) **Control** - to use at your discretion within the law
2) **Possession** - to hold and use or not use as in a lease
3) **Enjoyment** - to use without others infringing on your rights
4) **Disposition** - to sell, convey or will as you choose
5) **Exclusion** - to limit others from entry as you choose

The specific rights that are involved are almost endless. One common way to grasp this idea is to think of the rights an individual has in property as a **"Bundle of Rights."** This "bundle of rights" includes all of the rights the individual has in his property. He or she may dispose of all of these rights at one time, or a group of these rights, or only one of these rights.

Thus, if you own a piece of property, you may sell all of the rights you have to another party. This is the case in most real estate sales of residential property. You can transfer the group of **Possession Rights** to a tenant in a lease arrangement (we will go into leases in more detail in a later chapter).

Other common examples are the sale of **Mineral Rights** to property where the right to mine coal, petroleum or some other mineral is sold to a large company, but the balance of the "bundle of rights" to the property is kept by the owner.

An example of one right being granted to another is a common driveway where you give your next-door neighbor the right to use a part of your property to gain access to his garage. The property remains yours except for that one right of usage.

Limits to Property Rights

The "bundle of rights" that one has to one's property is not without limits. Although we "own" our property and have the right of control we are not completely free to do whatever we wish. Just as we deny an individual the right to yell "fire!" in a crowed theater, we must limit rights of ownership. These limits fall into two categories:

        1) **Rights of Other Persons**
        2) **Government Rights**

Rights of Other Persons

Our right of ownership allows us to do a number of things on our property, including the right to play a stereo. However, our neighbors have their right to the **Quiet Enjoyment** of their property. When the volume on the stereo gets so loud that we are disturbing our neighbors, we soon find that our right is limited by the property rights of others, and if necessary, the police may be brought in by the neighbor to enforce this right. It also includes landlord tenant relations and other rights that owners of an estate may have.

Government Limits to Rights

There are four rights that the government has that affect our private property rights. They are:

        1)   **Eminent Domain**
        2)   **Police Power**
        3)   **Taxation**
        4)   **Escheat**

Eminent Domain

The government may decide that it is in the best interest of the majority of the people to take ownership of a piece of private property even if the owner does not want to sell. The government must show that the taking is for the good of all, that a fair and equitable price is paid for the land, and the owner has his right to appeal the amount of compensation. This is called the power of **Eminent Domain** and is a right that the government has, while the administrative process for the taking is called **condemnation.** Common examples of eminent domain are when a city is building a school or a new road is being constructed. Some private landowners may be willing to sell and may do so through normal procedures. Those who refuse to sell, however, can be forced to do so by the city, state or federal governments via eminent domain.

Police Power

In order to protect the community, the government may limit the rights of the individual to do what he wishes on his property. This **Police Power** would be used to enforce any of the laws of the community. Some examples are laws dealing with environmental impact, wetlands usage and health codes. The two major examples of local exercise of police power limiting individual property rights are:

1) **Zoning Ordinances**
2) **Building Codes**

Zoning Ordinances - Most developed communities have adopted a form of community planning called **Zoning**. Thus, a city can decide on a set of rules that will establish separate areas within the city for manufacturing firms, retail stores, medical facilities, multifamily dwellings and single-family dwellings. These regulations often go into considerable detail as to what may be constructed on a piece of property and what that structure may be used for, including number of parking spaces required, minimum lot size, amount of front footage on the street, front and side setbacks, etc. (Each student should obtain a copy of the local zoning ordinances for personal study.)

City or town governments usually have a procedure whereby permission may be obtained to build, convert or otherwise use a parcel of property in violation of the zoning ordinances. Such permission is called a **Variance**. This variance may be obtained by contacting the **Local Board of Appeals** in the city or town and receiving its approval.

Building Code - The local city or town will have a set of standards that the various trades must adhere to when building or renovating property. The property owner and tradesmen (carpenters, plumbers, electricians, etc.) must adhere to these rules and regulations.

Taxation

Cities and towns finance their operations primarily through a tax on private property. Anyone who does not pay such a charge is subject to governmental action that may eventually lead to loss of ownership for nonpayment of taxes. The right of the city or town to levy and collect such taxes is called **Ad Valorem Taxation.** This means that the taxes are set "according to valuation" based on the assessed value of the property.

Escheat

If a person dies without a will disposing of his property, this is known as **intestate,** and if there are no known relatives to inherit the property, the ownership transfers to the state via a power called **Escheat.**

Glossary Quiz

1) A set of rules used to establish minimum workmanship standards by tradesmen in the construction of a building. _____

2) Process by which the government takes title to private property for the public good. _____

3) An article of personal property that has become real property by being attached to the realty. _____

4) An exercise of Police Power that limits property rights by defining what can be built within certain sections of a city. _____

5) A freezer that is installed in a building by a tenant who is opening a restaurant. _____

6) A mining company retains the right to the coal deposits under your property. These rights are called? _____

7) A supermarket has the right to build a store over an inner city highway. These rights are known as? _____

8) Town approval to build a two family in a one family zone would be obtained by permission of the _____

9) Approval to build a two family in a one family zone is called _____

10) Government right to take ownership of real estate when no rightful owner can be identified is called _____

Self Quiz A

1) A dishwasher that has been built into a set of kitchen cabinets is:
   A)   Personal property
   B)   A chattel
   C)   A fixture
   D)   Incorporeal

2) Charlie rents a retail store and installs counters and shelving as part of his retail business. These items are considered:
   A)   Trade fixtures
   B)   Personal property
   C)   Landlord's property
   D)   Chattels

3) When B bought his house, the dining room chandelier remained because it is:
   A)   A chattel
   B)   Personal property
   C)   A fixture
   D)   A trade fixture

4) A property owner has his property transferred to the state against his will by:
   A)   Eminent domain
   B)   Escheat
   C)   Prescription
   D)   Inheritance

5) Which of the following is considered personal property:
   A)   Wood burning stove
   B)   Gas furnace
   C)   Living room couch
   D)   Rose bush in the garden

6) Which of the following would be considered real property:
   A)   Dining room table
   B)   Shrub in a pot on the patio
   C)   Screen porch furniture
   D)   Kitchen ceiling fan

7) Fixtures are:
   A)   Personal property
   B)   Real property
   C)   Chattels
   D)   Incorporeal

8) Prior to putting his house on the market, Jones replaced the dining room chandelier. Which of the following is true?
   A)   Jones was within his rights because the original chandelier is a chattel.
   B)   Jones must replace the original chandelier
   C)   Jones was within his rights because the replacement was prior to marketing the property
   D)   Jones would have to negotiate which chandelier remained with the buyer.

9) Which of the following is an example of a chattel?
   A)   Oak tree in front yard
   B)   Kitchen table
   C)   Wall to wall carpet
   D)   Common driveway

10) When A's house is sold, the contract calls for her to take the wood stove with her. The wood stove:
   A)   is real property
   B)   is personal property
   C)   is a chattel
   D)   must remain because it is attached

11) The right of a city to restrict a certain area to single family homes is called:
   A)   A building code
   B)   Zoning
   C)   A variance
   D)   Escheat

12) If you wished to construct a two family in a one family zone you should:
   A)   Hire an approved contractor and begin construction
   B)   Take out a building permit for a one family
   C)   Obtain town approval through a Variance
   D)   Abandon your plan because town approval is not possible

13) When a property owner dies intestate and leaves no heirs, property transfers to the state via:
   A)   Possession Rights
   B)   Eminent Domain
   C)   Inheritance
   D)   Escheat

14) A building code regulation governing construction standards is an example of the government's right to limit private property rights by means of:
   A)   Eminent domain
   B)   Escheat
   C)   Police power
   D)   Encroachment

Answer Key

Glossary Quiz		Self Quiz A	
1)	Building Code	1)	C
2)	Condemnation	2)	A
3)	Fixture	3)	C
4)	Zoning	4)	A
5)	Trade Fixture	5)	C
6)	Mineral / Subsurface Rights	6)	D
7)	Air Rights	7)	B
8)	Board of Appeals	8)	C
9)	Variance	9)	B
10)	Escheat	10)	A
		11)	B
		12)	C
		13)	D
		14)	C

2 Estates

The following terms and concepts will be covered in this chapter. They will also be found in the glossary at the back of the text.

Terms And Concepts

Commercial Easement in Gross
Common Driveway
Concurrent Estate
Curtesy
Dominant Estate
Dower
Easement
Easement Appurtenant
Easement by Necessity
Easement by Prescription
Easement in Gross
Encroachment
Encumbrance
Estate
Fee Simple
Fee Simple Absolute
Fee Simple Defeasible
Fee Simple Determinable
Fee Simple on Condition Subsequent
Freehold Estate

Homestead
Joint Tenancy
License
Lien
Life Estate
Littoral Rights
Non-Freehold Estate
Personal Easement in Gross
Remainder Estate
Remainderman
Restrictive Covenant
Reversionary Estate
Right of Survivorship
Riparian Rights
Servient Estate
Tenancy by the Entirety
Tenancy in Common
Tenancy in Partnership
Water Rights

The "bundle of rights" and interests that an individual has in land is called an **Estate.**

Estates can be classified according to the length of time they last as in the case of **Freehold Estate** (indefinite period of time) or **Non-Freehold Estates** (definite period of time). Estates also deal with an individual's share of ownership in property where more than one person has title, known as **Concurrent Estates.**

Freehold Estates

Freehold estates last for an infinite period of time. This may be either for a lifetime or longer than a lifetime and because the owner possesses title, it can be passed on to heirs. The types of freehold estates are:

1) **Fee Simple**
2) **Fee Simple Determinable**
3) **Fee Simple on Condition Subsequent**
4) **Life Estate**

Fee Simple Estate

Fee Simple, also known as **Fee Simple Absolute**, is the highest form of estate possible. The owner has all of the rights possible and the estate is limited only by the rights of others and by government rights. The estate may be given away, sold or inherited and has no time limit.

There are types of *qualified* estates that depend on the occurrence or non-occurrence of a specific event. They are known as **Fee Simple Defeasible** and fall into two categories; **Determinable** and **Condition Subsequent.**

Fee Simple Determinable

Fee Simple Determinable is a fee simple defeasible estate with a condition attached which, if violated, causes the estate to **automatically** revert back to the person who created the estate (or the heirs). For example, Jones sells his land to Brown with the condition that Brown allow Jones's mother to live there. Brown subsequently evicts Jones's mother. Title automatically reverts back to Jones. The condition must be stated specifically in writing on the deed.

Fee Simple On Condition Subsequent

Fee Simple on Condition Subsequent is a fee simple defeasible estate with a condition attached which, if violated, gives the prior owner the right to reclaim the estate, but the process is **not automatic.** For example, Jones sells his land to Brown with the condition that Brown allow Jones's mother to live there. Brown subsequently evicts Jones's mother. Jones has the right to reclaim the property, but if he does not exercise that right, the property remains Brown's.

Life Estate

A life estate is an estate given by the grantor (seller) to the grantee (buyer) for life. Upon the death of the grantee, the property passes on to a third party who is known as the **Remainderman.** For example, A grants a life estate to B, with C named as remainderman. While B is alive, C is said to have a **Remainder or Remainder Estate** in the property. When B dies, C receives a full fee simple estate in the property.

The grantor may name him or herself as remainderman. In this situation the remainder interest in the estate is considered **Reversionary.** This same term applies to the situation where there is a limited interest in an estate which upon certain conditions can revert back to the original grantor as in a defeasible estate.

A **Homestead** is a life estate in real estate occupied as the family home. It is intended to protect the occupants against certain creditors during the occupant's lifetime. The homestead does not protect against taxes, mortgages or mechanic's liens but does protect against other personal debt such as credit cards and charge accounts.

Concurrent Estates

The various freehold estates we have covered may be held by one individual or by two or more individuals. When two or more hold estates together, they are said to have **Concurrent Estates.** Examples of concurrent estates are husband and wife owning a house or business partners owning a building.

There are several types of concurrent estates to be considered:

1) **Tenancy by the Entirety**
2) **Joint Tenancy**
3) **Tenancy in Common**

Tenancy By The Entirety

Tenancy by the Entirety is restricted to husbands and wives. They may not take title as tenants by the entirety prior to their marriage. Neither can sell his or her interest without the signature of the other. If one should die, the survivor owns the property in fee simple (**Right of Survivorship**). Thus, the property does not become part of the decedent's estate for probate purposes. If the two should become divorced, the tenancy by the entirety ceases and the two hold title as tenants in common (**No Right of Survivorship**).

Joint Tenancy

Joint Tenancy is a form of ownership where two or more persons own the same land with right of survivorship. One example might be where three business partners buy a store together, and if one dies he wants the remaining partners to own the land and building.

It is important to note that Joint Tenants have equal interests, including rights of possession, that begin at the same time and exist for the same duration. One joint tenant may not hold title in full while another holds a life estate or remainder estate. One joint tenant may convey his share to a new party, who then holds title as tenant in common (no survivorship) with the others who remain joint tenants to each other (right of survivorship).

Tenancy In Common

Tenancy in Common exists when two or more persons have separate interests or shares in a parcel of property with no right of survivorship. These interests may begin at separate times via the same or separate title, and each may dispose of his share without the prior approval of the other tenants in common.

Tenancy In Partnership

There are three forms of business ownership:

1) **Single Proprietor**
2) **Partnership**
3) **Corporation**

A partnership is formed when two or more individuals start a business for profit but, unlike a corporation it is not considered a separate legal entity apart from the owners and normally cannot own real property. Title to real property would have to be held by the owners of the partnership in either Joint Tenancy or Tenancy in Common.

Under the uniform Partnership Act this problem has been resolved. A form of concurrent ownership is allowed in most states called **Tenancy in Partnership** with its own advantages and disadvantages. Under this form of ownership there is right of survivorship and each partner has equal rights to use the property but only for partnership purposes. One partner may not assign or sell his or her share without approval of all the other partners. One important advantage is the fact that partnership property cannot be attached for the personal debts of one of the partners. Upon dissolution of the partnership the property must be sold since it was the partnership that owned the parcel and not any of the individual members.

As in any business venture it is important that all partners understand the implications of the contractual relationship entered into. A partnership is a form of ownership that brings together the resources of a number of people for the advantage of all members. It also brings problems, conflicts and misunderstandings relative to responsibilities, rights and sharing of profits and losses. The tenancy in partnership does not resolve any of these other problems nor details allowances to heirs in the case of death of a partner. It is wise to seek legal advice and draw up an Articles of Partnership Agreement to spell out how to resolve common and unforeseen events and the steps to follow in solving disputes.

Non-Freehold Estates

We have been discussing estates with a duration of a lifetime or longer (**Freehold Estates**). There is another category of estates that has a "bundle of rights" that exists for less than a lifetime and the owner doesn't have title to the realty (**Non-Freehold Estates**). An example of non-freehold estate is an apartment rental. A tenant has a specific group of rights that are acquired from the landlord by way of a rental agreement. These rights are temporary, depending on the tenant-landlord agreement, and do not carry forward for more than the lifetime of the tenant.

The different types of non-freehold estates will be dealt with in detail in a later chapter on leases.

Other Property Interests or Rights

In addition to the major areas already discussed, there are a number of other rights that will be encountered and should be covered.

Easement
An **Easement** is a right that one person has (**Dominant Estate**) in the land of another (**Servient Estate**). Easements can fall into two basic categories.

The first is called an **Easement Appurtenant** and needs two pieces of property to exist that may or may not be adjacent. An example of this sort of easement is the common driveway. The right to travel over another parcel of property is stated in the deed and that right "runs with the land".

The second is called an **Easement in Gross** and can be held by an individual or by a company. It is personal in nature and runs with the user not the land. When the user dies the easement ceases to exist. One example is a utility company's right to run wire or pipe across private property. **Commercial Easements in Gross** can typically be transferred easily while **Personal Easements in Gross** are not. An easement created when land is sold that can only be reached by crossing abutting land owned by the seller is called an **Easement by Necessity**. An easement established by 20 years of open, continuous and notorious use is called an **Easement by Prescription.**

Easements can be created by deed, prescription, or necessity.

Deed - A written document that transfers title.
Prescription - Open, continuous and adverse use for 20 years in
        Massachusetts - other states vary.
Necessity - Owner must be granted access over the land of another (a
        landlocked parcel is an example)

License

A **license** is a use that is permitted by an owner of a piece of property for a specific purpose. This right, which can be verbal, is revocable at any time by the owner. The licensee (user) does not accrue any permanent rights in the property. Examples of license include the permission to fish, hunt or camp on a parcel of property.

Dower and Curtesy

The rights that a husband (**curtesy**) or wife (**dower**) hold in the estate of the other are called dower and curtesy rights. In Massachusetts, either party had a one-third life estate in the real property of the spouse at the time of the spouse's death. Dower and curtesy would apply to property held in one name only (either husband or wife). If the property were held in any of the joint forms of ownership (tenancy by the entirety, joint tenancy, or tenancy in common), the provisions of that form of estate would apply rather than dower and curtesy.

Encroachment

Encroachment exists when any structure, addition, or attached fixture intrudes on the property of another. An example of encroachment is when a garage is built over the lot line and part is actually on the abutter's land. Another example is a screened porch that hangs over a neighbor's property.

Restrictive Covenant

Because the owner of real property has as part of his "legal bundle of rights" the right of control and disposition, grantors can put restrictive covenants in the deed that transfers property. A **Restrictive Covenant** in a deed is a prohibited use or a requirement that must be followed.

Some examples are: 1) no external antenna or clothes lines, 2) although zoning laws allow more, a deed may state that a parcel of land is limited to only one living unit, 3) houses must use cedar shakes for roofing, or painted only certain colors.

Most modern day restrictions are placed in deeds by developers of large projects to maintain the continuity of design for a neighborhood. Also, condominium projects will typically have a number of restrictions. Restrictions must be reasonable to be enforced by law.

Encumbrances and Liens

Any right or interest that A has in B's property that limits B's rights but still allows transfer of title by B to another party is an **Encumbrance**. If the encumbrance is financial, it is called a **Lien**. Some encumbrances are liens. All liens are encumbrances. A common driveway is an encumbrance but not a lien. A mortgage is an encumbrance that is a lien.

Water Rights

Water Rights fall into two basic categories, **Littoral** and **Riparian.** Rights that a property owner has to abutting standing bodies of water such as lakes, ponds, and oceans are littoral. Rights that a property owner has to flowing bodies of water, as in the case of rivers and streams, are considered riparian.

An example of littoral rights can be found in the situation of abutters to ponds or lakes. If a lake is less than 10 acres it is owned and controlled by the abutters, and any lake over 10 acres is owned by the state. If more than 20 acres, the abutters must allow public access. Ponds completely within the boundaries of one owner's property are exempt.

With rivers or streams there is a differentiation in rights based on whether the body of water is navigable or non-navigable. If navigable, the abutters own only to the banks of the stream and the state owns the stream. If the stream is non-navigable, the abutters own to the center of the stream.

On the other hand, abutters to tidal waters have a less clear picture of their rights, and this makes it important to read an owner's deed for clarification. some deeds show that ownership extends to the mean high water mark while there may be some that show ownership extending to the mean low water mark. In addition to this, there may be local regulations that control public access.

Glossary Quiz

1) The right of the husband to a share of his wife's estate (in Massachusetts, rights are one-third of what the wife owned at the time of her death) _____

2) When the property of one intrudes on the property of another (e.g., porch overlaps neighbor's property line) _____

3) The highest form of estate - the holder possesses all of the rights possible, limited only by government rights and rights of others _____

4) Method of establishing an easement by open, continuous, and notorious use for twenty years _____

5) A type of concurrent estate (two or more persons) restricted to husbands and wives only (provides for right of survivorship) _____

6) A life estate established for the occupant of the family home _____

7) Tenant A has the right to cross B's land to go to the beach. A's estate is said to be _____

8) In the above situation B's estate is said to be _____

9) Requirements that prohibit you from parking a trailer on land you have purchased are called _____

10) An encumbrance on your property caused by a mortgage of $100,000 is called a _____

Self Quiz A

1) A property owner was denied permission to build a garage too close to his lot line because this would
   A) constitute Encroachment
   B) violate the Building Code
   C) be against Zoning Ordinances
   D) result in an Easement

2) A grants property to B for B's lifetime, and upon B's death the property transfers to C. During B's lifetime C holds which of the following estates?
   A) Life Estate
   B) Fee Simple Estate
   C) Concurrent Estate
   D) Remainder Estate

3) A freehold estate that automatically reverts back to the grantors or their heirs if a condition is violated is:
   A) Fee Upon condition
   B) Fee Simple Absolute
   C) Life Estate
   D) Fee Simple Determinable

4) John and Sally are married and own real estate with right of survivorship. Which of the following is not available to them?
   A) Tenancy by the Entirety
   B) Tenancy in Common
   C) Joint Tenancy
   D) Ownership as Partners

5) Harry's garage is two feet over the property line on Mary's land. This is an example of:
   A) An Encroachment
   B) An Easement
   C) A Lien
   D) A Fixture

6) Joe has the deeded right to cross Bill's land to reach a pond. This is an example of:
   A) An Encroachment
   B) Littoral Rights
   C) An Easement
   D) Riparian Rights

7) Dick has certain rights to the use of a stream that borders his property. These rights are known as:
   A) Riparian Rights
   B) Prescriptive Rights
   C) Encumbrance Rights
   D) Littoral Rights

8) Which of the following is the best type of estate to receive.
   A) Life Estate
   B) Fee Simple
   C) Fee Upon Condition
   D) Fee Simple Determinable

9) If you wanted title to automatically revert back to the prior owner if a stated condition was violated, you would use:
   A) Life Estate
   B) Fee Simple
   C) Fee Upon Condition
   D) Fee Simple Determinable

10) To ensure that two individuals owned property equally, you would specify:
   A) A Concurrent Estate
   B) A Life Estate
   C) A Fee Simple Estate
   D) A Fee Upon Condition

Self Quiz B

1) Which form of estate is not available to two brothers:
   A) Concurrent Estate
   B) Tenancy by the Entirety
   C) Joint Tenancy
   D) Tenancy in Common

2) If one of two brothers owning property together intends his interest to go to his spouse upon his death, he should use:
   A) Tenancy in Partnership
   B) Tenancy by the Entirety
   C) Joint Tenancy
   D) Tenancy in Common

3) "A" dies and his share of jointly owned property passes to his spouse. Which of the following is true? A and his spouse held title as:
   A) Joint Tenants or Tenants by the Entirety
   B) Joint Tenants or Tenants in Common
   C) Tenants by the Entirety or Tenants in Common
   D) Tenants in Common

4) "A" owns a parcel of property and is planning to marry. When A dies he wishes his property to pass to his wife for her lifetime and upon her death to pass to A's son. Which of the following is not true?
   A) During the wife's ownership the son is a remainder man
   B) Upon the wife's death, the son has a fee simple interest
   C) Upon A's death his wife has a fee simple interest
   D) A's wife may not convert the life estate to a fee simple interest.

5) If an owner violates a side line setback and builds a deck to within two feet of the lot line, this is an example of:
    A) A Zoning Violation
    B) An Encroachment
    C) An Encumbrance
    D) An Easement

6) Property may transfer without the owner's permission by means of:
    A) Deed or Adverse Possession
    B) Deed or Foreclosure
    C) Escheat or Adverse Possession
    D) Adverse Possession or Inheritance by Will

7) If A's property with a Dominant Estate Right of Way over B's Servient Estate sells to a third party, which of the following is true:
    A) The Right of Way terminates if B does not agree to continue
    B) The Right of Way transfers to the new owner
    C) The third party must negotiate the Right of Way with B
    D) The Right of Way would remain with A

8) "A" has a mortgage with the Usury Credit Union. Which of the following is true? The mortgage is:
    A) A Lien but not an Encumbrance
    B) An Encumbrance and an Encroachment
    C) An Encumbrance but not a Lien
    D) A Lien and an Encumbrance

9) The rights that an owner has with property on a lake are:
    A) Riparian Rights
    B) Littoral Rights
    C) Easement Rights
    D) License Rights

10) Your next door neighbor has a deeded Right of Way over your property to reach his barn. your neighbor has:
    A) Servient Rights
    B) Dominant Rights
    C) Encroachment Rights
    D) Prescriptive Rights

Answer Key

	Glossary Quiz	Self Quiz A	Self Quiz B
1)	Curtesy	C	B
2)	Encroachment	D	D
3)	Fee Simple	D	A
4)	Prescription	B	C
5)	Tenancy by the Entirety	A	A
6)	Homestead	C	C
7)	Dominant	A	B
8)	Servient	B	D
9)	Restrictive Covenants	D	B
10)	Lien	A	B

3 Condominiums, Cooperatives, and Time Share

The following terms and concepts will be covered in this chapter. They will also be found in the glossary at the back of the text.

Terms And Concepts

Bylaws
Capital Reserve
Common Areas
Condo Budget
Condo Fee
Condo "Super Lien"
Condo Trust / Association
Condominium
Cooperative
Dockominium
Elderly
Handicapped
Low or Moderate Income

Master Deed
Master Insurance Policy
M.G.L. c. 183A
Operating Reserve
Percent of Common Ownership
Rules and Regulations
Time Share
Unit Deed
Unit Square Footage
6 (d) Certificate

The idea of owning a "piece of the whole" is not new in Real Estate. There is historical evidence that going back to at least Roman times, society has established ways to allow a buyer to purchase a part of a parcel of real estate as his own when he could not purchase the total parcel for one reason or another.

In recent years, there has been a revival of this form of ownership through three different concepts, i.e.:

1)   **Condominiums**
2)   **Cooperatives**
3)   **Time share**

Each one offers benefits of ownership such as tax advantages and appreciation (increase in value) that are not available to those who rent instead of own. The increase in the value of real estate has put the ownership of homes out of reach of many people.

The Condominium, Cooperative and Time Share forms of ownership place the ownership of a piece of real estate with all its ownership advantages within reach of a buying public that otherwise could not afford to become property owners.

These areas of real estate brokerage have grown to a point where many in the field will specialize exclusively (i.e. condominium development and brokerage or time share sales). Even if you do not plan to specialize, the real estate professional of the 1990's and beyond will encounter a growing level of activity in these fields and should become knowledgeable in the terms, concepts, practices and procedures for the formation, conversion and brokerage of condominiums, cooperatives and time share units.

Condominiums

The most common example of this type of "piece of the whole" ownership in Massachusetts is known as **Condominium Ownership**.

A condominium buyer purchases his unit (apartment) which he then owns as if it were his house. The buyer also has a partial interest, along with all other unit owners, in everything that is not a separate unit, (**common areas**), i.e. halls, elevators, lobby, roof, exterior walls, pool, yard, etc.

This approach is also used in commercial real estate where a buyer purchases his office unit individually and then, along with other unit owners, has a partial interest in common areas, i.e., lobby, elevators, heating equipment, roof, exterior walls, parking lot, etc.

The condominium concept is still growing and has expanded into "**Dockominiums**", where a unit owner buys a boat slip or dock at prices of $20,000 to $100,000 or more.

"Condominium" refers to a form of ownership and not to an architectural style or type of structure. Therefore each of the following can be a "Condominium":

1. One floor apartment in a typical apartment building.
2. Two or more story "townhouse" attached side by side.
3. Five separate cottages each unattached from the others.
4. Retail or office space within a commercial building.

In order to understand this field and to be better prepared to represent buyers and sellers in condominium brokerage, we need to become familiar with many new terms and concepts. Some of these are:

Budget	Master Insurance Policy
Bylaws	Percent of Common Ownership
Common Areas	Rules and Regulations
Condo Fee	Unit Deed
Trust/Association	Unit Square Footage
Master Deed	6 (d) Certificate

Condominium Formation

Massachusetts General Law c.183A was passed in 1983 to provide the legal structure to govern the formation and management of condominiums in the Commonwealth of Massachusetts.

Master Deed

A condominium is created by recording what is known as a **Master Deed** at the County Registry of Deeds where the real estate is located. This Master Deed shall contain the following:

1. Land description of property where building is located.
2. Building description, including number of stories, number of units and major construction materials.
3. Unit designation of each unit including location, area, number of rooms, common area access.

4. Description of Common Areas and unit percent of interest in them.
5. Set of floor plans certified by registered architect, professional engineer or land surveyor.
6. Statement of purpose of buildings and unit use.
7. Method for amending the Master Deed.
8. Name of the Corporation, Trust or Association formed to provide unit owned management of the condominium.

The Master Deed is recorded once at the local Registry of Deeds and receives a Book and Page reference which is then referred to for the sale of all units in the future. The detailed procedure of recording deeds at the local registry and the "Book and Page" system will be more fully covered in a subsequent chapter.

Unit Deed

In addition to the **Master Deed** which is filed to establish the total condominium, each unit (apartment or office) must have a **Unit Deed** to convey each separate condominium from one owner to the next.

Massachusetts General Law c. 183A requires that the unit deed contain:

1. Indication that the unit is a condominium and controlled by Massachusetts General Law c183A
2. Land description of the overall Condominium, including Master Deed Book and Page reference
3. Unit designation from Master Deed
4. Statement of intended use, including any restrictions
5. Percent of Interest in Common Areas

Common Areas

The Unit owner receives title to the individual unit he/she has purchased plus an interest in the **Common Areas** along with other unit owners.

The common areas referred to are defined by Massachusetts General Law c. 183A to include:

1. The foundations, columns, girders, beams, supports, party walls, common walls, main walls, roofs, halls, corridors, lobbies, public stairs and stairways, fire escapes and entrances and exits of the buildings.
2. Installations of central services such as power, light, gas, hot and cold water, heat, refrigeration, air conditioning and incinerating.
3. The elevators, tanks, pumps, motors, fans, compressors, ducts, and in general all apparatus and installations existing for common use.
4. The land on which the building is located.
5. The basements, yards, lawns, gardens, recreational facilities, parking areas and storage spaces.
6. The premises for the lodging of custodian or persons in charge of the condominium.
7. Such community and commercial facilities as may be provided for the master deed as being owned in common.

8.   All other parts of the condominium necessary or convenient to its existence, maintenance and safety, or normally in common use.

Bylaws

The unit owners association managing and regulating the condominium must have bylaws in accordance with Massachusetts General Law c.183A that include the following:

1.   The method of providing for the necessary work of maintenance, repair and replacement of the common areas and facilities and payment therefore, including the method of approving payment vouchers.
2.   The manner of collecting from the unit owners their share of the common expenses.
3.   The procedure for hiring all personnel, including whether or not a manager or managing agent may be engaged.
4.   The method of adopting and of amending administrative rules and regulations governing the details of the operation and use of the common areas and facilities.
5.   Such restrictions on and requirements respecting the use and maintenance of the units and the use of the common areas and facilities, not set forth in the master deed, and designed to prevent unreasonable interference with the use of their respective units.

Condominium Fee

Each unit owner has a percentage interest in all common areas that is set forth in the Master Deed. The percentage interest is the relationship of the unit to the total of all units. The law states that this shall be the relationship of unit fair market value to the total of all unit fair market values. As a practical matter, most percents of common interest are determined by **Unit Square Footage** compared with total unit square footage. Therefore, if Unit A contained 1000 square feet of area and there were 20 identical units, the percent of common interest would be calculated as follows:

$$\frac{\text{Unit A sq. ft.}}{\text{Total unit sq. ft.}} = \frac{1,000}{20,000} = .05 \text{ or } 5\%$$

This would mean that A, the owner of Unit A would be responsible for 5% of all common area expenses. Typically, these expenses would include such items as:

1)   Liability and Building Insurance
2)   Common Area cleaning and maintenance
3)   Landscaping
4)   Snow Removal
5)   Property Management, including collecting fees and paying bills.

Assuming a projected **Condominium Budget** of all expenses totaled $12,000 for the year, Unit A owner with 5% common interest would be responsible for 5% × $12,000 or $600 annually.

The unit owners' management association would typically collect Unit A's portion monthly at $600 per year or $50 per month. This would be known as Unit A's monthly condo fee.

They would be known as the **Condo Association** and would be elected by and from the unit owners.

The management association may elect to collect fees monthly, quarterly or annually as the unit owners decide. Any profits or losses at the end of the year would belong to the unit owners in the same percentage as their percent of ownership.

Any outstanding condominium fees must be paid to the condominium association prior to selling a unit or such outstanding fees will form a lien on the property. To insure that such outstanding fees are paid, Massachusetts General Law c. 183A Section 6(d) requires a statement of the organization of unit owners setting forth the amount of unpaid common expense assessed to the unit owner. This document known as the "6(d) Certificate" clears the unit when it is recorded at the registry with the unit deed.

These outstanding common expenses form a lien on the property with priority over all other liens except municipal liens and first mortgages. A detailed discussion of mortgages and other liens will be taken up in later chapters.

Condo Associations with a small number of unit owners often decide to manage the affairs of the condominium themselves with volunteer unit owners. However as the number of units grows and the affairs of the condo association become more complex, it is very common to hire an outside service as a Condominium Management Company. When this happens the Condo Management Company fee is added to the Condo Budget and the expense is carried by each unit owner.

Rules and Regulations

Condominium Associations will usually prepare a set of **Rules and Regulations** controlling some of the activities of unit owners and their guests. Some of the more common items affected might include parking regulations and fines, use of "For Sale" signs on the premises, use of decks or common areas to dry towels or other clothing, use of swimming pool or tennis courts, permission for pets (including size limitations).

Such Rules and Regulations are not usually recorded at the registry. However, the real estate broker and salesperson should become familiar with them. The Master Deed, Bylaws and Rules and Regulations become known as the "Condominium Documents", which should be made available to prospective buyers.

Miscellaneous Brokerage Items

Closing Requirements

In addition to normal closing requirements, when a parcel of property passes papers, a condominium requires:

1. **6(d) Certificate** - This is a statement required by Massachusetts General Law c. 183A Section 6(d) - thus "6(d) Certificate." It states the unit owner condominium fee balance of payment and is necessary to provide unit title free of any condo fee lien. This certificate is obtained from the Condominium Association Management Office and is usually the responsibility of the broker or salesperson to obtain.

2. **Master Insurance Policy** - Most lending institutions require that a statement covering the overall condominium building or buildings be prepared showing amounts of coverage and showing the new unit owner and the new unit owner's bank as the loss payee in the event of damage. This certificate of or copy of the Master Insurance Policy is obtained from the Insurance Company handling the policy on the total condominium and is usually the responsibility of the broker or salesperson to obtain.

Condo Financing

Buyers of condominiums are often surprised to find their bank will allow them to buy more house than condominium. In calculating how much a buyer can afford, most lenders will include the condo fee as a monthly expense. Therefore, when calculating how much of a buyer's monthly income is available to carry a mortgage, we have to include the condo fee on a condo but not on a single family house.

Condo Conversion

By 1985, the practice of converting existing rental housing to condominiums became so widespread that the state declared a "Declaration of Emergency" and filed an amendment to Massachusetts General Law c.183A. This amendment was specifically designed to regulate the conversion of existing rental housing to condominiums and to attempt to offer some protection to the growing number of tenants who were being displaced by condominium conversion. Special protection was established for elderly, low-and moderate-income, and handicapped tenants.

This conversion amendment covers conversion to either condominiums or cooperatives. We have not discussed cooperatives as yet, but will do so shortly.

If any city or town had passed conversion restrictions, they would take precedent over this amendment. If none had been passed, then these restrictions apply. For example, some communities had passed regulations controlling or even forbidding the conversion of rental housing to condominiums.

Special protection is provided for the following classes of tenants:

1. **Elderly** - 62 years of age or older.
2. **Handicapped** - person entitled to housing accommodations who is physically handicapped as defined in Massachusetts General Laws chapter 22, Section 13A
3. **Low or Moderate Income** - total prior twelve-month income of all unit occupants is less than 80% of area median income as set forth by H.U.D. (U.S. Department of Housing and Urban Development)

Major Conversion Provisions

Any building containing four or more housing units that has been occupied by tenants during the prior year is covered. The owner of such a building must give all tenants a notice of intent to convert to condominium or cooperative containing the following:

1. Owner has filed or intends to file a Master Deed converting the property to a condominium.
2. The tenant shall be given a period of time to vacate based on status as elderly, low to moderate income, handicapped or other.
3. The tenant shall be given a chance to purchase the unit he or she occupies at terms equal to or better than those offered to the general public.

Any notices given must honor any existing leases that exist between landlord and tenant.

The procedure for offering the unit for sale to the tenants calls for the owner to provide a Purchase and Sale agreement to the tenant signed by the owner. The tenant has a minimum of 90 days to sign the Purchase and Sale Agreement and accept the offer.

Time To Vacate

If the tenant elects not to purchase the unit, he shall have one year from the owner's notice to vacate. In the case of elderly, handicapped, and low- to moderate- income tenants, the period to vacate is two years.

The owner is required to assist any tenant in the protected categories (i.e., elderly, handicapped, low-to-moderate income) in finding comparable housing. If such comparable housing cannot be found, the time to vacate is increased from two to four years. Rent during this period can only be increased by an amount controlled by the Consumer Price Index (C.P.I.) as published by the U.S. Department of Labor.

5 YEARS

Moving Reimbursement

Any tenant who elects not to purchase the unit shall be reimbursed by the owner for moving expenses. Reimbursement for these actual expenses shall not exceed $750 or in the case of elderly, handicapped, or low- or moderate - income tenants, $1,000. Money is to be paid to the tenant within `10 days of the tenant's moving.

Any owner violating these conversion regulations can be subject to both fines and imprisonment.

A real estate broker or salesperson involved in condominium sales and/or condominium conversion obviously needs to be aware of the complexities of this field and the necessity to recognize when it is prudent to seek good legal advice when your brokerage activities include condominiums or cooperatives.

Condo Super Lien

In April 1993 a change in Massachusetts General Law c. 183 became effective improving a Condo Association's right to collect unpaid condo fees in the case of foreclosure. This change, referred to as the **Condo "Super Lien"** allows the condo association to collect up to six month's overdue condominium fees after taxes and municipal debts have been paid but before any mortgage obligations are paid. This is true even if the condominium association lien is recorded after the mortgage at the Registry of Deeds.

Before this change, all unpaid condo fees came after the first mortgage. In many cases, due to falling condo real estate values, condo's were selling at foreclosure and there was not enough equity to pay off the mortgage. Unpaid condo fees were then the responsibility of the other condo owners. This change improves the position of all condo owners by putting the first six months delinquent condo fees after taxes and municipal fees but before the first mortgage. This change in the condo law also gives the association priority status for court costs and attorney's fees. However, specific notification requirements must be followed. The change also addresses new requirements for Capital Reserve funds, record keeping and financial reports.

Capital Reserves vs. Operating Reserves

Considerable confusion has evolved regarding the distinction and treatment of **Capital Reserve** and **Operating Reserve** funds that needs to be clarified.

Many condominium developers or associations established **Operating Reserve** accounts when a condominium project was first established; either new construction or apartment conversion.

This typically amounted to two to three months condo fee and gave the new condo association a fund of operating capital to work from in the early days of a condominium project when a number of unforeseen expenses might arise. Owners were also typically told they would receive this operating reserve back when they sold.

Many, if not most, condo associations eliminated this separate operating reserve account and transferred those operating reserve balances into their normal association operating account after the condo project was fully sold out and the association had been in control for a period of time. The developer who told the unit buyer they would receive their operating reserve funds back when they sold had now moved on and the association was in control.

The next development involved the separate concept of a "**Capital Reserve**" account. Many condo associations decided that funding capital improvements, such as resurfacing the parking lot or redecorating the lobby, should not come out of the normal operating account or by means of a special assessment. That would make the current owner responsible for the total cost even if they have just purchased. Therefore; a separate Capital Reserve account was established for this purpose.

A capital reserve account was established and each month a certain amount added to the monthly condo fee would be collected for future condo improvements. This would be an owner's share of using these common facilities and would not be returned to the owner when the unit was sold. Capital reserve accounts frequently amount to $1,000 to $2,000 per unit and more.

The confusion arises when purchase and sale language refers to "Reserve Account" without distinguishing between "Operating Reserves" or "Capital Reserves".

You then have the scenario where at a closing:

A) The seller wants his two months operating reserve returned by the buyer as the developer promised - but the developer is gone and the buyer didn't realize he would be asked to pay this or,

B) The "Reserve Account" referred to in the purchase and sale agreement is not clarified. The seller intended to give the "Operating Reserve" he paid of two months condo fee at $125.00 per month or $250.00 to the buyer but, the Condo Association reports the only reserve account they maintain is a "Capital Reserve" account and the unit's share is now $1800. That is what the buyer expects to receive.

You do not want to be in the position of defending against the charge that as a real estate professional you "knew or should have known" the status of the reserve accounts and therefore should be held accountable.

Therefore what can be done to clarify this reserve situation?

When listing a condominium, determine with the seller and the condominium association or condo management company the status of any "Operating Reserve" or "Capital Reserves". Next determine if the seller expects this reserve to be paid to the seller by the buyer at closing. See that this information is specified by category and dollar amount on the listing, the offer, and the purchase and sale agreement.

You also have to make sure all parties are aware of the reserve situation including seller, buyers, attorneys and other real estate brokers or sales associates.

Even if a purchase and sale agreement is clear about the treatment of a reserve, if the seller or buyer were not, you can have a dissatisfied customer or client who doesn't feel properly treated.

Cooperatives

The cooperative form of ownership has similarities to condominium ownership. However, there are some decided differences

The cooperative buyers do not receive a deed to this unit as a condominium buyer does. Rather, a cooperative is formed by creating one ownership entity (usually a corporation) which buys the total building and finances the entire complex with one mortgage at a bank or other lending institution. Once the total cooperative is thus formed and financed, the individual unit owner buys shares in the corporation and in return receives a proprietary lease for his unit good for the life of the corporation. The cooperative is financed as one package and also is taxed that way. There is one property tax assessed against the total cooperative. The taxes along with the expenses are collected from individuals through the collection of fees.

Major differences therefore, of the cooperative form of ownership compared to condominium ownership include:

1. Buyers purchase stock in the corporation.
2. Buyers receive a proprietary lease for the life of the corporation - not a fee simple deed to the unit as in a condo.
3. The Cooperative Corporation secures one mortgage for the total complex compared to condominium owners who each finance their own unit separately.
4. The cooperative is taxed as one entity for the total complex, while each condominium unit is taxed separately and such taxes are collected separately.

One risk to the cooperative form is that the individual unit owner is dependent on the other unit owners for payment of mortgage and taxes. In the condominium form, the unit owner pays the bank and the city or town directly for his unit and is relatively free from the action of other unit owners.

In a cooperative, however, these bank and tax payments are made by the cooperative as a total entity. Therefore, if sufficient cooperative owners do not make their payments to the cooperative in a timely manner, the cooperative could be unable to make the mortgage payment or tax payment and all cooperative owners would be adversely affected, including those owners who had made payments properly to the cooperative.

One other area of difference is that the sale of a unit owner's shares in the cooperative to another party is usually subject to the approval of the corporation Board of Directors. This limits the right of disposition of stock by the shareholder or unit owner.

Cooperatives are not as common in Massachusetts as in other states, but they do exist and the real estate broker and salesperson should be familiar with some of the fundamental concepts involved in cooperative ownership.

Time Sharing

The time sharing form of ownership is primarily found in vacation properties. The time share property is divided into weeks throughout the year, and the buyer purchases one or more weeks. The buyer then has the right to use that property for that week each year. Those rights can be obtained by deed and transferred by deed or by lease. If a buyer wishes to vacation on Cape Cod each year for two weeks in the summer, he could buy weeks 26 and 27 of a time share. He would use the unit during those weeks and would share his unit with the owners of other weeks throughout the year. Taxes and expenses are calculated by the time share management association and collected from each time share owner.

In this manner, a buyer who could not afford to buy vacation property in a conventional manner can afford one or more weeks of vacation ownership through the time share form of ownership.

There are usually fees assessed to the time share owner by the time share management association for cleaning and maintenance between weekly occupancy. The management association will also replace furnishings periodically (most time share units come fully furnished) and these expenses are distributed to all weekly owners.

Another service that is available to time share owners is an exchange organization. For a fee, a time share owner can exchange his week or weeks for a given year for a comparable week or weeks in most any other location. These exchange opportunities are so extensive now that you could select a different location each year and vacation in most locations around the world. The prices of time share weeks will obviously vary with the area and the time of year. A week on Cape Cod in January is not like a week on Cape Cod in July; therefore, the market value will vary considerably. Conversely, a January week in ski country might be more valuable that one in July.

Time share brokerage tends to be a specialty form of brokerage and the real estate broker or salesman in more conventional brokerage fields might not encounter time share property. However, it is a benefit for the real estate student to be aware of some of the terms and fundamental concepts involved in this form of ownership.

Glossary Quiz

1) The part of the condo budget that the unit owner is responsible for.

_____

2) Statement from Condominium Owners' Association stating outstanding fees or other charges due from an individual unit owner.

_____

3) Deed recorded to show transfer of an individual condominium apartment/office from one individual to another.

_____

4) Ratio of unit square footage to total of all unit square footage.

_____

5) Deed recorded when condominium is formed.

_____

6) Everything in a condominium that is not individually owned as a unit.

_____

7) Buyer takes title to one or more weeks of ownership each year.

_____

8) Annual forecast of monies necessary to manage the Condominium Common Expenses

_____

9) Condominium concept applied to boats.

_____

10) Number of square feet of space within an individual condo unit.

_____

Self-Quiz A

1) When a condominium is first created, the following documents are recorded at the Registry of Deeds:
   A) Cooperative Schedule of Stockholders
   B) Unit Deed conveying ownership from one owner to another
   C) 6(d) Certificate
   D) Master Deed including a set of floor plans

2) Which of the following does not have to be included in the Master Deed of a Condominium?
   A) Description of Common Areas
   B) Unit designation including square footage
   C) Manner of collecting condo fees
   D) Set of floor plans

3) Which of the following is contained in the Condominium Bylaws?
   A) Method of providing for necessary maintenance
   B) Land description of the condominium
   C) Method of amending the Master Deed
   D) Schedule of unit owners

4) Ownership in a cooperative provides the owner with which of the following:
   A) Master Deed
   B) Stock in the corporation
   C) Time Share Deed
   D) Unit Deed

5) Which of the following would not be considered a part of the condominium Common Areas?
   A) Parking lot
   B) Elevator
   C) Roof
   D) Unit 2A

6) In the event of a Condominium conversion, which of the following statements is true?
   A) An elderly tenant must be given one year to vacate
   B) Conversion requirements do not apply to Cooperatives
   C) Tenants have 90 days to decide to purchase when a building is being converted to Condominiums
   D) Tenants pay for their own moving expenses if they elect to relocate and not purchase their units

7) Harry bought two weeks' ownership of a unit. He bought:
   A) A Condominium
   B) A Time Share
   C) A Cooperative
   D) An Apartment

8) Mary has use of her apartment by buying stock in a corporation.
This is a :
A) Condominium
B) Time Share
C) Cooperative
D) Unit deed

9) In dealing with handicapped tenants when converting to condominiums, an owner must:
A) Give 30-day notice to vacate
B) Pay moving expenses up to $1000
C) Retain as tenant indefinitely if tenant chooses
D) Sell to tenant at a reduced price

10) The arrangement for condo parking violations and fine collection is found in which of the following:
A) Rules and Regulations
B) Bylaws
C) Master Deed
D) Unit Deed

Self-Quiz B

1) When the transfer of a condominium unit ownership takes place, which of the following does not have to be present:
A) Unit Deed
B) Master Insurance Policy update
C) 6(d) Certificate
D) Master Deed

2) Condominium bylaws contain
A) Land Description of Property
B) Method for collecting Condo Fee
C) Master Deed Book and Page Number
D) Set of floor plans

3) Condominium Master Deed contains all of the following, except:
A) Set of Floor Plans
B) Unit Designation of Each Unit
C) Method for Amending the Master Deed
D) Method for Replacing Common Area Items

4) In a condominium conversion project, which of the following is true:
A) Existing Tenants have 90 Days to Vacate
B) Elderly Tenants have One year to Vacate
C) Elderly and Handicapped Tenants have 2 years to Vacate with an extension possible
D) All tenants have One Year to Vacate

5) A Unit Deed conveys:
   A) Common Areas
   B) Proprietary Lease
   C) Stock in corporation
   D) Separate Unit to Grantee

6) Condominium Common Items do not include
   A) Unit Appliances
   B) Pool Equipment
   C) Lobby Furniture
   D) Laundry Room Equipment

7) An owner of a cooperative
   A) Owns His Unit in Fee Simple
   B) Owns a Share in the Corporation
   C) Owns a Percentage of the Common Areas
   D) Mortgages his Unit with a Bank or Mortgage Company

8) The condominium fee is usually calculated by:
   A) Multiplying the Percent of Common interest times the projected budget
   B) Dividing the projected budget by the number of units
   C) Adding the monthly mortgage payment to the unit taxes
   D) Adding the unit monthly principal, interest and taxes

9) Having a Fee Simple Interest in a parcel of property for the same two weeks each year, would be most indicative of which of the following:
   A) Tenancy from Period to Period
   B) Time Share Unit
   C) Condominium
   D) Cooperative

10) Given a projected annual budget of $30,000 and a condo Unit of 1,000 sq. ft. in a 10 Unit Building with five 1,000 sq. ft. units and five 2,000 sq. ft. units, what is the subject units quarterly condo fee?
   A) $3,000
   B) $500
   C) $2,000
   D) $1,000

Answer Key

	Glossary Quiz	Self Quiz A	Self Quiz B
1)	Condo Fee	D	D
2)	6(d) Certificate	C	B
3)	Unit Deed	A	D
4)	Percent of Common Ownership	B	C
5)	Master Deed	D	D
6)	Common Area	C	A
7)	Time Share	B	B
8)	Condo Budget	C	A
9)	Dockominium	B	B
10)	Condo - Square Footage	A	B

4 Leases

The following terms and concepts will be covered in this chapter. They will also be found in the glossary at the back of the text.

Terms and Concepts

Actual Eviction	Net Lease
Assignment	Non-freehold Estate
Constructive Eviction	Option
Demise	Percentage Lease
Descent	Periodic Tenancy
Devise	Rent
Escalated Lease	Right of Possession
Estate for Term	Reversionary Rights
First Right of Refusal	Sale and Leaseback
Flat Lease	Sandwich Lease
Freehold Estate	Security Deposit
Graduated lease	Step-Up Lease
Gross Lease	Straight Lease
Ground Lease	Sublet Lease
Hold Over Tenancy	Tenancy
Index Lease	Tenancy from Period to Period
Lease	Tenancy at Sufferance
Lease Option	Tenancy at Will
Lease Purchase	Tenancy for Years
Leased Fee Estate	Tenant
Lessee	Term
Lessor	Triple Net Lease
	Waste

Freehold vs. Non-Freehold Estates

In Chapter 2 we discussed **Freehold Estates** as those estates that last for an indefinite period of time (i.e. more than a lifetime). For example, the property owner who holds a fee simple title to his property has a freehold estate.

This chapter will deal with **Non-Freehold Estates.** These estates are of limited duration (less than a lifetime) and include the landlord-tenant relationships that the real estate professional must be familiar with in renting residential or commercial property.

Leasehold (Non-Freehold) Estates

In a leasehold (non-freehold) estate the property owner keeps most of the rights to his property but conveys the **Right of Possession** (right to occupy) to the tenant. This right of possession is conveyed to the tenant in a contract known as a **Lease** in return for consideration known as **Rent**. The property owner (landlord) is the **Lessor** and the tenant is the **Lessee**. The duration of the lease is the **Term**. The property is said to be **Leased** or **Demised**.

The tenant's rights revert back to the landlord at the termination of the lease. The landlord has **Reversionary Rights** and a **Leased Fee Estate.**

In the transfer of a non-freehold estate the title to the property remains with the owner. He is not transferring title to his real property to the tenant. Therefore, the law views the transfer of the non-freehold estate as personal property as opposed to real property. (**A lease is personal property**)

Types of Leasehold Estates

There are four major types of non-freehold estates with which we should be familiar (these are also known as leasehold estates or tenancies):

1) **Estate/tenancy for years**
2) **Estate/tenancy from period to period**
3) **Estate/tenancy at will**
4) **Estate/tenancy at sufferance**

Note: Either term, **Estate** or **Tenancy,** may be used, thus an estate for years is the same as tenancy for years.

Estate/Tenancy for Years

This form of tenancy is for a specific or definite term and has a specific or definite end date. (also referred to as an "**Estate for Term**") Although tenancy for years usually covers a term of more than one year, it can be for less than a year. The critical feature is that it have a specific end date.

Example: A ten-year lease for a department store beginning January, 1996 and ending December 31, 2005.

Example: An apartment lease beginning September 1, 1996 and ending May 30, 1997.

No notice is required to terminate the lease. It terminates at the end of its term. Extension of the lease requires a new negotiation.

Estate/Tenancy from Period to Period

This form of tenancy has no specific end date (**Periodic Tenancy**). The period may be any time period but is usually month-to-month or year-to-year. The tenancy is for a month or a year, depending on the period agreed to, and either party may end the tenancy at the end of the period. If neither party ends the tenancy, it continues for another period (month or year). The tenancy may continue in this manner indefinitely.

Example: Mr. and Mrs. Jones lease a five-room apartment for one year. The lease has a clause in it stating that if neither party notifies the other by sixty days prior to the end of the lease that they wish to end the lease at the end of the year, it automatically is renewed for one more year. The same provision would apply at the end of the second year and each year there after until either landlord or tenant takes action to end the tenancy. When a tenant with a tenancy for years stays beyond the tenancy end date, a **Holdover Tenancy** is created and the tenancy for years becomes a tenancy or estate from period to period.

Estate/Tenancy at Will

Either party may end the tenancy at any time by giving proper notification to the other party. There is no specific duration. Either party must give the other notice equal to the time between rent payments. That notice must be given prior to the first day of the rent period. In Massachusetts the minimum notice that can be given by either party is one month.

Example: John rents an apartment on a tenant-at-will basis with rent payable monthly on the first day of each month. If he wishes to leave on the last day of April, he must give one month's notice as of March 31. If he waits until April 2 to give his notice, he is legally obligated for one more month.

Estate/Tenancy at Sufferance

If a tenant remains after the term of his lease has expired or after he has received proper notice to vacate, the tenant is a **Tenant at Sufferance.** The landlord should be careful to take the proper legal steps in dealing with a tenant by sufferance.

The law recognizes an oral lease agreement but only as a tenant-at-will agreement. Therefore, if the parties wish the lease to have more force than a tenant-at-will agreement, the lease should be in writing. Remember that a tenant-at-will agreement can be terminated by either party at any time by giving the other party proper notification.

Types of Leases

There are various types of lease arrangements between landlord and tenant as to payment of rent. Some of the more common types are:

1) **Gross Lease**
2) **Net Lease**
3) **Percentage Lease**
4) **Graduated Lease.**

Gross Lease

In a **Gross Lease** (also known as a **Flat** or **Straight Lease**) the tenant pays the landlord a specified rent and the landlord is responsible for paying all expenses.

Example: Jones, as tenant, leases a 1,000 square-foot office for $18.00 per square foot per year, or $18,000 per year. Out of that $18,000 received by Smith (the landlord), he must pay the property taxes and other expenses. Jones's only obligation is to pay the agreed-upon rent.

A gross lease where rent changes as the lessor's taxes or operating costs change is known as an **Escalated Lease**.

Net Lease

With the **Net Lease** the tenant is required to pay for some or all other expenses in addition to the rental fee. Some of these expenses might include but are not limited to utilities, insurance, maintenance and taxes.

It is important that all parties to the lease agreement understand what they will be responsible for paying and the items should be clearly indicated. The key factor to remember when the term "net lease" is used, is that payments in addition to the rent will be required.

Example: Jones, as tenant, agrees to lease a 1,000-square-foot office on a net lease that calls for Jones, the tenant, to pay all taxes, fire insurance, heat, light and telephone, plus pay Smith, the lessor, $5.00 per square foot per year or $5,000 per year.

A major difference is that any increase in taxes or other expenses are paid by the landlord (lessor) in a Gross Lease, while they are paid by the tenant (lessee) in a Net Lease.

A lease where the tenant pays all expenses in addition to a periodic rent (i.e. taxes, insurance, utilities) is known, as a net, net, net or **Triple Net Lease**. This is a very common form of lease in commercial leases. (A tenancy is offered at $20.00 per sq. ft. per year-triple net - the tenant pays for taxes, insurance, utilities. All increases are the tenant's responsibility - not the landlord's).

Percentage Lease

The **Percentage Lease** calls for the rent to be calculated as a certain percent of the gross sales of the tenant. Sometimes there is a combination of a fixed rent plus a percentage of sales. This then causes the rent payment to go up as sales go up.

A gross lease or a net lease may be structured as a percentage lease. In a percentage lease the landlord assumes some of the risk of the tenants business success. If the tenants business increases, the rent increases.

Graduated Lease

A **Graduated Lease** (also known as a **Step-up Lease**) specifies an increasing rent over the term of the lease. This is often done to allow a tenant a lower rent at the beginning of a lease when a business is first getting established.

EXAMPLE: A three-year lease with a per-square-foot rental of
Year 1 = $ 6.00 per square foot per year
Year 2 = $10.00 per square foot per year
Year 3 = $14.00 per square foot per year

Additional Types of Leases - In addition to the above more commonly used forms of lease, there are some other forms that are less used but we should be aware of them.

Index Lease- Rent increases or decreases periodically based on some index agreed to in advance by the lessor and the lessee (i.e. Consumer Price Index).

Ground Lease- Lessor leases land to the lessee and the lessee improves the land (i.e. Constructs a building). Due to the nature of the lease and the lessee investment, Ground Leases are commonly net leases (tenant pays taxes, insurance and expenses) and long term (50 to 99 years, plus options).

Lease Purchase- A lessor and lessee enter into an agreement to rent for a period of time, then the lessor will transfer ownership to the lessee. This is often used when the tenant does not have the down payment necessary to obtain financing. This form of lease purchase may also be structured as a lease with an option to buy; not a contractual obligation to buy.

Sandwich Lease-When a lessee in a conventional lessor - lessee relationship leases the subject property to a new tenant, the lessee becomes the sublessor, the new tenant becomes the sublessee. The new lease agreement becomes a "**Sandwich Lease**" between the property owner and the new tenant.

Sale and Lease Back- Often used as a financial strategy by a property owner to sell to an investor and then lease the same property back on a rental or leasehold arrangement. The result is to convert an existing asset to cash while maintaining control over the original property. There also may be some tax advantages to this arrangement.

Obligations of the Lessor and Lessee

According to the laws of contracts, when two parties enter into an agreement, they are expected to fulfill their part of the contract. When dealing with leased or rented premises, we are also bound by other concerns which, although not spelled out in the lease, are expected.

The penalty is quite severe for landlords who willfully withhold services that were agreed upon in a lease agreement. A person can be fined up to $300 or jailed up to six months for withholding heat, electricity, water, hot water, or janitorial services, etc., as the lease provided. In addition, a person who violates the tenant's rights to utilities or quiet enjoyment of the premises pursuant to Massachusetts General Law, Chapter 186, Section 14, shall also be liable for actual and consequential damages or three months' rent, whichever is greater, and the costs of the action, including reasonable attorney's fees. Since the tenant, who along with possession of the premises is entitled to "quiet enjoyment," the law provides the same punishment for a landlord who violates this right. A landlord may not enter a tenant's apartment (this would include an employee of the landlord) without permission and proper notification. In addition, the landlord is expected to provide a safe, and habitable apartment free and clear of any state or local sanitary or building code violations.

The tenant, on the other hand, is paying to have all these rights in the lessor's property and, therefore, a lessee's major responsibility is to insure timely payment of the rental fee. Beyond this obligation, the lessor has every right to expect the tenant to take care of the property - not in the sense that a tenant would be required to paint the house, but so as not to commit **Waste**. Waste is a willful act that would hurt or change the structure of the premises. As an example, a tenant could not remove a wall between the kitchen and dining room to obtain more space.

A tenant who does not live up to his lease obligations may be sued for damages or **Actual Eviction**. A landlord who does not live up to his lease obligations to maintain the property in habitable conditions may be sued for **Constructive Eviction**. The tenant may abandon the premises and refuse to pay rent until the premises are habitable.

One other area that is a cause for concern is the **Security Deposit**. A landlord may require an amount of not more than one month's rent to be held as security. The landlord must pay the tenant 5% interest or the same interest that the bank is currently paying on the deposit, whichever is less and it is paid annually. Payment must be made within 30 days of the anniversary date or if the tenancy is terminated before that time, all accrued interest must be paid within 30 days. The security deposit, which must be held in an escrow account in a Massachusetts bank, cannot be co-mingled with other funds of the landlord. The landlord must notify the tenant of the name, address and account number of the bank in which the monies are held and is required to return the deposit within 30 days of termination minus any documented amounts for repairs (landlord must have proof of the condition of the premises at the beginning of the tenancy and repairs cannot include anything attributed to normal wear and tear). If a **last month's** rent is held, 5% interest or bank interest is to be paid on this amount also, but does not need to be held in escrow and is different and separate from the security deposit.

One exemption to note relative to security deposit requirements under the law is **vacation rentals** of **100 days** or less. The landlord may have more than the thirty day maximum to return the security deposit. The amount of time to return the deposit is negotiable but must be reasonable. As an example; a landlord might use sixty days to return the deposit which would not be considered unreasonable since this would be time for the phone or other bills to come in for the rental period.

In addition to the security deposit and last months rent a landlord may also require a reasonable **key and lock** deposit.

Options

Very often a lease agreement contains a provision that allows the lessee (tenant) to extend the lease at the end of the term. The lessee is not bound to do this, but he has the right to extend, and if he chooses to exercise this right, the lessor (landlord) must comply. The lessee would possess an option to renew or extend his lease.

Options are basically agreements between two parties that give one party the right to do something in the future. If one party exercises his option, the second party is bound. The critical point is that one party may or may not exercise the option, but whatever his decision, the second party must comply.

Another type of option used in this area is the option to buy. A person may pay for an option to buy a piece of property at a certain price and terms within a specified time period. If the optionee also leases the property during the option time period, this would be termed a **Lease-Option**. Terms of a lease-option are negotiable and may or may not include part of the monthly payment to be credited towards the purchase price.

In any case, there must be some form of consideration to have a binding option and in the eyes of the law an option (just as a lease) is considered personal property and unless otherwise stated in the agreement may be sold.

An option must also state a price and/or terms of the sale and have a specified time limit. If any or all of these parts are missing what you have is an agreement somewhat closer to a **First Right of Refusal**. In this situation the seller would obtain a bona fide offer on the property and then give to the current lessee first chance to purchase the property at that price.

Assignment Versus Sublease

Unless otherwise stated in a lease, the tenant has control over the leased premises and can sell the interest he owns to a third party. In an assignment the lessee does not retain any reversionary interest in the premises. While in a sublet the lessee does retain some interest in the property, whether it be part of the premises or a portion of the term of the lease.

To be classified as an **Assignment**, the lessee would sell the balance of the term of the lease to a third party. For example, if you rented an apartment for one year and after six months your company transferred you, the obligation of the lease still exists. Allowing someone else to take over the premises and the responsibility of paying the rent for the remaining six months would be an assignment.

In the case of a **Sublease**, the lessee sells a part of the lease term or the use of part of the premises. To illustrate, using the example from the last paragraph let's assume you are transferred for only three months. If you negotiate with someone else to take occupancy and responsibility for the rent just for the three months that you are gone and you take the apartment back for the remainder of the lease period upon your return, this would be a sublet.

Sale of Property and Leases

When property is sold, the new owner is bound by any lease agreements that exist. Therefore, if you are involved in the sale of rental property, you should determine whether or not leases exist between the owner and tenants and make certain that the buyer is aware that he will be bound by those leases. It is advisable to make reference to the leases in the purchase and sales agreement so that there is a written agreement that the leases exist and that the buyer understands he must honor those agreements when he takes title to the property. A lease for more than seven years is valid against the lessor only if it is recorded at the Registry of Deeds. This would include, for example, a lease for four years with an option to renew for four more years.

Ninety-Nine-Year Lease

In order for a lease to have more binding force than a tenant at will, it must be in writing. A lease also must be specific about when it begins and when it ends. When an extremely long-term arrangement is desired, parties sometimes satisfy the requirement to be specific as to the end date by writing the lease for 99 years. However, there is one additional consideration. Massachusetts considers a lease of more than 100 years to have the effect of an estate in fee simple as to matters concerning devise and descent as long as there are at least fifty years remaining. To avoid this situation, many leases are written for ninety-nine years to gain the maximum length of time without crossing the 100 year limit.

Other Considerations

All states have different laws pertaining to the upkeep and requirements relative to sale and rental of property. It is important for professionals to become familiar with these regulations to protect not only themselves but their clients.

As an example, in Massachusetts there are very detailed requirements in the areas of lead paint, discrimination and smoke detectors when renting or selling real estate. For detailed treatment of these and other fair housing and consumer protection issues, please refer to Chapter 10 Consumer Protection and Chapter 11 Fair Housing.

In addition, it would also be advisable to review the actual state and local laws and obtain advice from legal counsel.

Property Management

Many real estate companies have a property management division within their organization dealing with this one specialized area. Although there are a lot of people who manage their own income property, we find individuals, investors, condominium organizations, and other groups that would prefer to leave this task to a professional.

Property managers enter into a contract with the owner of a piece of property which creates an agency relationship and a fiduciary responsibility. Payment for services can be a percent of the gross income, a fee, or a combination.

Duties of the manager in general are to generate income and to take care of the property. To do this though, there are many varied tasks the agent may be required to perform under the terms of the contract. Some of these responsibilities are:

1. Advertise, screen and select tenants, collect rents
2. Pay the expenses incurred on the property
3. Evictions
4. Maintenance and repairs
5. Account for funds and necessary reports

A good property manager will always be in demand. It is important to the owners of these large investments to be able to find someone who can be trusted.

Glossary Quiz

1) An estate of indefinite duration (more than a lifetime) _____

2) A lease where the tenant agrees to pay the expenses on the leased property, plus a fixed amount to the lessor _____

3) A contract for the rental of real property _____

4) The party to whom real property is rented (tenant) _____

5) Right of one party to do or not to do something at a future date _____

6)   Duration or length of time of a lease   _____

7)   A lease where the amount of rent increases over the
         term of the lease   _____

8)   The owner of property being rented (landlord)   _____

9)   Lease where the tenant pays a fixed amount of rent and
the landlord pays all expenses)   _____

10)   Lease where the amount of rent is a percentage of sales
for that period   _____

Self-Quiz A

1)   A tenant who remains after the end of his lease is considered
         A)   Tenant at will
         B)   Tenant at sufferance
         C)   Tenant by the entirety
         D)   Tenant from month to month

2)   A summer rental agreement for the period July 1, 1995 to August
30, 1995 would be considered which of the following forms of
tenancy?
         A)   Tenancy for years
         B)   Tenancy at will
         C)   Tenancy from period to period
         D)   Tenancy at sufferance

3)   Which of the following statement is true?
         A)   A non-freehold estate conveys title
         B)   A fee simple estate is considered a non-freehold estate
         C)   A non-freehold estate is considered personal property
         D)   A tenant at will agreement is a freehold estate

4)   Under which form of lease is the landlord's income received most
likely to remain constant?
         A)   Net lease
         B)   Gross lease
         C)   Percentage lease
         D)   Graduated lease

5)   Which of the following does not refer to a lessor-lessee relationship?
         A)   Tenancy at will
         B)   Tenancy at sufferance
         C)   Tenancy from month to month
         D)   Tenancy in common

6)   Tenant B takes over the balance of Tenant A's lease with the landlord's permission. Which of the following is true?

    A)   Tenant A has sublet the property
    B)   Tenant A and B are tenants in common
    C)   Tenant A has assigned the lease to Tenant B
    D)   Tenant B is a tenant at sufferance

7)   Following the sale of leased property, the lease

    A)   Is null and void
    B)   Must be renegotiated
    C)   Is binding if under 7 years' duration and unrecorded
    D)   Is binding on all parties if more than 7 years' duration and unrecorded

8)   The type of business where the rent would be the largest percent of total expense is:

    A)   Parking lot
    B)   Supermarket
    C)   Restaurant
    D)   Discount store with a net lease

9)   A contract that conveys right of possession but not title is:

    A)   Deed
    B)   Purchase and Sale Agreement
    C)   Listing Agreement
    D)   Lease

10)   Tenant A sublets to Tenant B, Tenant B becomes:

    A)   Assignee
    B)   Lessor
    C)   Sub-Lessee
    D)   Tenant in Common

Self-Quiz B

1)   A tenancy for years is

    A)   Real Property
    B)   Personal Property
    C)   Neither Real nor Personal Property
    D)   Either Real or Personal Property

2)   A tenant paying monthly rent plus utilities would have a

    A)   Gross Lease
    B)   Percentage Lease
    C)   Net Lease
    D)   Tenancy at Will

3)   A lease where the lessor would be least affected by a tax increase would have:

    A)   Net Lease
    B)   Percentage Lease
    C)   Graduated Lease
    D)   Gross Lease

4) The lessee with the least rights is:
   A) Tenant at Sufferance
   B) Tenant at Will
   C) Tenant in Common
   D) Gross Tenant

5) When rental property is sold, which of the following is true?
   A) The leases must be renegotiated with the new owner
   B) The grantee must honor the leases
   C) The leases become void
   D) The tenants become tenants at will

6) A restaurant owner wishes to rent land and build at his expense.
   He would use:
   A) A Lease with an Option
   B) A Long-term Lease
   C) A Leaseback Agreement
   D) A Ground Lease

7) A tenant renting a room would most likely have which form of lease:
   A) Gross Lease
   B) Net Lease
   C) Graduated Lease
   D) Percentage Lease

8) Annual rent will most likely increase under:
   A) Gross Lease
   B) Net Lease
   C) Graduated Lease
   D) Percentage Lease

9) If a tenant rents a room in his apartment to a friend, which of the following
   is true:
   A) He is assigning tenancy rights
   B) He is subletting tenancy rights
   C) He is creating a Tenancy at Sufferance
   D) He is voiding his lease

10) If the intent of a lease is to vary rent up or down with gross sales of a
    business we would use:
    A) Gross Lease
    B) Next Lease
    C) Percentage Lease
    D) Graduated Lease

Answer Key

Glossary Quiz		Self Quiz A	Self Quiz B
1)	Freehold Estate	B	B
2)	Net lease	A	C
3)	Lease	C	A
4)	Lessee	A	A
5)	Option	D	B
6)	Term	C	D
7)	Graduated lease	C	A
8)	Lessor	A	C
9)	Gross, flat, or straight	D	B
10)	Percentage lease	C	C

5 Contracts / Purchase and Sale Agreement

The following terms and concepts will be covered in this chapter. They will also be found in the glossary at the back of the text.

Acceptance	Laches
Assignee	Legal Title
Assignment	Legality
Assignor	Liquidated Damages
Bilateral Contract	Listing Agreement
Bill of Sale	Mortgage Deed
Caveat Emptor	Mortgage Note
Competency	Novation
Consent	Offer
Conservertorship	Offeree
Consideration	Offeror
Counteroffer	Option
Deed	Power of Attorney
Deposit	Purchase and Sale Agreement
Disclosure	Specific Performance
Earnest Money	Statute of Frauds
Equitable Title	Statute of Limitations
Estoppel	Suit for Damages
Executed Contract	Unilateral Contract
Executory Contract	Valid
Expressed Contract	Void
First Right of Refusal	Voidable
Implied Contract	
Lease	

Contracts

In general terms, a contract is merely an agreement between two parties to do something. Legal action can be taken if one of the parties does not fulfill the terms of the agreement. The real estate practitioner deals day to day with a variety of contracts. Some of the standard types of contracts you will encounter in the real estate profession include:

Listing Agreement
A contract between a seller and a real estate firm to sell property.

Buyer Agency Agreement
A contract between a buyer and a real estate firm to assist the buyer in purchasing property.

Purchase and Sale Agreement
A contract between a buyer and a seller to purchase a piece of property for some consideration.

Lease
A contract between a landlord and a tenant agreeing to rent property for a specified amount of money and time.

Deed
A contract between grantor and grantee conveying title to property for some consideration (sometimes referred to as a title deed).

Mortgage Note and Mortgage Deed
When financing is created for the purpose of purchasing realty, a lending institution will require the execution of these two instruments. The mortgage note is a promissory note to pay and the mortgage deed is a contract that transfers interest in the real estate to the bank subject to the mortgagor repaying the loan.

Option
An agreement between two parties where one party has the right to do or not to do something within a specified time. (Typically includes a set price and other terms)

First Right of Refusal (or Right of First Refusal)
Similar to an option except a price is usually not specified. An example would be a tenant who has a first right of refusal to match any accepted offer if the landlord sells the property.

General Contract Classifications

There are several general classifications that apply to contracts.

Expressed vs. Implied

An **Expressed Contract** is a contract where the agreement between the parties is specific and usually in writing. A verbal contract can be expressed if the agreement is detailed in words. A verbal expressed contract is very difficult to prove and therefore to enforce. In Massachusetts the statute of frauds requires that a contract for the sale of real estate (purchase and sale agreement) be in writing, and cannot be verbal.

An **Implied contract** is a contract where the agreement of the parties is determined by their actions without the specific wording of agreement either verbally or written.
An automobile owner who orders gasoline at a gas station has implied that he will pay the posted price even though there was no specific agreement to do so.

Bilateral vs. Unilateral

A **Bilateral Contract** is an agreement where one party agrees to do something and a second party agrees to do something else in return.

A listing agreement (either written or verbal) is a bilateral contract where the broker agrees to advertise, show the property and produce a buyer; in return the seller agrees to pay a commission.

A **Unilateral Contract** exists when one party agrees to do something if the other party does something else but the second party has not committed to do anything.

Posting a reward for finding a lost animal is a unilateral contract. If someone finds the animal and returns it the party offering the reward is bound to pay it but the party that found the animal at no time agreed to do anything.

Executed vs. Executory

An **Executed Contract** is a contract where both parties have completed everything that each agreed to perform. A purchase and sales agreement is fully executed after the property has transferred to the buyer and the seller has received full payment. Just the signing of a contract does not necessarily constitute execution.

An **Executory contract** is a contract where two parties have agreed but some things have yet to be completed. A purchase and sales agreement between the time when buyers and sellers have signed but the closing has not yet taken place is considered executory. There is a contract but not all terms have been completed.

Elements of a Contract

As a real estate professional, you will be constantly dealing with a variety of these types of contracts. Therefore, some knowledge of the basic elements of any contract is necessary.

Of the contracts listed, the purchase and sale agreement is the most important to the real estate broker and salesperson and will be dealt with in detail later in the chapter.

Any contract, whether for the purchase of property or for any other purpose, must have certain basic elements to be valid. These basic elements are described in the following paragraphs.

Offer and Acceptance

There must be a "meeting of the minds" between the two parties. Agreement on nine out of ten items is not sufficient. Agreement on all items is necessary. The party making the offer (buyer or seller) is the **offeror**; the party receiving the offer (buyer or seller) is the **offeree**. An offer and/or acceptance must be communicated to be valid and binding.

Consideration

There will be something of value exchanged for something of value. This usually takes the form of a tangible item exchanged for cash. The size of the consideration is not important. Therefore, a contract to sell a car for $5.00 is just as valid as a contract to sell a car for $2,000.00. Although the consideration is usually money, it need not be. Valid consideration may be something other than money, as in an exchange (my car for your stereo) or for a promise to do something (my T.V.

for your promise to drive me to California next summer) or a combination of a tangible item for a tangible item plus a promise to do something (my property for $50,000 cash plus a promise to pay a mortgage).

Legality

A contract must deal with an agreement within the law. An agreement between partners in an illegal gambling operation would not be valid, and therefore, neither party could seek enforcement or remedy through the courts.

Competency

Both parties must be competent to enter into a contract. Some of those who would not be considered competent would be minors (under 18), insane persons, or one who is drunk or senile. In matters of real estate, one must be careful of minors, especially as tenants in signing leases. A contract between an adult and a minor is a valid contract. That is, it has binding force. However, it is voidable at the will of the minor. The adult may not break the contract, but the minor may with some exceptions.

Another area of competency in real estate matters in senility in the elderly. If, for example, an elderly widow is selling property and there is a question of her competency, a broker would be wise to suggest that a **power of attorney** or **conservatorship** (a guardian) be established through advice of legal counsel. The power of attorney does not have to be granted exclusively to an attorney. Any relative, friend or advisor, as well as a lawyer, may be given the power of attorney to act for an individual. It is recommended that the legal power to represent be limited in purpose and duration. For example, a power of attorney may be granted by me to you to act in my behalf for ninety days for the purpose of selling my property for not less than $110,000.

Consent

The main purpose here is to establish that no duress is being applied and that all parties are acting of their own free will. The normal procedure in real estate matters is to have a notary public witness the contract and take the acknowledgment of the parties that this is their free act and deed.

Not only does consent deal with duress but other areas as well. Fraud or misrepresentation of a material fact with intent to deceive will make a contract voidable. Also, any honest mistake in the identification of the parties involved or the subject of the contract can make a contract voidable only if the mistake is mutual. (This is not to include a mistake in or the lack of knowledge relative to law.)

Unenforceable Contract

A Contract can be deemed unenforceable for the following reasons:

Statute of Limitations - a legal time limit has been established to take action to enforce a contract. The matter in question has exceeded this time limit and therefore is not actionable.

Laches - similar to statute of limitations but the time limit is not set by statute. The court determines that action was not taken to enforce the contract in a "reasonable' period of time.

Estoppel - A previous action or statement can be used to hold a party accountable even if later proved to be in error. Mortgage balance stated by a bank or water bill owed to a town would be examples. A new owner who relied on these documents could not be made accountable if they later proved to be the bank or town's error. The action by the bank or town to hold the new owner accountable in such a case could be stopped by **Estoppel**.

Termination of an Offer

Because we deal to a great extent in real estate with offers and counteroffers, we should spend some time examining when an offer exists and when it ceases to exist. An offer from either buyer or seller ceases to exist under several conditions.

Death of the Offeror

An offer extended on Tuesday afternoon cannot be accepted Wednesday morning if one of the offerors has died on Tuesday night. Upon the death of the offeror on Tuesday night, the offer ceases to exist and, therefore, is not there to be accepted by the offeree

Time Limit

It is recommended practice to make an offer good for a specified period (for example, until 6:00 p.m. on Thursday, September 28, 1996). If the offeree decides to accept on Friday, it is too late because the offer ceased to exist at 6:00 p.m. on the day before, and the offeree cannot accept something that no longer exists.

Offer Revoked Prior to Acceptance

A makes an offer to B on Monday. On Tuesday, A reviews finances and notifies B that he cannot afford the property so he is withdrawing his offer. On Wednesday, B decides to accept A's offer. No contract, because when B decided to accept, A had already withdrawn the offer and it did not exist for B to accept.

Acceptance

A extends offer to B. B accepts and we now have a contract. Because of the acceptance, the offer ceases to exist. A may not withdraw his offer because it now has become a contract by virtue of B's acceptance.

Counteroffer

A counteroffer will void any previous offers in existence. This happens quite often in real estate as two parties negotiate back and forth over price or conditions of sale. Neither party is obligated to accept the terms of a previous offer once a counteroffer has been made.

Valid -Void - Voidable

In dealing with contracts, we must distinguish among the terms that follow.

A **valid contract** is one that has binding force on the parties, as in the majority of contracts where the legal qualifications have been met.

A **void contract** is one where no binding force exists as in an agreement on an illegal partnership.

A **voidable contract** is one where binding force exists, but one party may make the contract void if he wishes. One good example is the contract between an adult and a minor. It is valid and has binding force between the two parties. However, the minor has the option of voiding the contract. The contract is valid but voidable by the minor. It is not void. (In Massachusetts the age of majority is 18)

Purchase and Sale Agreement

So far, we have been discussing elements of any contract with some examples relating to real estate issues. Now we shall look at one specific real estate contract - the purchase and sale agreement.

Of the various contracts we said we would deal with in real estate (i.e., listing, buyer agency agreement, purchase and sale, lease, deed, mortgage), the purchase and sale agreement is the one that is most significant in the real estate professional's business life.

The purchase and sale agreement must establish a "meeting of the minds" of the buyer and the seller on a very complex set of items. (Many standard forms cover thirty to thirty-five paragraphs.) It is not uncommon for the broker to draw up the purchase and sale agreement which then may be reviewed by the client's attorney.

A broker who does not develop the ability to prepare a proper purchase and sale agreement will find himself with dissatisfied clients, fines, law suits, and a large percentage of his time spent in the unproductive process of straightening out problems that should have been resolved at the outset.

There are numerous versions of the purchase and sale agreement that can be used in the real estate profession. Your local Board of REALTORS® may recommend one or the real estate office with which you associate yourself will probably have a specific version they would prefer that you use.

Whatever form is used, there are some basic elements that should be contained in any purchase and sale agreement.

Name of the parties - full legal name, including address, is recommended: Harry S. Jones and Mary L. Jones of 21 High Street, Reading, Middlesex County, Massachusetts.

Description of the land - a full legal description is recommended, or a reference to the book and page at the registry where a prior legal description may be found. Typical format is: "Property at 10 Main Street, Melrose, Middlesex County, Massachusetts, containing 10,500 square feet of land, more or less, and buildings thereon. Said property is further described at the Middlesex South Registry of Deeds in Cambridge, Massachusetts, in Book _____ Page_____ and Date _____.

Price/Consideration - the law states that there must be some form of consideration. Although this does not have to be money, that is the normal consideration: You sell your house for $185,000 cash.

Deposit - there must be some initial consideration (**earnest money**) to make the purchase and sale agreement binding. The amount of this deposit, and any subsequent deposit, should be specified in the agreement, as well as who will hold the deposit. The deposit should be sufficient to protect the seller if the buyer should fail to fulfill his agreement. Who holds the deposit is determined by the contractual agreement of the buyer and seller. Sometimes the seller or the seller's attorney holds the deposit, but most often the broker does. If the broker does hold the deposit, the law requires that he keep a separate bank account for such money. This is not his money and may not be mixed with any of his personal or other business funds. Such an account is called an **escrow account**. The escrow is usually an account opened by the agency for this purpose and is a noninterest-bearing business account. This does not preclude the parties in the contract to negotiate that a deposit be put in an interest-bearing escrow account. The interest-bearing escrow account is used quite often in today's market due to the large selling prices of homes and the length of time it takes to close. Confusion may exist as to which party is to receive the interest if nothing is stated in the contract, which makes it important to clarify this in writing in the beginning, since it is a negotiable item. In the case of a salesperson working for a broker, you are required by law to turn over any monies received for deposit or payment, to that broker for disposition.

Date - the date that the parties actually signed the agreement should be specified. The date of transfer of title to the buyer should also be clearly spelled out, including day, time, and location of the passing: "To be conveyed on or before 2:00 p.m., January 11, 1996, at the Middlesex South Registry of Deeds, Cambridge, Massachusetts."

Signatures - all parties named as buyers or sellers should sign the agreement. If, for example, husband and wife owned property jointly and the husband signed the agreement but not the wife, the wife could not be required to sign the deed. A purchase and sale agreement can only be enforced against those who signed it.

In addition to these basic elements of the purchase and sale agreement, the real estate professional should be aware that many other contingency clauses may be added. Some of these are:

1)   The seller's responsibility to convey a clear and marketable title.
2)   The right of the seller to use purchase money to clear title.
3)   The right of the buyer to obtain approval for financing.
4)   Various rights of the buyer to inspect, i.e., pests, structural, mechanical, hazardous chemicals, lead paint, etc.
5)   Disclosure by the seller to the buyer regarding details about the subject property.
6)   Miscellaneous contingencies to the contract agreed upon between the seller and buyer.

Miscellaneous Purchase and Sale Agreement Concepts

Realty Versus Personalty

A contract for the sale of real estate is a **purchase and sale agreement**. A contract for the sale of personal property is a **bill of sale**.

Agreement in Writing

A contract for the sale of real estate in Massachusetts must be in writing to be enforceable. It must be in writing to be valid. This does not have to be one document but may take the form of an exchange of correspondence. The law that requires that all real estate contracts be in writing to be enforceable is known as the **Statute of Frauds.**

Equitable Title Versus Legal Title

When a purchase and sale agreement is signed, the buyer is said to have acquired equitable title to the property because he has established rights to the property, although his legal title is not established until papers are passed and the seller gives the buyer a deed to the property.

Breach of Contract

In the event that either party does not live up to part of the purchase and sale agreement, there are several legal alternatives. Either party may take court action to force the other party to live up to the commitment (**specific performance**). Either party may take legal action to have the defaulting party pay for any expenses incurred because the contract was not honored (**suit for damages**). If it is the buyer who will not live up to part of the contract, and depending on the detailed terms of the purchase and sale agreement, the seller may retain the buyer's deposit as **liquidated damages.**

Assignment

Most contracts, unless specifically prohibited, are assignable. This means one of the parties to a contract may turn his interest over to a third party. The **assignor** does not necessarily void himself or herself of a contingent liability to fulfill the terms of the contract and an **assignee** also cannot be held liable except if so stated. The agreement between assignor and assignee that precipitates the transfer of rights under the contract is a separate arrangement.

Novation

Instead of substituting a new party to the existing contract (assignment), a whole new contract may be substituted for the original contract. This process of substituting a "new" contract is called **novation.** A bank may allow a promissory note by a new individual to replace a promissory note by an original debtor.

Caveat Emptor

The term **caveat emptor** means "let the buyer beware," and means that the seller and the seller's agent, the broker, do not have an obligation to reveal information to the buyer if the buyer does not inquire. For example, if the roof leaks and there are termites in a piece of property, under the principle of caveat emptor, if the buyer does not ask specifically about these items, the seller and broker do not have an obligation to tell him about those defects.

However, with increasing legislation, the principle of caveat emptor has given way to the concept of "full disclosure" and "consumer protection, " to a point where the broker can be held legally liable for failing to disclose known defects.

In our state this has taken the form of the **Massachusetts Consumer Protection Act**, commonly referred to simply as **Chapter 93A** (see chapter 10).

Glossary Quiz

1) The party extending an offer to another (either buyer or seller) _____

2) A remedy at law by which the court will force one to fulfill his part of a contract _____

3) A principle in law that means "let the buyer beware" _____

4) Force applied to make someone act against his will _____

5) Having legal binding force but able to be broken at the option of one of the parties _____

6) A written contract between two parties for the sale of personal property _____

7) Having legal binding force _____

8) An agreement (written or oral) between two parties to do something _____

9) Establishment of a third party to hold funds for two parties _____

10) A written contract between two parties for the sale of real property _____

Self Quiz A

1) The signing of a Purchase and Sale Agreement by all parties conveys which of the following?
    A)   Equitable title
    B)   Legal title
    C)   An executed contract
    D)   A unilateral contract

2) A Seller and Broker have signed a listing contract. Which of the following statements is true?
    A)   This is an expressed contract
    B)   This is an implied contract
    C)   This is an executed contract
    D)   This is a unilateral contract

3) An adult landlord signs a lease with a minor tenant. Which of the following statements is true?
    A)   The lease is voidable by the landlord
    B)   The lease is void.
    C)   The lease is voidable by the tenant
    D)   The lease is valid

4) An offer is signed by the offeree an hour after the offeror dies. The contract is :
    A) Valid
    B) Void
    C) Voidable
    D) Revoked

5) The offeror in a unilateral contract cannot:
    A) Sue for specific performance
    B) Reject a counter offer
    C) Revoke the offer before acceptance
    D) Impose a time limit

6) A contract between a property owner and a broker to sell the property in return for a commission is a:
    A) Purchase and Sale Agreement
    B) Mortgage
    C) Listing Agreement
    D) Deed

7) If the buyer withdraws, deposit money given to the salesperson should:
    A) Be returned to the buyer by the salesperson
    B) Be given to the broker for disposition
    C) Be given to the seller by the salesperson as damages
    D) Be retained by the salesperson until the parties agree on disposition

8) Which is not necessary for the sale of personal property?
    A) Offer and acceptance
    B) Consideration
    C) Legality
    D) Written Contract

9) An acknowledgment is taken when a contract is signed to:
    A) Prevent Caveat Emptor
    B) Convey legal title
    C) Protect against duress
    D) Transfer equitable title

10) After A's offer of $95,000 to B is rejected, B offers to sell his house to A for $97,000 B is the:
    A) Offeror
    B) Offeree
    C) Grantor
    D) Grantee

Self Quiz B

1) A Bilateral contract:
    A) May be an expressed contract
    B) Must be in writing
    C) Does not require competency
    D) Does not require consideration

2)   A buyer asks the court to order the seller to honor the Purchase
     and Sale Agreement, which would best describe the situation:
     A)   Suit for damages
     B)   Suit for specific performance
     C)   Suit to forfeit the deposit
     D)   Suit for civil enforcement

3)   Which of the following is not true for a real estate contract:
     A)   Must be in writing
     B)   Must be legal
     C)   Must have cash consideration
     D)   All parties must be competent

4)   Under an executed contract, which of the following is true:
     A)   Must be in writing
     B)   All parties have performed their duties
     C)   Contract is executed when all parties have signed
     D)   Must be notarized

5)   A lease signed by a minor tenant would best be described as:
     A)   Unilateral
     B)   Valid
     C)   Void
     D)   Voidable by the Minor

6)   A signed Purchase and Sale Agreement gives the buyer:
     A)   Legal Title
     B)   Implied Rights
     C)   Equitable Title
     D)   Voidable Rights

7)   In a $200,000 purchase of real estate with a $150,000 mortgage and a $500
     check with the offer toward a $10,000 deposit to be held in escrow until
     closing, the earnest money amount is:
     A) $200,000
     B) $50,000
     C) $10,000
     D) $500

8)   In the contract for personal property, which of the following is not
     required:
     A)   Must be in writing
     B)   Must have consideration
     C)   Must have legality
     D)   Parties must have competency

9)   When a house is listed, but not sold yet the contract is:
     A)   Implied
     B)   Executed
     C)   Executory
     D)   Unilateral

10) When a Purchase and Sale Agreement has resulted in a subsequent sale and recording of a deed, which is not true about the contract:
A) It is bilateral
B) It is expressed
C) It is executed
D) It is executory

Answer Key

Glossary Quiz		Self Quiz A	Self Quiz B
1)	Offeror	A	A
2)	Specific Performance	A	B
3)	Caveat Emptor	C	C
4)	Duress	B	B
5)	Voidable	A	D
6)	Bill of sale	C	C
7)	Valid	B	D
8)	Contract	D	A
9)	Escrow	C	C
10)	Purchase and Sale Agreement	A	D

6 Transfer of Title/Deeds

The following terms and concepts will be covered in this chapter. They will also be found in the glossary at the back of the text.

Terms And Concepts

Abstract of Title
Acceptance
Accretion
Acknowledgment
Adverse Possession
Attorney in Fact
Attorney at Law
Avulsion
Bargain and Sale Deed
Base Line
Book
Certificate of Title
Chain of Title
Codicil
Condemnation
Condemnee
Condemnor
Consideration
Contract for Deed
Covenant Against Encumbrances
Covenant of Further Assurance
Covenant of Quiet Enjoyment
Covenant of Right to Convey
Covenant of Seisen
Covenant of Warranty
Deed
Deed in Trust
Deed Restrictions
Deficiency
Delivery
Descent
Devise
Devisee
Devisor

Eminent Domain
Erosion
Escheat
Escrow Agent
Et Al
Et Ux
Excise Stamps
Executor
Executor's Deed
Executrix
Foreclosure
General Warranty Deed
Government Survey
Grantee
Grantee Index
Grantor
Habendum Clause
Installment Contract
Intestate
Involuntary Alienation
Judicial Deed
Land Contract
Land Court Certificate
Legal Description
Lis Penden
Lot and Block
Meridian
Metes & Bounds
Page
Plat
Point of Beginning (POB)
Prescription
Probate Court
Quit Claim Deed

Range Line
Range Strip
Recording
Registered Land
Registry of Deeds
Residual
Section
Sheriff's Deed
Special
Statute of
 Frauds
System
Tax Deed
Tax Stamps
Testate
Testator
Title Reference
Title Search
Torrens System
Township
Township Line
Township Strip
Transfer by Descent
Trustee
Trustee's Deed
Trustor
Vendee
Vendor
Voluntary Alienation
Warranty Deed
Will

Deeds

There are a number of ways that title (ownership) of real estate can transfer from one party to another.

The most common method is to transfer title by deed. This is especially true for those planning to enter the Real Estate Brokerage profession. We shall give the transfer by deed the most attention. However there are a number of other methods of title transfer we need to become familiar with. Title transfer may include the owner's consent (**Voluntary Alienation**), such as a **Deed**, or title transfer may take place without the owner's consent (**Involuntary Alienation**) such as **Foreclosure** by a bank for nonpayment of a mortgage. After examining the transfer by Deed we shall look at other types of transfer.

A **Deed** is a written instrument that transfers ownership of real property from one party to another.

This transfer of ownership takes place between two parties: the **Grantor**, who is transferring title or ownership to the new owners; and the **Grantee**, who is receiving the title or ownership. The grantor is said to convey title to the grantee via the deed. The **Massachusetts Statute of Frauds** requires that the deed be in writing. Although the grantor has the legal right to prepare the deed, the vast majority of deeds are prepared by attorneys.

The filing and control of deeds is the responsibility of the individual county within which the property lies. Each deed is filed or recorded at the **County Registry of Deeds** and is assigned a specific **Book and Page Number**, which are known as that parcel of property's **Title Reference**.

If a deed has a title reference of Book 8302, Page 28, then at the Registry of Deeds for that County, take Book 8302 from the shelf and turn to Page 28; Page 28 will be the subject deed.

Each time property is conveyed from one owner to another, a new deed is drawn and recorded at the Registry of Deeds in a new book and page. Therefore, a piece of property that is sold three times will have three deeds recorded three times with three title references, one for each deed recorded.

The most common form of deed used in Massachusetts is the **Quit Claim Deed**. In order to better understand the Massachusetts Quit Claim Deed we need to examine the **Warranty Deed, Special Warranty Deed and Quit Claim Deed**. Then we shall examine some of the many other forms of deeds available.

Another form of transfer, called an **Installment Contract,** is used for the sale of real property where the seller (**vendor**) enters into an agreement with the buyer (**vendee**) that allows payments for the property to be made over a period of time; sometimes over a number of years.

The buyer is allowed possession or occupancy of the property while the installment payments are being made and during that time has equitable title. When all payments have been made the buyer receives legal title through a deed from the seller. (Also known as an **Contract for Deed** or a **Land Contract**)

General Warranty Deed

A **General Warranty Deed**, (also known as a **Warranty Deed**) provides the buyer or grantee with the highest form of protection by the seller, or grantor. The grantor guarantees the title to the grantee against all claims extending back in time prior to the grantor's ownership.

The covenants (promises) made by the grantor to the grantee include:

1) **Covenant of Seisen** - Grantor warrants that they hold title and they convey it to the grantee.

2) **Covenant of Right to Convey** - Grantor warrants that they have the right to convey title to the grantee.

3) **Covenant Against Encumbrances** - Grantor warrants there are no encumbrances (including easements and liens) unless stated in the deed.

4) **Covenant of Quiet Enjoyment** - Grantor warrants that the grantee shall enjoy quiet enjoyment and will not be disturbed by a third party claim due to a defect in title (Does not protect against loud neighbors).

5) **Covenant of Further Assurance** - Grantor warrants that they will take any future action necessary to correct any title defect.

6) **Covenant of Warranty** - Grantor warrants they will defend title to the grantee against the claims of anyone (including claims arising from time prior to the grantor's ownership).

The General Warranty Deed has the greatest risk to the grantor and the greatest protection to the grantee when compared to the other forms of deed.

Special Warranty Deed

A **Special Warranty Deed** guarantees the grantee against any defects (called a cloud on the title) or claims which arose during the grantor's period of ownership and not before.

Quit Claim Deed

A **Quit Claim Deed** conveys whatever interest the grantor has in the property but makes no warranties or guarantees as to what they include.

In Massachusetts the Quit Claim Deed, which is the most frequently used form of Deed, is treated as a Special Warranty Deed. Because of the extensive title search used as well as court interpretation the grantor is required to defend title against any claim made during the grantor's term of ownership. However it is still labeled a "Quit Claim Deed".

Other Forms of Deed

There are a variety of other forms of deeds that are used for special purposes and often limit the liability of the grantor. Some examples are as follows:

Deed in Trust- A Deed in Trust is used when a grantor (**Trustor**) transfers title to set up a trust controlled by a **Trustee** for the benefit of a beneficiary.

Trustee's Deed- After a trust has been established using the Deed in Trust, if the trustee conveys title they use a Trustees Deed.

Bargain and Sale Deed- A Bargain and Sale Deed contains no expressed warrantees but implies that the grantor holds title and possession. Used in some areas for foreclosure and tax sales.

Judicial Deeds-Judicial Deeds are used by court appointed officials and are known by the activity the court has asked them to carry out and carry no warrantees.

Executor's Deed- Deed used by the executor of an estate to sell the estates property at the discretion of the court or with the court's permission.

Tax Deed- Deed used to convey property taken by the government for nonpayment of taxes.

Sheriff's Deed- Deed used when foreclosed property is sold by a sheriff by court order.

The use of other forms of deed from state to state will often be known by the purpose of the conveyor or the title of the grantor such as **Administration Deed, Guardian's Deed, Gift Deed, Commissioner's Deed** or **Referee's Deed in Foreclosure.**

Elements of a Deed

In order to be valid a deed must have the following elements:
1) Grantor (Seller)
2) Grantee (Buyer)
3) Consideration (Usually Money)
4) Granting Clause
5) Habendum Clause (Defines Ownership)
6) Limitations (Deed Restrictions)
7) Legal Description (Describes Property)
8) Signature of Grantors (Sellers Sign)
9) Delivery and Acceptance (Buyer/Grantee)
10) Acknowledgment (No Duress)
11) Recording (County Registry of Deeds)

Acknowledgment and Recording are recommended to be fully effective but not necessary for Deed to be valid. (This will be explained later)

Grantor
The **Grantor** or grantors of the deed are the owners (sellers) of the property and should all be identified. Sometimes "**et ux**" or "**et al**" will be used meaning "and wife" and "and others" respectively. The grantor must be competent.

If the grantor is a minor, as in other contracts, the deed will be **voidable**. If the grantor is mentally impaired, as in the case of alcohol or other drug influence, the deed will be **Void**. If the grantor is mentally incompetent, the deed is void and property can only be conveyed by court order.

Grantee

The **Grantee** is the buyer and must be named and identifiable for the deed to be valid. (Cannot be fictitious)

Consideration

Consideration is "Something of Value". It must be stated that some consideration was received in return for the conveyance of the property. The consideration is usually money and is stated in the deed.

However the amount does not have to be stated and does not have to be money as in:

"consideration of $1.00 and other valuable consideration"

Granting Clause

The **Granting Clause** must state that the Grantor intends to convey certain rights to the Grantee.

If less than full fee simple is being conveyed such as a life estate it should be stated here:

"Grants to John Q. Buyer for the duration of his natural life."

If there is more than one grantee, their joint interest should be stated here:

"As Tenants by the Entirety" or as "Joint Tenants"

Habendum Clause

Habendum means to "have and to hold"; follows the granting clause and re-affirms the granting clause. The Habendum Clause would be the place to state any interest other than fee simple such as condominium interest or time sharing interest.

Legal Description

There must be sufficient description to identify the property being conveyed. What actually constitutes sufficient description may take many forms. There are three types of property description commonly used:

> 1) **Metes and Bounds**
> 2) **Lot and Block**
> 3) **Government Survey**.

Metes And Bounds

This form of land description is used most often in Massachusetts. It describes land by identifying the perimeter of a lot via length of a side in feet (145'), plus location of the lot line either by compass point (N38'10") or by monument (an iron pipe or oak tree or stone wall).

Lot And Block

This type of property description refers to a map or plat that has been placed on file with the county by a developer. The plat identifies each parcel or lot within a block and assigns numbers to them. The individual deed may reference "Lot 17, Block 23" on that particular plat as legal description for the property. (See last page of chapter)

Government Survey

This form of description is used principally in the mid-western and western states. It involves a grid of north-south lines called **Range Lines** and east-west lines called **Township Lines**. Using these lines as identification, the land is then subdivided into **Townships**, **Sections**, and **Subsections**. It is useful to be aware of this type of property description for general information. But the Massachusetts real estate broker or salesperson will not be dealing with government survey descriptions.

The various types of legal description will be discussed in more detail later in the chapter.

Signature of the Grantors

All grantors named in the deed must sign the deed. The grantees must be named but do not have to sign. A grantor may give a **Power of Attorney** to someone to sign for them. The Power of Attorney must be in writing and specify that the individual is authorized to sign the deed. The Power of Attorney is usually given to a lawyer but can be given to someone who is not a lawyer such as a relative or friend. In these cases the individual is referred to as an **Attorney in Fact** as opposed to an **Attorney at Law.**

Delivery and Acceptance

The transfer of title is not complete until the deed signed by the grantors is delivered to the grantee and accepted by the grantee.

Acceptance can be actual or implied. The deed may be delivered directly to the grantee or the deed may be delivered to a representative, as to an escrow agent. Massachusetts recognizes recording at the Registry of Deeds as evidence of acceptance. A deed must be delivered while the grantee is alive. The deed may not be held until after the grantee's death and then delivered.

Acknowledgment

Acknowledgment of the deed by a Notary Public is required in Massachusetts for a deed to be recorded. A deed does not have to be acknowledged to be valid. Acknowledgment involves affirmation that the grantor is known to the one taking the acknowledgment and requires a statement that the signing of the deed by the grantor is their free act and deed and is not being signed under any force or duress.

"Do you John Q. Seller acknowledge that this is your free act and deed" Anything less than an unqualified "Yes " to this question can stop the entire transfer of title.

Recording the Deed

In order to provide protection against claims and disputes over ownership, the deed should be recorded at the County Registry of Deeds where it will be placed on file and be assigned a book and page number. In order to record a deed, the signature of at least one of the grantors must be acknowledged before a notary public or justice of the peace. Although the law does not require it, it is good practice to have the signatures of all grantors acknowledged. The acknowledgment is merely a statement by the grantor that this is their free act and deed and not made under any duress or outside pressure.

A deed is said to be valid when signed and delivered, but to be fully effective it must be recorded, which requires acknowledgment.

The importance of recording a deed should not be underestimated. A recorded deed takes precedence over an unrecorded deed. This allows someone doing a title search to be able to rely on the chain of title as reflected at the registry of deeds. It also prevents the possibility of an unrecorded deed appearing at a future date and casting a cloud on the title.

As an example, let's assume "A" transfers a piece of land to "B". "B" does not record the deed. Later, "A" dies and wills all of his or her estate to "C". The will acts as a deed and transfers all the property "A" owns to "C". "C" promptly records this. "C" now has legal title to property and "B" cannot make a future claim.

Torrens System

Massachusetts has developed a court system of settling land disputes called the **Torrens System**. If a dispute or question arises concerning title to a piece of property, the issue is taken to a land court where evidence is examined and the court issues a ruling that "A" now holds clear title. A **Certificate of Title** is issued as documentation that this is now a good and clear title. No prior claim may be raised after the Certificate of Title is issued. This is now referred to as **Registered Land** and the certificate is also referred to as a **Land Court Certificate.**

This certificate must be present at all future transfers of ownership. If it becomes lost, the land court must be petitioned for a new certificate, which can take weeks or months. The broker should make certain that any seller of property that has been land courted has the Certificate of Title in his/her possession and that they bring it with him/her to the passing of papers.

Property that has had a Certificate of Title issued is recorded in a separate filing system at the Registry of Deeds and can be recognized by the comparatively low book number (usually under 1,000).

A typical title reference for registered land might be Book 385, Page 29; while a typical title reference for property that has not received a Certificate of Title might be Book 11,793, Page 20. This will vary with each Registry numbering system as you go from county to county but in general terms, property that has a Certificate of Title will have a low book number.

A Sales Associate should learn to recognize low book numbers when listing property so that the question of the sellers having the Certificate of Title can be discussed early in the listing-showing-selling-passing cycle.

Title Search

In a typical real estate transaction, the mortgage bank will ask an attorney to perform a **Title Search** on the property before loaning money to the new buyer. The bank attorney may perform the title search him or herself or hire a specialist or title examiner to perform the title search.

In searching a title, the examiner will go to the appropriate County Registry of Deeds and, using the filing system at the registry, will prepare a **Chain of Title** often going back into the 1800's. This will list all of the owners of the property from that time up until the present owner. Then each deed that transferred ownership from one owner to another over the years is referred to and examined to assure that the title was properly transferred up to the present time and that in fact the title is free and clear and therefore acceptable as security for the bank loan and for the buyer to purchase. Other documents on record, in addition to deeds, such as mortgages and other liens will also be examined.

To use the filing system at a registry of deeds it is important to get the title reference of the current owner's deed. As noted previously, each deed has a book and page number which directs the searcher to a specific book logged at the registry of deeds and a particular page within the book. Each deed will have another title reference in the body of the document that will give the book and page number of the previous deed held by the grantor. In this fashion, the title examiner can follow each transfer going as far back as necessary. If you do not have a title reference to begin with, you may use what is called either the grantor or the grantee index. These indexes list the names in each category by date of transfer. Once you find the name of the party to the transaction you are researching, the file will list the book and page number of the deed you are looking for. The **Abstract of Title** is a summary of the history and status of ownership of a parcel of property including: the chain of title, the details of each consecutive conveyance, liens, other encumbrances and the current status of each. An Abstract of Title is usually prepared by an attorney or a title examiner.

History of Ownership

Some of the typical things an attorney might check for in a title search are:

1) Did all of the grantees receiving title in one transaction sign as grantors in the next (or was their interest properly accounted for through a will or inheritance law)?

2) Were all mortgage notes or other liens discharged (paid off) over the years?

3) Did the form of title transfer properly over the years (or, for example, did someone receiving a life estate in one transaction convey a fee simple estate to someone else)?

4) Does the legal description of the property correspond from one transaction to another?

5) Was each of the deeds properly executed and therefore valid (executed, signed and delivered)?

6) Are there any other legal claims to the property or is there a court case pending on the property as noted by the filing of a **Lis Penden**?

A **Lis Penden** is a recorded legal document that gives notice that legal action has begun that may affect the subject property.

Deed Versus Bill of Sale

Ownership of real property is transferred from one person to another by means of a **Deed**. Ownership of personal property is transferred from one person to another by means of a **Bill of Sale**.

Tax Stamps

When Property is conveyed from one party to another by means of a deed, Massachusetts requires **Excise Stamps** to be purchased and affixed to the deed. These tax stamps are paid for by the seller and the money to pay for them is usually deducted from the seller's proceeds by the bank attorney at the passing of papers. The attorney then purchases the stamps and they are affixed to the deed when it is recorded at the Registry of Deeds.

The amount of the tax stamps is figured at a rate of $2.28 per $500 of the sell price. This amounts to $4.56 per $1,000 of sell price when the sell price is in even $1,000 increments.

Example 1: The sell price $142,000. The sell price is at an even $1,000 level. Therefore, tax stamps of $2.28 per $500. can be calculated at $4.56 per $1,000.

$$142 \times 4.56 = \begin{array}{r} 142 \\ \times\, 4.56 \\ \hline 852 \\ 710 \\ \underline{568} \\ 647.52 \end{array} = \$647.52$$

Problem 1: A house sells for $198,000. What will the excise tax stamps cost?

Example 2: The sell price is $193,500. If the sell price is at a $500 increment, calculate the tax at $4.56 per thousand for the $1,000 figure and add $2.28 for the other $500. $193,500 sell price equals 193 x 4.56 plus 2.28.

$$\begin{array}{r} 193 \\ \times\, 4.56 \\ \hline 1158 \\ 965 \\ \underline{772} \\ 880.08 \end{array} \qquad \begin{array}{r} 880.08 \\ +\ 2.28 \\ \hline \$882.36 \end{array} \begin{array}{l} \text{tax on} \\ \text{tax on} \end{array} \begin{array}{r} \$193,000 \\ +\,500 \\ \hline \$193,500 \end{array}$$

Problem 2: What are the tax stamps on a piece of property that sells for $104,500?

Example 3: The sell price $187,620. Round sell price up to nearest $500 to determine base for tax calculation (always round up, never down).

$$
\begin{array}{r}
188 \\
\times 4.56 \\
\hline
1128 \\
940 \\
\underline{752} \\
857.28
\end{array}
$$
= \$857.28 tax stamps

Problem 3: What are the tax stamps on a house that sells for \$162,100? (Don't forget to round up to the nearest \$500).

Legal Description

Earlier in the chapter we stated that the three types of legal description were:

1)   **Metes and Bounds**
2)   **Lot and Block**
3)   **Government Survey**

Now lets look at each in more detail.

Metes and Bounds

The "Metes and Bounds" method of property description goes back to early colonial times and is most prevalent on the East Coast and the North East in particular. Massachusetts, as one of the original colonies uses the "Metes and Bounds" method as the predominant method of description. The "Lot and Block" and "Government Survey" methods evolved later and are more common in other parts of the country.

In the Metes and Bounds method you begin at one point and actually "walk" the perimeter stating distances, compass direction and specific boundaries as you proceed. The Metes and Bound method begins at a particular point called the **Point of Beginning (POB)** and walks the perimeter ending up back at the POB.

Example:

Land in Anytown with the buildings thereon being Lot 3 on Plan of House Lots in Anytown belonging to John Q. Owner, dated May 1888, recorded in Middlesex South District Registry of Deeds, Plan Book xx, Plan xx, and bounded as follows:

NORTHWESTERLY: by lots 1 and 2 on said plan, one hundred (100) feet
NORTHEASTERLY: by land of Mary Q. Public, fifty (50) feet
SOUTHEASTERLY: by lot 4 on said plan, one hundred (100) feet; and
SOUTHWESTERLY: by Main Street, fifty (50) feet.

Containing 5000 square feet of land, according to said plan.

Lot and Block

The **Lot and Block** method uses a survey of a parcel that is broken down into individual lots and recorded at the Registry of Deeds (Recorded Plat, Plan or Plat Map).

Following this Plat Map, lots can be legally referred to by their position on the Recorded Plat. For example on the plat of North Shore Estates at the end of the chapter, a legal description could be:

"Lot 6, Block D of the North Shore Estates Plan Recorded…"

It is not necessary to walk the perimeter as with a Metes and Bounds description.

Massachusetts may use a combination of Metes and Bounds as well as reference to a Recorded Plan.

For example: **"The land with buildings thereon situated at 100 Hometown Street, Boston, Suffolk County MA being Lot 12 on a plan recorded with Suffolk County Registry of Deeds Book 1111, Page 11 and bounded and described as follows:**

Easterly by Hometown Street, 100 Feet: Southerly by lot 12 as said plan one hundred Forty and 54/100 (150.54) feet and so forth.

In this example you see metes and bounds reference to specific distances and compass direction plus the reference to the parcel as a part of a recorded subdivision plan.

Government Survey System

The **Government Survey System** (also known as the **Rectangular Survey System**) was established by the federal government in the late 1700's. This method is the predominant method of land description in the Mid West and West Regions of the United States. In Massachusetts you will not encounter this method of land description but we should be familiar with some of the basic concepts.

The government survey method establishes a grid of East West lines six miles apart called **Base Lines** and a grid of North South lines 6 miles apart called **Meridians**, where they meet establishes a six mile by six mile parcel that is call a **Township**.

Each Township (6 miles by 6 miles) is subdivided into 36 one mile by one mile parcels called **Sections**.

First we will explain how a Township is described and then how the Sections and Partial Sections within a Township are described.

Township

A Township is described in terms of its location to specific Township Lines and Base Lines.

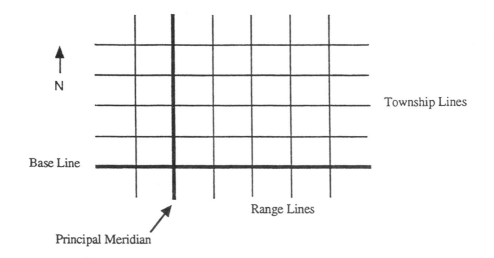

The Township Lines run East and West, six miles apart and are parallel to the Base lines.

The Range Lines run North and South, six miles apart and are parallel to the Principal Meridian.

Each Principal Meridian has a name or number and is crossed by a Base Line.

The distance between two Township Lines is six miles and is a Township Strip. It is referred to in relationship to its Base Line

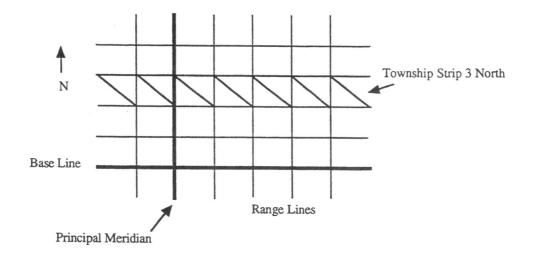

The Township strip shown above would be called Township strip 3 North. It is six miles wide, it is between Township lines 3 and 4 North of its Base Line and is Township Strip 3.

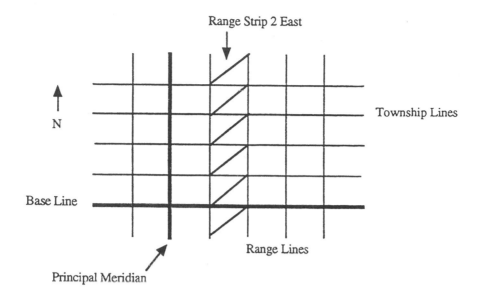

The Range strip shown above would be called Range strip 2 east. It is six miles wide, it is between Range lines 2 and 3 east of its Principal meridian and is Range Strip 2.

To identify the Township we refer to the Township Strip and the Range Strip. The Township where the two strips cross is then identified

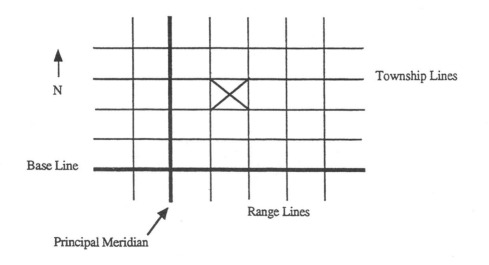

The Township shown above would therefore be identified as in Township Strip 3 north of the Base line and in Range strip 2 east of the Meridian. Abbreviated this would read T3N, R2E Principal Meridian.

Section

Each Township therefore is 6 miles by 6 miles or 36 sq. miles. A township is then divided into 36 one mile by one mile parcels called sections that are numbered 1 to 36 with number one in the N.E. corner and section 16 reserved by law for the township school section. Each 1 mile by 1 mile section contains 640 acres.

N

6	5	4	3	2	1
7	8	9	10	11	12
18	17	16	15	14	13
19	20	21	22	23	24
30	29	28	27	26	25
31	32	33	34	35	36

W   E

S

After locating the section, the individual parcel being described is referred to by dividing the section into 4 equal parts and then that parcel into 4 equal parts, and so on, until the subject parcel is legally defined.

Therefore, the following parcel in Section 6 of the Township above would be described as follows:

"N 1/2 of the S.E. 1/4 of the N.W. 1/4 of the section 6, Township 3 North, Range 2 East of the third Principal Meridian."

It would be located by finding the third Principal Meridian, locate the 3rd township strip north of the Base line and the 2nd Township strip east of the third Principal Meridian to establish the Township. Within Section 6 of the Township (640 acres) the property would be in the N.W. 1/4 of section 6 (160 acres). That parcel would be subdivided into 4 parts and the subject property would be in the S.E. 1/4 of that subdivision (40)Acres. The north 1/2 of that parcel as (20 Acres) is the property being described.

NW 1/4 40 A	NE 1/4 40 A	
SW 1/4	20 Acres	NE 1/4 160 Acres
SW 1/4 160 Acres		SE 1/4 160 Acres

" N 1/2 of the SE 1/4 of the NW 1/4 of Section 6, T3N, R2E Principal Meridian"

Involuntary Alienation

The most common transfer of title from one party to another is by Deed which includes the owner's consent and is therefore called **Voluntary Alienation**. There are several methods of title transfer that do not include the owner's consent and are therefore called **Involuntary Alienation**.

1) **Adverse Possession**
2) **Eminent Domain**
3) **Escheat**
4) **Foreclosure**
5) **Natural Forces**

Adverse Possession

An individual gains title to property by occupying land openly, notoriously, adversely and continuously for a period of twenty years. **Adverse Possession** will result in a transfer of title while **Prescription** results in an easement or Right of Way after 20 years of open, notorious, adverse and continuous use. Under Adverse Possession, it is necessary to go through land court to obtain confirmation of title to the property. (Adverse Possession and Prescriptive Rights are 20 years in Massachusetts, while other states vary.)

Eminent Domain

Eminent Domain has been discussed previously under government limits to property rights. When the government decides that it is in the best interest of the common good, they may take title to property via a power called eminent domain. Consent of the property owner is not necessary. This procedure is used when property must be taken for school or road construction as examples. The process of taking private property for public use by Eminent Domain is called **Condemnation.** The agency taking the property is the **Condemnor** and the property owner is the **Condemnee.**

Escheat

As mentioned earlier, this is the right of the state to take title to property when the owner dies intestate and there are no heirs.

Foreclosure

The bank (or other lien holder) may force the sale of property when the property owner does not live up to the terms of the original contract. A good example of this is found in the mortgage note where the borrower, or mortgagor, uses the real estate as security for the note.

After a foreclosure sale where all debts have been satisfied and expenses incurred are paid, any monies in excess of these costs are considered **Residual** and belong to the debtor. In contrast, if the sale does not cover the debts and expenses of the foreclosure, we have what is termed a **Deficiency.** The mortgagor is still held accountable for this deficiency judgment.

The order of debt payment is usually:

1) Government
2) First mortgage holder
3) Other lien holders in order of recordation
4) Residual/Deficiency

Natural Forces

Nature may add or take away property, this is very common in a seacoast state such as Massachusetts. When land is added to land bordering rivers, lakes and ocean it is call **Accretion.** When land is lost gradually it is called **Erosion.** A sudden loss such as through a storm or earthquake is called **Avulsion.**

Transfer by Will

A will is a written document disposing of property after a person's death. This includes real estate. If an individual leaves a will he has died **Testate** and is known as the **Testator.** If he does not leave a will he has died **Intestate** and individual state laws determine how the property will be distributed to the heirs. Transfer by the laws of inheritance without a will is called **Transfer by Descent.**

The Probate Court is the judicial body that processes and approves the transfer of property by means of a will. The **Executor** (male) or **Executrix** (female) is named in the will and is in charge of processing the required documents. If no executor or executrix is named in the will, the Probate Court will appoint an **administrator** to fulfill that function.

Property transferred by a will is said to be **Devised.** The donor is the **Devisor** and the recipient is the **Divisee.** A change to a will is a **Codicil.**

Glossary Quiz

1) Process whereby a notary public or justice of the peace witnesses a signature and attests that the signer has stated that the signing is his "free act and deed" (intended to protect against duress) _____

2) Process of filing a deed at the Registry of Deeds. Deed is assigned a title reference. (book number and page number) _____

3) Court system of settling land disputes in Massachusetts. Results in the court issuing a Certificate of Title to establish clear title. _____

4) Something of value exchanged for an article. In real estate, usually money, but may be a promise to perform a future act. _____

5) County agency that records, files and controls deeds, liens, and other paperwork relating to title of real property. _____

6) Document issued by the land court that documents the court decision and the property owner's title. _____

7) When referring to a deed it includes signing by grantor and delivering to grantee.

_____

8) Written instrument that transfers ownership of real property from one party to another.

_____

9) Form of deed that conveys grantor's interest to grantee; grantor will not defend title against claim brought by any owner other than himself; most common deed in Massachusetts.

_____

10) Property that, under the Torrens System, has been to land court, received a judgment, and now has a Certificate of Title documenting the land court decision.

_____

Self Quiz A

1) Legal title to real property is conveyed by means of:
   - A) A Purchase and Sale Agreement
   - B) A Bill of Sale
   - C) An Abstract of Title
   - D) A Deed

2) Which of the following statements regarding a deed is not true?
   - A) A deed must be signed by the Grantor
   - B) A deed must be recorded to be valid
   - C) A deed must be acknowledged to be recorded
   - D) A deed must contain a granting clause

3) Book 12,105, Page 48 might be an example of:
   - A) Metes and Bounds
   - B) Lot and Block
   - C) Title Reference
   - D) An Abstract of Title

4) A piece of property selling for $190,000 with bank financing of $152,000 will pay excise tax stamps in the amount of:
   - A) $693.12
   - B) $346.56
   - C) $866.40
   - D) $433.20

5) If a house sells for $121,200 the tax stamps will cost:
   - A) $551.76
   - B) $275.88
   - C) $280.44
   - D) $554.04

6)   A valid deed does not require:
      A)   Granting Clause
      B)   Signature of the Grantee
      C)   Property Description
      D)   Execution

7)   A Grantee receives the most protection by receiving:
      A)   Purchase and Sale Agreement
      B)   Special Warranty Deed
      C)   Quitclaim Deed ——— CLEAN TITLE
      D)   Warranty Deed

8)   A grantor in Massachusetts who agrees to defend title to real property against claims arising during his ownership is using:
      A)   A Quitclaim Deed
      B)   A Warranty Deed
      C)   Title Insurance
      D)   A Certificate of Title

9)   A land court decision under Massachusetts Torrens System results in a:
      A)   Quitclaim Deed
      B)   Warranty Deed
      C)   Special Warranty Deed
      D)   Certificate of Title

10)   A summary of the history of ownership of a piece of property is known as:
      A)   An Abstract of Title
      B)   A Chain of Title
      C)   A Title Search
      D)   An Equitable Title

Self Quiz B

This Self Quiz is based on the Plat of the North Shore Estates at the end of the chapter.

1)   Which of the following lots has the least frontage on East Street?
      A)   Block D, Lot 1
      B)   Block E, Lot 3
      C)   Block E, Lot 1
      D)   Block D, Lot 2

2)   Which of the following has more than 15,000 square feet of land area?
      A)   Block D, Lot 6
      B)   Block C, Lot 2
      C)   Block B, Lot 5
      D)   Block D, Lot 8

3) Which of the following has less than 100 foot frontage on North Street?
    A) Block B, Lot 1
    B) Block D, Lot 3
    C) Block D, Lot 8
    D) Block B, Lot 5

4) On which of the following lots would a house face Northeast?
    A) Block C. Lot 1
    B) Block D, Lot 10
    C) Block E, Lot 2
    D) Block B, Lot 1

5) Lot 1 in Block B, at the corner of Bay and North Streets, is on which corner of Block B?
    A) Northeast
    B) Southwest
    C) Southeast
    D) Northwest

6) Which lot has the most frontage on North Street"
    A) Block D, Lot 3
    B) Block C, Lot 1
    C) Block B, Lot 1
    D) Block B, Lot 4

7) How many lots are shown on Block E?
    A) 3
    B) 5
    C) 7
    D) 11

8) Which of the following lots has frontage on two streets?
    A) Block D, Lot 2
    B) Block B, Lot 1
    C) Block D, Lot 9
    D) Block C, Lot 1

9) Which lot has the longest depth?
    A) Block D, Lot 11
    B) Block D, Lot 8
    C) Block B, Lot 4
    D) Block C, Lot 2

10) How many lots are shown with less than 100-foot frontage on East and Elm Streets?
    A) 3
    B) 9
    C) 4
    D) 0

Self Quiz C

1) Which of the following is not required for a valid deed?
   A) Signatures of all Grantors
   B) A Granting Clause
   C) Signatures of all Grantees
   D) Legal Description

2) Title to real property may not be transferred by
   A) Escheat
   B) Inheritance
   C) Deed
   D) Prescription

3) A Valid Deed does not require
   A) Recording
   B) Granting clause
   C) Legal Description
   D) Grantors Signatures

4) In Massachusetts a deed that conveys only the interest that the grantor possesses is best described as:
   A) Quitclaim Deed
   B) Warranty Deed
   C) Land Court Deed
   D) Fiduciary Deed

5) Which is not required for a Deed to be valid:
   A) Delivery to the Grantee
   B) Signature of the Grantor
   C) Granting Clause
   D) Recording at the Registry

6) The least protection is provided to the grantee by:
   A) Limited Warranty Deed
   B) Quitclaim Deed
   C) Land Court Deed
   D) Warranty Deed

7) A Deed is not valid until it is:
   A) Signed and Notarized
   B) Recorded
   C) Signed and Delivered
   D) Acknowledged and Recorded

8) To protect against the Grantor signing under duress, a Deed is:
   A) Recorded
   B) Acknowledged
   C) Witnessed
   D) Signed

9)   Title may be transferred against the owner's will by means of:
    A)   A Will
    B)   A Deed
    C)   Escheat
    D)   Eminent Domain

10)   Tax stamps are paid for by
    A)   Grantor
    B)   Grantee
    C)   Title Attorney
    D)   Mortgage Company or Bank

Answer Key

Problems

1. $902.88
2. $476.52
3. $741.00

	Glossary Quiz	Self Quiz A	B	C
1)	Acknowledgment	D	B	C
2)	Recording	B	B	D
3)	Torrens System	C	D	A
4)	Consideration	C	A	A
5)	Registry of Deeds	D	C	D
6)	Certificate of Title	B	C	B
7)	Execution	D	A	C
8)	Deed	A	B	B
9)	Quitclaim Deed	D	D	D
10)	Registered Land	A	D	A

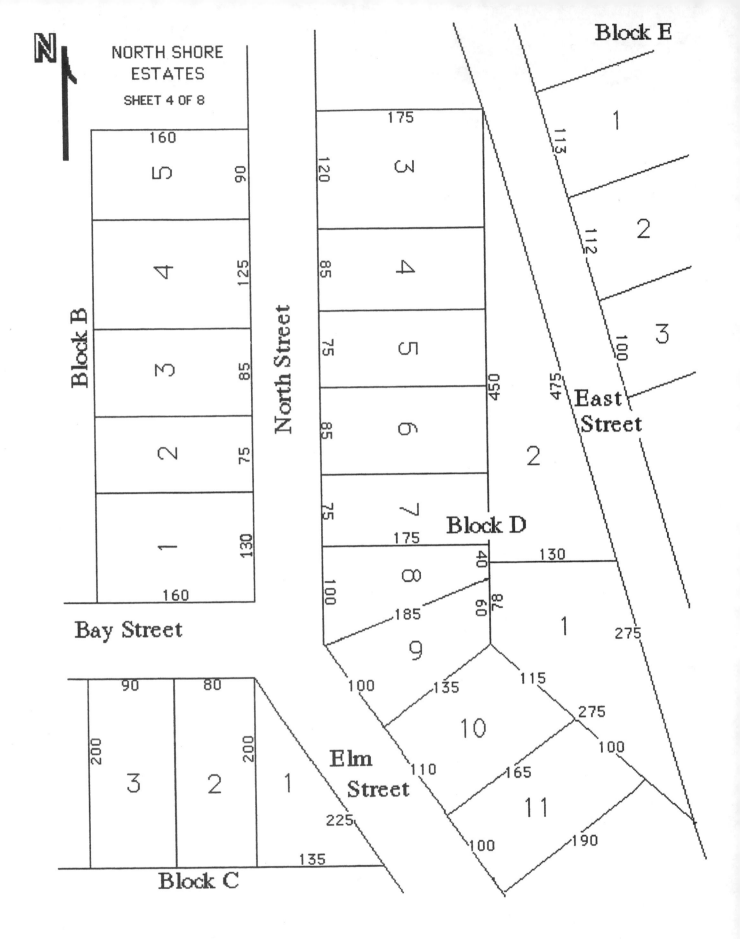

NORTH SHORE
ESTATES
SHEET 4 OF 8

Block E

Block B

North Street

East Street

Bay Street

Block D

Elm Street

Block C

Transfer of Title/Deed   6-22

7 Financing and Mortgages

The following terms and concepts will be covered in this chapter. They will also be found in the glossary at the back of the text.

Terms and Concepts

Alienation clause
Amortization
Balloon mortgage
Blanket mortgage
Certificate of Reasonable Value
Commercial Bank
Construction Mortgage
Conventional mortgage
Defeasance Clause
Demand mortgage
Direct Reduction mortgage
Disclosure Statement
Equity
F.H.A. mortgage
Home Equity Loan
Impound Account
Impound Payment
Investment
Junior mortgage
M.G.I.C. mortgage
Mortgage

Mortgage buydown
Mortgage deed
Mortgage note
Mortgagee
Mortgagor
Negative Amortization
Open end mortgage
Package mortgage
Point
Pre-qualify
Primary mortgage market
Prime rate
Purchase money mortgage
Regulation Z
Reverse Annuity
Right of rescission
Secondary mortgage market
Shared Equity
Truth-in-lending
V. A. Mortgage
Variable rate mortgage
Wraparound mortgage

Role of Financing

In the vast majority of real estate transactions, the buyer does not have enough money to pay cash for the property. The buyer must turn to some other party to borrow the funds for a part of the purchase price. This third party is usually a bank or mortgage company. In this chapter we will investigate the role of the bank and mortgage company in providing financing for real estate transactions and how the real estate broker or salesperson plays a part in this process.

Real Estate Cycle

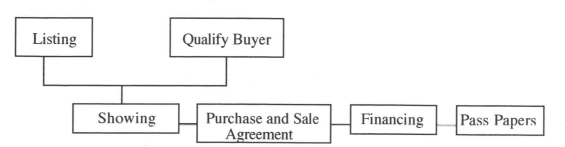

The financing step in the real estate cycle takes place after the purchase and sale agreement is signed and prior to the passing of papers. The sequence of events proceeds as indicated in the diagram at the bottom of the previous page.

Listing

A property owner hires a broker to sell his property for a real estate commission. At this time the broker lists all of the pertinent information about the property. (See chapter on Brokerage.)

Qualify Buyer

The broker or salesperson identifies the prospective buyer's needs, likes or dislikes and reviews financing, including typical down payment, taxes, interest rates, and other carrying costs. The buyer's income and the lender's qualifying ratios are reviewed to determine how much the buyer can borrow.

Currently much of this process has been replaced by **pre-qualifying** at a bank or a mortgage company. This is a process where a potential home buyer meets with a mortgage loan originator and reviews financial information such as a loan amount, interest rate alternatives and points, plus buyer's personal information such as down payment, income and other consumer debt. After analysis by the loan originator, a pre-qualification letter is given to the buyer stating what mortgage amount he or she can afford.

Showing

A potential buyer is offered the property by the broker or salesperson and usually taken on a tour of the property.

Purchase and Sale Agreement

A written contract is drawn up and signed by the buyer and seller. The purchase and sale agreement should cover all of the items that the parties have agreed to, including a financing clause that will be discussed shortly.

Pass Papers

When the financing has been arranged and the bank attorney has searched the title and the deed and mortgage papers have been prepared, the parties are ready to "pass papers." The buyer, seller, bank attorney, and usually the broker meet at a location of the bank attorney's preference. The seller signs the deed, which the attorney then records at the Registry of Deeds.

Financing Procedure

The financing arrangements are between the borrower (buyer) and the lender (bank or mortgage company). However, in many cases the buyer would like some assistance in arranging the financing. It is in the best interests of all parties for the real estate professional to be prepared to provide this service. This usually involves being up to date on the availability of money and the interest rates being charged by the banks in your community and in surrounding communities. Then, if a buyer does not have a specific bank in mind and asks for a recommendation, you will be in a position to state who currently is accepting mortgage applications and what they are quoting for interest rates.

Mortgage Application

The first step in obtaining financing is to fill out a mortgage application form. When a purchase and sale agreement has been signed and the buyer is ready to move on to the financing step, you should be prepared to help the buyer find a loan program to fit his or her needs.

Many loan originators from banks or mortgage companies will meet with buyers at the buyer's home, your real estate office or the loan originator's office. At this time they will qualify the buyer and take the loan application.

Bank Approval Cycle

The bank has two separate steps to approving a loan:

1) It must approve the property.
2) It must approve the borrower.

The property is usually inspected by an independent real estate appraiser and an appraisal report is completed. The borrower is approved from the information on his application following verification from a credit report. If the bank feels that the property and the borrower are both sound, it approves the loan and sends out a mortgage commitment letter, which confirms to the buyer that the loan has been approved. This commitment letter usually specifies the amount of the loan, the interest rate and the number of years of the loan (for example, $120,000 at 10 percent interest for 30 years). The terms of the note will be based on market conditions at the time of the loan.

Purchase and Sale Agreement Financing Clause

The buyer will be able to buy the property only if he/she can obtain the financing needed. Therefore, a clause should be included in the purchase and sale agreement that indicates that the contract is "subject to" the buyer's obtaining the required financing. The amount of the required loan should be specified and a "not to exceed" figure for interest rate and number of years should be included (for example, "subject to a mortgage commitment of not less than $120,000 at not more than 10 percent interest for 30 years"). The buyer is then protected in the event he cannot obtain his financing for some reason. He cannot be expected to fulfill his part of the contract and can receive his deposit back.

From the seller's point of view, we want to know as soon as possible whether or not the buyer can obtain his financing. If he cannot, the seller must return the deposit and put the property back on the market. It is, therefore, a good idea to put a time limit in the purchase and sale agreement financing clause for the buyer to arrange financing (for example, "mortgage commitment to be obtained on or before March 16, 1997").

Mortgage Note and Mortgage Deed

In Massachusetts, the contract between the borrower and the bank involves two documents:

1) Mortgage Note
2) Mortgage Deed

The **mortgage note** is the written promise of the borrower to pay the money borrowed back to the bank at a specific rate of interest over a specific period of time.

The **mortgage deed** (referred to as the **mortgage**) is a conditional conveyance of the property to the bank subject to the borrower's right of redemption.

This means that the buyer or borrower actually deeds (transfers title to) the property to the bank. The bank may not deed the property to anyone else as long as the buyer continues to make his mortgage payment in accordance with the terms of the mortgage note. To insure that the buyer (borrower) lives up to this arrangement, the mortgage note and mortgage deed (signed by the buyer) are recorded at the Registry of Deeds immediately after the deed conveying the property from seller to buyer is recorded. Then the property cannot be conveyed to a new owner without satisfying the mortgage note and deed.

The **mortgagor** is the party borrowing money with property as security (buyer or borrower) and the **mortgagee** is the party lending the money with property as security.

Lending Institutions and Money

The money market by nature is a dynamic and rapidly changing market at best. Recent history has shown that interest rates and terms for home mortgages can change on almost a daily basis. Conditions that set the stage for these fluctuations are quite varied and not only include the law of supply and demand but government policy and regulations that are set up to guide lending institutions.

Money for mortgages is in competition with other investments such as government bonds, stocks, mutual funds, or certificates of deposit. Whether it be the people who put money into savings accounts or the private investor who purchases mortgages in the secondary mortgage market, they will be looking for the best return possible. This ultimately affects the rates to the home buyer.

The **prime rate**, the rate at which a lending institution charges its best customers on short-term notes, will also have an effect on the home mortgage market. When the cost of these types of loans changes, the interest rates on most all other types of financing are sure to follow.

Another factor that influences the cost of money is the **federal discount rate**. This is the rate charged by the Federal Reserve Bank to its member banks. When the federal government wants to increase economic activity, it will lower the discount rate. With the lower rates, banks will tend to borrow more money which in turn increases the supply of money on the market, the intended result. The reverse of this policy would slow the market down as in times of a fear of inflation. The prime rate will usually float around two percent above the federal discount rate. All federally chartered commercial banks and some state banks are members of this system.

Different institutions have different rules they must abide by and also have different goals. The following will give you some examples.

Saving and Loan Associations

These institutions are set up to deal with the long-term lending requirements for real estate sales. Organizations that fall into this category currently write the largest amount of home-loan mortgages in the country.

Savings and loan associations must be chartered by the state or federal government and are governed by the Federal Home Loan Bank Board. They will also insure depositor funds through the Federal Savings and Loan Insurance Corporation (FSLIC) up to $100,000.

Savings and loan associations are usually owned by stockholders.

Commercial Banks

Although commercial banks do write loans for real estate, this area is of secondary importance. Most of this type of bank's work is done with short-term instruments, such as checking accounts, auto or personal property loans, short-term business loans, and home improvement loans. These types of loans help keep the bank "liquid" which is important since a large amount of deposits are "on demand."

Commercial banks are required to be chartered by the state or federal government and will insure depositor funds through the Federal Deposit Insurance Corporation (FDIC).

Mutual Savings Banks

In this type of organization, no stock is issued, and it is owned by the depositors. These banks, which are similar to a savings and loan associations, prefer the more stable real estate loan, such as conventional, F.H.A. and V.A. These institutions are located mostly in the Northeast with loans being insured by the FDIC.

Cooperative Banks

A cooperative bank considers depositors as shareholders in the institution. Members can deposit money and buy shares in different increments. Loans are usually only made to shareholders, which a person may become by depositing a token sum of $1.00 to $5.00.

Credit Unions

This institution is created by members of corporations, associations, or other organizations for the members' benefits. It is considered cooperative by nature and has the member depositing funds in accounts with better-than-average interest rates. Originally dealing mainly with consumer loans, credit unions are now competing on a limited basis in the areas of short-term business loans and first mortgages on real estate.

Mortgage Companies

Mortgage companies or brokers have taken on a significant role in the mortgage industry in recent years. These organizations originate loans on real estate for other investors. Acting similar to an intermediary for pension funds, insurance companies, or private individuals, mortgages are placed on property and then serviced by the mortgage company for a fee.

Life Insurance Companies

These organizations loan money from premiums, usually on large commercial or business ventures. Life insurance companies do have a portion of their "portfolio" tied up in other areas of real estate, mainly through mortgage companies.

Private Lenders

There are also private investors who are willing to loan funds provided they are secured by real estate. These investors will act like a bank in loaning money; it may be in a first or a junior position, and often times charge a higher rate of interest. The higher rate of interest is due to the fact that some of these investors deal in problem financing where risk is greater.

A seller who "takes back" a purchase money mortgage would also be considered a private lender (See next section).

Types of Mortgages

All mortgages are not the same. There are different types of mortgages that we should be familiar with in order to provide both the buyer and the seller with advice and guidance in the real estate transaction. Some of the more common types of mortgages are:

Conventional Mortgage	M.G.I.C. Mortgage
V.A. Mortgage	Direct Reduction Mortgage
F.H.A. Mortgage	Construction Mortgage
Blanket Mortgage	Balloon Mortgage
Purchase Money Mortgage	Shared Equity Mortgage
Junior Mortgage	Negative Amortization Mortgage
Open-end Mortgage	Package Mortgage
Wraparound Mortgage	Demand Mortgage
Variable Rate Mortgage	Reverse Annuity Mortgage

Before we discuss the various types of mortgages, it should be noted that a specific mortgage may be more than one of the types listed. Thus, when buyer A arranges his financing at a bank, he may have a conventional mortgage that is also a direct reduction mortgage and a blanket mortgage all at the same time.

Conventional Mortgage

A conventional mortgage is a mortgage with no guarantee or insurance from the federal government (no V.A. or F.H.A. protection). The buyer applies to the bank for a mortgage loan. After review of the buyer and the property, the bank agrees to loan the money. The buyer and the bank enter into the mortgage contract with no federal government agency insuring or guaranteeing the loan. The interest rate is determined by the bank based on the mortgage application and the supply and demand of money at the particular time.

V. A. Mortgage

The V. A. mortgage is also known as the G.I. mortgage. The V.A. mortgage guarantee program began in 1944 as a means of assisting World War II veterans to buy and finance a house. For a veteran to be eligible, he must obtain a Certificate of Eligibility through the local Veterans' Administration Office. Although the name implies that the Veterans' Administration loans the money, the bank actually makes the loan and services the account as if it were a conventional mortgage. However, the Veterans Administration **guarantees** the loan to the bank in the event of a foreclosure and loss. The loss guarantee is limited to a specific amount which changes with market conditions. Check for current limits.

There are other requirements set forth by the Veterans Administration that must be fulfilled before a loan can be made under this program. Not only does the veteran himself have to qualify, but the property does also. It must be an owner-occupied, one to four unit dwelling which has obtained a **Certification of Reasonable Value** (CRV) through a V.A. appraisal and passed a termite inspection. The Certificate of Reasonable Value is a document issued by the V. A. which is based on an appraisal and is intended to insure the veteran that the price being paid for a piece of property is reasonable.

The major advantages to the V.A. mortgage are that there are no prepayment penalties, it is assumable, and it is still possible to finance with no down payment.

Formerly the V.A. did not limit points charged but the veteran could pay only one point and the V. A. set the rate for the V. A. loan. Recent changes now allow the rate charged and the points charged to move with the supply and demand of the market as do other rates and may now be paid by the veteran.

F.H.A. Mortgage

The Federal Housing Administration was established in 1934 as part of the National Housing Act and is now a branch of the Department of Housing and Urban Development (HUD). The F.H.A. mortgage was a means to stimulate the housing market by protecting lenders against default on a mortgage and is available to all who qualify. The major difference between a V.A. and a F.H.A. mortgage is the fact that the F.H.A. insures the loan rather than guaranteeing it. For this insurance policy through the F.H.A., the borrower must pay one-half of 1 percent of the average annual balance of the loan as an insurance premium. A 30 year term is most common and an F.H.A. appraisal of the property must be obtained (a V.A. appraisal is acceptable).

The F.H.A. regulates most all areas of the program except the interest rate. This is now a point of negotiation between the approved lender and borrower. The main advantage to the F.H.A. mortgage is the low down payments permitted by lending institutions because of the insurance over the years due to the insurance against loss. This advantage has become less important over the years due to the competition from private mortgage insurance companies (PMI).

M.G.I.C. Mortgage (one form of Private Mortgage Insurance PMI)

The Mortgage Guarantee Investment Corporation is one of several private mortgage insuring companies that modeled themselves after that government V.A. and F.H.A. programs. The lender supplies the money to the borrower. The borrower pays a slightly higher interest rate and the bank "sells" some of its risk to M.G.I.C. There are two distinct advantages of M.G.I.C. over V.A. and F.H.A. First the paper work required from the borrower and broker is minimized. The standard bank application is usually sufficient. Secondly, the time from bank application to mortgage commitment is much shorter than V.A. or F.H.A. The M.G. I.C. commitment can usually be obtained in the same time as the conventional mortgage (two to three weeks). The V.A. and F.H.A. mortgage commitment seldom takes less than thirty days and often forty-five to sixty days.

Direct Reduction Mortgage

With a direct reduction mortgage, the total monthly payment of principal and interest combined remains constant throughout the life of the loan. At the beginning of the mortgage, the interest payment is much larger than the principal. As the mortgage progresses, the ratio shifts, and at the end of the loan the principal is much larger than the interest. Most residential home mortgages are the direct reduction type. The process of repaying a loan by making systematic payments over a period of time is called **amortization**. (See table at end of chapter.)

Construction Mortgage

A construction mortgage finances construction of a new home. The money is advanced to the builder in partial payments as the work advances and certain stages of completion are reached.

Blanket Mortgage

With a blanket mortgage, two or more parcels of property are offered by the borrower as security for the mortgage loan. This occasionally happens when a buyer must pass papers on his new house and has not passed papers on his old house. The bank will loan the money necessary for both houses with a blanket mortgage where both houses are security for the loan. Then when the old house is sold, the proceeds are applied to the blanket mortgage. The bank then holds a conventional mortgage on the new house alone.

Purchase Money Mortgage

The buyer does not have sufficient funds to pay the agreed sell price for a piece of property including money from the bank, so he gives the seller an I.O.U. for a part of the sell price. In return, the seller will hold a mortgage on the property after it has been deeded to the buyer to secure the loan. This mortgage will be recorded after the bank's mortgage and, therefore, becomes a junior, or second, mortgage, also known as a "take-back". A first mortgage held by the seller would also be a Purchase Money Mortgage.

Junior Mortgage

A junior mortgage is any mortgage that does not have first claim on a piece of property. For example, A sells to B. B has a $60,000 first mortgage with the XYZ Savings Bank and owes a $5,000 second mortgage to the seller. The $5,000 second mortgage is a junior mortgage. In this example the Junior Mortgage is also a Purchase Money Mortgage. A second mortgage from a bank would be a Junior Mortgage but not a Purchase Money Mortgage.

Open End Mortgage

With an open end mortgage the approved loan amount is not taken by the borrower all at once. In the case of the home purchase where the buyer intends to perform extensive improvements, he may borrow the bulk of the money at the time the house is purchased and then increase the amount borrowed as he needs it to pay for subsequent improvements. The borrower pays interest only on the amount borrowed. The total amount borrowed (including original amount plus later amounts) may not exceed the total amount approved initially.

Wraparound Mortgage

In creating the wraparound mortgage the seller of a parcel of realty will also become a lender. The payments from the new mortgage, usually for a larger amount and a higher interest rate, will be used to service any existing debt still secured by the property. The seller will receive payments from the buyer on the wraparound mortgage and take a portion of this payment to keep current any other existing debt. This type of mortgage is used when existing debt cannot be paid off or if rewriting the first mortgage would result in prohibitively higher interest rates.

It is also important to note that this may violate an **alienation clause** in an existing mortgage. The alienation clause, also known as the **due on sale clause**, states that if someone other than the original maker of the current note obtains an interest in the realty, the bank can call the note due and payable at its discretion.

Variable Rate Mortgage

The variable rate mortgage was first introduced to the market to help buyers qualify for financing and to insure that the bank would not be tied to a fixed rate for the term of the loan. Although there are many variations of the V.R.M, the basic concept allows the borrower to finance the property at lower-than-average fixed rate terms at the beginning, and as time passes, the rate would increase. The amount of rate and payment increases or decreases during the life of a note would be dictated by market conditions and parameters set up in the original note. (Also known as an Adjustable Rate Mortgage - ARM)

Balloon Mortgage

A balloon mortgage is one that culminates with a final payment which is larger than any preceding payments. As in the case of an interest-only note, the final payment would include any accrued interest and all of the principle. Many borrowers have found themselves in trouble when a balloon payment becomes due and payable; therefore, caution is advised when this type of financing is used.

Shared Equity Mortgage

In the shared equity mortgage the borrower and the bank agree to share the increase in value for the subject property. This is in contrast to the more common arrangement where the bank receives the return of the principal plus the agreed upon interest but any increase in value or equity belongs to the owner.

Negative Amortization Mortgage

In a negative amortization mortgage the monthly payment agreed to does not cover the interest charged. The difference is added to the amount due so the amount of the mortgage due increases rather than decreases as is the case in the standard mortgage.

Reverse Annuity Mortgage (RAM)

This mortgage allows the elderly to use the equity in a home by reversing the normal mortgage process. According to a pre-arranged schedule, which can vary, the mortgage company makes payments to the borrower over a period of time which increases the balance of the amount owed on the piece of property. This allows the borrower to have a stream of income to live on and it is paid back at a later specified date or upon an agreed upon event. The debt may be paid back by an insurance annuity or the proceeds of an estate.

Package Mortgage

This form of mortgage allows the buyer to finance not only the real estate, but items usually considered personal property. The stove, refrigerator, washer and dryer, or other items would be used to help secure the note to the lender. This form of mortgage is useful in the sale of furnished homes or condos.

Demand or Call Mortgage

The lender has the right to call this type of note due and payable at his or her discretion. Typically, the market conditions are reviewed annually and the mortgagor is offered the choice of paying off the principal outstanding or keeping the mortgage at a new and higher interest rate for another year.

Mortgage Buydown

To assist the buyer in qualifying or to make the terms of the sale more attractive, the buydown can be used. With this feature, the buyer or seller will pay to the lending institution an amount of money, up front, to decrease the monthly payments to the buyer. The amount paid for the "buydown" will usually be based in part on the present value of the loss the bank will incur because of the lower than normal monthly payments they will receive. It is common to pay a bank a "point" (one percent of the amount borrowed) to reduce the first year's interest rate. The banks ability to pay calculation then allows the borrower a larger mortgage.

Home Equity Loan

This type of loan gives the homeowner an open line of credit with the bank. The maximum amount of money that can be borrowed will usually be no more than seventy or eighty percent of the value of the house minus any first mortgage outstanding.

As an example, let's assume you owned a house appraised at $150,000 with an $85,000 first mortgage and the bank would allow you to use your "equity" (the difference between what an owner owes and the value of the property) up to seventy percent of value; $105,000. Based on these figures, the bank would give you an open line of credit up to $20,000. This loan would be secured by the property.

The amount approved will also be influenced by the buyer's income and other debt.

Points

A point is a charge that the lender (usually the bank) makes to the borrower (the buyer) when the loan is made. A point is 1 percent of the amount loaned and is usually paid by the borrower to obtain a more favorable interest rate. A bank may charge more than one point.

"Assuming vs. Subject to"

A buyer who **"assumes"** a previous mortgage agrees to pay the mortgage. The previous owner remains liable if the new buyer fails to pay.

A buyer who buys **"subject to"** a previous mortgage does not agree to pay it. However, the previous mortgage remains as a prior lien on the property and nonpayment could result in foreclosure.

Defeasance Clause

A **Defeasance Clause** is a clause used in a lease or a mortgage to cancel a certain right when a specific condition has been met. One of the best examples of a defeasance clause is in a mortgage where the conditional granting to the bank is canceled when the mortgage is fully paid.

Impound Account

An **Impound Account** is a trust account established to collect funds for the future needs of a parcel of real estate. Banks often establish Impound Accounts for taxes and insurance fees. An **Impound Payment** would be the periodic payment into such Impound Accounts. Tax escrow funds held by the bank are held in Impound Accounts.

Secondary Mortgage Market

Lending institutions can be broken down into two groups. The first group, which is more familiar, is the **primary mortgage market** and can be classified as those organizations which make loans to the consumer. They are called the originators of the loans. These institutions quite often find it beneficial to sell the notes owned by them at a discount to obtain funds which can be loaned out at a higher interest rate. A borrower may never know this has been done since it doesn't change the terms of the original agreement and the originator will still service the loan.

The organizations which buy these notes are known as the **secondary mortgage market**. There are three major organizations in the secondary mortgage market.

The **Federal National Mortgage Association** (FNMA or "Fannie Mae"), once a government organization, is now privately owned and considered a quasi-governmental agency. FNMA purchases F.H.A., V.A. and conventional mortgages from the primary market using funds raised through the sale of notes, debentures, and/or bonds.

The **Federal Home Loan Mortgage Corporation** (FHLMC or "Freddie Mac") also purchases F.H.A., V. A., and conventional mortgages to be used as security for sale of bonds to raise more funds. Freddie Mac deals with institutions insured by the federal government and mostly with conventional loans on single family houses.

The **Government National Mortgage Association** (GNMA or "Ginnie Mae") is a government-owned organization which assists Fannie Mae in secondary market purchases. When market conditions are particularly difficult, Ginnie Mae will join with Fannie Mae and purchase mortgages that are low-interest and high-risk at the full rate. Ginnie Mae guarantees payment and makes up the difference between the full market rate and what the mortgage would have been discounted to, if purchased under better market conditions. The name for this arrangement is the **tandem plan**.

Truth in Lending

As we have discussed previously, there is a definite move towards increased consumer protection within real estate. One force in this regard is the truth-in-lending law, which is federal legislation known as **Regulation Z**.

This law affects those who loan money as a normal business activity (banks, credit unions, department stores, etc.). Thus, an individual who sells his home and loans money to the buyer to assist in the financing would not be required to comply with the truth-in-lending law.

These creditors (those loaning money) must comply with the truth-in'-lending law when they extend credit to individuals but not when they extend credit to businesses. The law is designed to protect the individual consumer rather than businesses; therefore, businesses are exempt.

There are three major areas to the truth-in-lending law as it affects real estate:

1) **Disclosure**
2) **Right of Rescission**
3) **Advertising**

Disclosure

The lender must provide the borrower with a **disclosure statement** before the borrower makes any financing commitment.

The disclosure statement must itemize:

1) **Finance charge** - the dollar amount of all charges to the borrower including application fee, interest, service charges, penalties, points, etc.

2) **Percentage rate** - the annual interest rate expressed as a yearly percentage on the unpaid balance.(APR)

Right of Rescission

A borrower may change his mind and rescind, or cancel, his loan agreement up to three days after contracts have been signed.

The right of rescission requirement applies to one to four family owner-occupied dwellings currently occupied by the borrower. Therefore, a refinance, second mortgage, or a first mortgage on a dwelling the borrower currently owns and occupies, is covered by the three-day right of rescission requirement. However, the purchase of a house is exempt because the borrower is not the current owner-occupant.

Under a "financial emergency," a lender does have the ability to waive the right of rescission but this is the exception, not the rule. "Financial emergency" is left to the lender to determine.

In a refinance, it is not uncommon for the borrower to be paying interest on two notes during the three-day right of rescission period. A lender usually will not pay off the original note or mortgage until the time period has expired.

Advertising

Basically this provision requires any credit advertising to include all details if any are included. A lender may no longer advertise "$500 down" or "$300 per month" without listing all details. One exception to this is the annual interest rate (for example, 9 percent interest APR), which may be advertised without giving all other details.

Glossary Quiz

1) A one-time charge for loaning money equal 1% of the loan   _____

2) One lending money with property held as security (bank)   _____

3) A mortgage secured by two or more parcels of property   _____

4) A mortgage that is not insured or guaranteed by the federal government   _____

5) Notification from lender to borrower of the financing terms and charges of a loan   _____

6)   Any mortgage that takes second priority to another
        mortgage on the property   _____

7)   Written promise to pay money borrowed against
        property as security   _____

8)   Conditional conveyance of property held as security
        for a loan   _____

9)   A mortgage given by the seller to the buyer to assist
        in purchasing the property   _____

10)   The right of a borrower to cancel a financing agreement
        within three days after receiving a disclosure statement
        from the lender   _____

Self Quiz A

1)   Two buyers have signed a conditional conveyance to a bank which will not
        be exercised as long as they make their payments on time. They have
        signed A:
        A)   Purchase and Sale Agreement
        B)   Mortgage Note
        C)   Mortgage Deed
        D)   Quitclaim Deed

2)   The funds for a V.A. Mortgage are provided by the:
        A)   Bank or Mortgage Company
        B)   Veteran's Administration
        C)   Sellers
        D)   Junior Mortgage

3)   The cost of searching title is paid by the:
        A)   Broker
        B)   Mortgagee
        C)   Sellers
        D)   Mortgagor

4)   The interest that the owner of property has above the balance of the
        mortgage debt is known as the:
        A)   Mortgage Note
        B)   Mortgage Balance
        C)   Equity
        D)   Market Value

5)   The maximum a bank may charge in granting a V.A. guaranteed loan is:
        A)   1 Point
        B)   2 Points
        C)   0 Points
        D)   No limit

6) The Truth-in-Lending law applies to which of the following situations?
   A) A bank when loaning money to a Buyer for the purchase of an owner-occupied single-family house
   B) A Seller when loaning money to two partners when buying a business.
   C) A Seller who is taking back a second mortgage from a Buyer in the purchase of his new home when the Seller is being transferred by his company.
   D) A business when loaning money to another business.

7) A conventional mortgage of $60,000 on a house that sells for $90,000 requires the Buyer to pay two points. The Buyer will pay:
   A) $600
   B) $900
   C) $1200
   D) $1800

8) Which of the following statements about a variable rate mortgage is correct?
   A) Allows the borrower lower interest rate in the first year of the mortgage.
   B) Makes it more difficult for the Buyer to qualify.
   C) Always results in a balloon mortgage.
   D) The Buyer's interest rate will increase but not decrease.

9) The secondary mortgage market:
   A) competes directly with the primary mortgage market for clients.
   B) Buys mortgages and helps stimulate the real estate market.
   C) Sells mortgages to the primary mortgage market for a small fee.
   D) Is the main originator of funds to first-time home buyers.

10) Which of the following statements would not violate the Regulation Z advertising regulation if stated by itself in an ad?
    A) No money down
    B) "10% A.P.R."
    C) "Payments only $1000 per month"
    D) "$5000 down $1000 per month payment"

Self Quiz B

1) The interest rate on a conventional mortgage is determined by:
   A) V.A.
   B) F.H.A.
   C) Lending Institution
   D) Federal Reserve Bank

2) The interest rate on a V.A. mortgage is determined by:
   A) V.A.
   B) F.H.A.
   C) Lending Institution
   D) Federal Reserve Bank

3) Which of the following statements is true concerning a V.A. mortgage?
   A) The V. A. determines the number of points the bank may charge.
   B) The V.A. determines the number of points the veteran may pay.
   C) The V.A. guarantees the mortgage to the bank.
   D) The V.A. provides the mortgage funds to the veteran.

4) When passing papers the buyer will be required to sign:
   A) Mortgage Note and Mortgage Deed
   B) Mortgage Deed, but not the Mortgage Note
   C) Title Deed
   D) Mortgage Note, but not the Mortgage Deed

5) In a sale and leaseback, which of the following is true?
   A) The Lessor becomes the Grantor
   B) The Lessor becomes the Lessee
   C) The Grantor becomes the Lessee
   D) The Lessee becomes the Grantor

6) Which of the following statements is true concerning the secondary mortgage market?
   A) Fannie Mae sells to the mortgage company
   B) The primary mortgage market sells to the secondary market
   C) The lending institution buys mortgages from the secondary market
   D) Fannie Mae guarantees the loan to the bank

7) Which of the following statements is true regarding Regulation Z?
   A) Applies to a business borrowing money from a bank
   B) Applies to an individual borrowing money from anyone
   C) Applies to a business borrowing money from anyone
   D) Applies to an individual borrowing money from a bank

8) If a buyer pays $80,000 cash and the seller takes back a mortgage note for $10,000 on a $90,000 condo, the $10,000 mortgage can be described as:
   A) Purchase Money Mortgage
   B) Junior Mortgage
   C) Assumable Mortgage
   D) Balloon Mortgage

9) A mortgage protected by two parcels of property would be:
   A) Wraparound Mortgage
   B) Insured Mortgage
   C) Blanket Mortgage
   D) Open End Mortgage

10) Which of the following statements is most likely to be true concerning fixed rate loans?
   A) A bank will hold fixed rate mortgages in their own portfolio
   B) A mortgage company will hold variable rate mortgages in their own portfolio
   C) A bank will sell fixed rate mortgages to F.N.M.A.
   D) A bank will sell fixed rate mortgages to a mortgage company.

Answer Key

Glossary Quiz		Self Quiz A		Self Quiz B	
1)	Point	1)	C	1)	C
2)	Mortgagee	2)	A	2)	C
3)	Blanket Mortgage	3)	D	3)	C
4)	Conventional Mortgage	4)	C	4)	A
5)	Disclosure Statement	5)	D	5)	C
6)	Junior Mortgage	6)	A	6)	B
7)	Mortgage Note	7)	C	7)	D
8)	Mortgage Deed	8)	A	8)	A
9)	Purchase Money Mortgage	9)	B	9)	C
10)	Right of Rescission	10)	B	10)	C

Amortization Table per $1,000

YEARS	6%	7%	8%	9%	10%	11%
15	8.44	8.99	9.56	10.15	10.75	11.37
20	7.16	7.75	8.36	9.00	9.66	10.33
25	6.44	7.07	7.72	8.40	9.09	9.81
30	6.00	6.65	7.34	8.05	8.78	9.53

8 Real Estate Brokerage

The following terms and concepts will be covered in this chapter. They will also be found in the glossary at the back of the text.

Terms and Concepts

Accountability
Agency
Agent
Attorney in fact
Broker
Buyer agent
Care
Client
Co-Mingling of funds
Confidentiality
Customer
Disclosure
Disclosed dual agent
Dual agent
Escrow Agent
Estoppel Agent
Exclusive Office Listing
Exclusive Right to sell
Expressed Agency
Fiduciary
General Agency
General power of attorney
Implied Agency

Imputed Notice
Independent contractor
Law of agency
Listing
Loyalty
Multiple listing
Net listing
Notice
Obedience
Open Listing
Option listing
Power of attorney
Principal
Procuring cause
Puffing
Realtor
Seller agent
Single agent
Special power of attorney
Sub-agent
Tristram's Landing
Undisclosed dual agent

Broker

A real estate **broker** is any individual who, for consideration, sells, buys, rents, exchanges, or negotiates options on real property. (This is a general definition. A more complete one is included in the Chapter on License Law). The majority of real estate brokers deal with the sale of real property. Therefore, the issues we shall discuss will be primarily addressed to the sale of real property. We should keep in mind, however, that these principles do apply to other brokerage areas. A broker may specialize in many areas in addition to residential sales such as rentals, property management, commercial, industrial, exchanging, investment counseling, developing, and education, to name a few. It should be noted that although the broker will be referred to as an individual, the broker may in fact be a partnership or corporation.

Law of Agency

The **law of agency** is that part of our contract law that governs the relationship between a **principal** who hires an **agent** to represent him and the agent who is hired to be the representative of the principal. Most agency relationships in the past have been between the seller as the principal and the broker as agent. However, the buyer may hire a broker as a representative. The broker is then the agent of the buyer who is the principal in the principal-agent relationship. This increase in buyer's brokerage is a recent one in Massachusetts and will be covered in more detail in a later chapter on Massachusetts state sensitive issues.

Therefore, the **principal** is the individual who hires the agent (could be either the buyer or the seller). The **agent** is the broker who is hired by the principal (either the buyer or the seller). The relationship between the principal and the agent is known as **agency.** The agent must act in the best interest of his principal at all times. This is known as a **fiduciary relationship** which means a position of trust and confidence.

The relationship between the principal and agent must also be clear in client-customer terms.

The one who has hired the agent to represent him is the **client** (buyer or seller). The third party to whom service is provided is the **customer.**

For example, when Seller Sally hires Agent Al to sell her house and Buyer Bob purchases the property, Seller Sally is the principal and Agent Al is the agent. Seller Sally is also Agent Al's client and Buyer Bob is Agent Al's customer.

Seller Sally hires Agent Al to sell to Buyer Bob

Client ------------**Agent**----------------Customer

The roles will change in a buyer's brokerage relationship.

Make sure you know who is your client and who is your customer and what your fiduciary duties are to each!

Buyer Agency

The concept of a **buyer broker** is a recent one in Massachusetts. The real estate broker needs to be very certain to establish who is his principal and therefore his client. The fiduciary relationship between agent and principal becomes much more complicated when some agents represent the seller, some agents represent the buyer and in a co-broke situation we may have a buyer's broker and a seller's broker involved in the same transaction.

Single Agency

The most common agency is **a single agency**. That is, the broker represents one party, seller or buyer. Seller S hires broker agent A to sell his property. Single agency also exists when buyer B hires agent A to find a house.

Dual Agency

The law allows agent A to be a **dual agent,** that is to represent both buyer and seller.

Seller S has hired agent A to sell his three family house and Buyer B has also contracted with Agent A to find him a good piece of investment property. If B buys S's property; agent A has represented both the buyer and seller. This would then be **dual agency** and is allowable under the law. Dual agency must be disclosed and informed consent in advance from each must be in writing according to Massachusetts License Law. If both parties do not consent to the broker's representation of both the buyer and seller in the same transaction we have **undisclosed dual agency** and this is illegal.

Note: Although the payment of a fee usually follows the agency relationship, this is not essential. Payment of a fee does not establish an agency relationship.

For example a Buyer Broker fee may be paid in full or in part from the Selling Broker's fee. The Buyer Broker fee may also be paid by the Buyer. This may be outside the transaction or out of the sale proceeds. All of these arrangements are subject to negotiation between the parties; Seller, Listing Broker, Buyer and Buyer Broker.

Sub-Agents

When a listing agent co-brokes with other brokers, a sub-agency is established. The initial agency must be agreed to between the Principal (the seller) and the Agent (the broker). The Agent must consent to the agency and often times uses other real estate agents in a cooperative or co-broke arrangement. The co-broke agent has an agency relationship with the listing broker and is the **sub-agent** of the seller.

The following represents several of the agency relationships possible with a listing agent, a cooperating sub-agent and a buyer's broker.

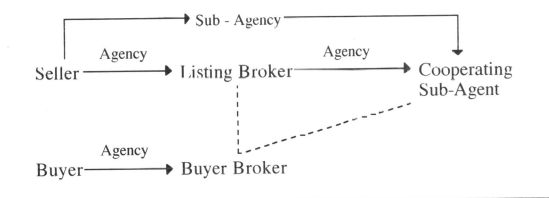

Types of Agency

There are a number of types of agency relationship between a principal and an agent:

1) **General Agency** - an agency relationship covering a broad range of matters. A property manager managing an apartment complex would be a general agent for the apartment owner principal. The relationship of a real estate broker and the sales-associates selling real estate within that office would be a general agency. The agent is representing the principal in a broad range of matters; more than a single matter. (also known as Universal Agency)

2) **Special Agency** - agency where the agent is hired to perform an individual or specific act such as to sell a house. A listing agreement between a seller as principal and a broker as agent to sell a parcel of property would be a special agency and the broker would be a special agent. (also known as Limited Agency)

3) **Estoppel Agency** - an agency established when a third party has reason to believe that due to the actions of two parties that an agency relationship exists. Even if an agency relationship does not formally exist if two parties allow it to appear by their actions that there is an

agency relationship, the courts may find there is an agency by estoppel (ostensible agency). The court can then estoppel the principal from denying the agency.

Facilitator / Transactional Broker

A Transactional Broker or Facilitator is a Broker who does not represent either the Seller or the Buyer. The Transactional Broker acts as a middleman (Facilitator) to see that the transaction moves smoothly through its various stages to a successful conclusion at the closing with no Agency relationship to either the Seller or the Buyer. No Seller Agency, no Buyer Agency, no Dual Agency.

Power of Attorney

A **Power of Attorney** is a legal document that authorizes an individual to act for another. You do not have to be a lawyer to be appointed as a Power of Attorney although most Powers of Attorney will be granted to an **Attorney at Law.** When appointed through a Power of Attorney an individual becomes an **Attorney in Fact.**

The Power of Attorney may cover all of a principal's matters in a General or Universal Power of Attorney or may be limited to a range of matters in a Special or Limited Power of Attorney.

An elderly person turning all of their affairs over to the family lawyer or a relative would establish a General (Universal) Power of Attorney.

A property owner turning control of their real estate holdings to another would establish a Special (Limited) Power of Attorney.

Creation of an Agency

An agency relationship can be either **expressed** or **implied**. An expressed agency is created by mutual consent between a principal and agent. This can be in writing or orally (not in writing).

A written listing contract between a seller and a broker is an expressed agency. A verbal agreement between a seller and a broker is an expressed agency. A listing agreement in Massachusetts does not have to be in writing. It can be verbal. However, a written listing agency is highly recommended so that each party clearly understands the terms of the agreement.

A written or verbal agreement between a buyer and a broker is an expressed agency. (Buyer-Agency Agreement)

If a principal and agent have not agreed to an agency relationship (either in writing or verbally) but by their actions indicate they have established an agency then they may establish an implied agency and be held accountable.

For example, a Seller's Sub-Agent who acts in the interest of the Buyer " they are asking $200,000 but I suggest offering $180,000 because the property has been on the market for several months" may be found to have created an **Implied Buyer Agency** and therefore be in a **Dual Agency** relationship that would require Dual Agency disclosure.

Imputed Notice

Imputed Notice is knowledge by an agent that is binding on the principal due to the principal-agent relationship even though the principal does not have first hand knowledge. Ex. Notice under a purchase and sale agreement as to a buyer's ability to obtain financing.

Types of Listings

There are several basic types of listings with which we should be familiar:

1) **Open listing** - more than one broker has been given the listing. The broker who sells the property receives the total commission. The seller retains the right to sell the property without paying a commission.

2) **Exclusive office listing** - only one broker is given the listing. The seller retains the right to sell the property without paying a commission (also known as **exclusive agency**).

3) **Exclusive right to sell** - one broker is given the listing. The seller agrees to pay the broker's commission no matter who sells the property (including a direct sale by the seller without the broker).

4) A **Net listing** is any of the three basic types of listings where the seller states what he wishes to receive and the broker keeps everything over that amount. (For example, a seller wants $140,000 for his property. If the broker finds a buyer who will pay $180,000, the broker keeps $40,000.) **Net listings are illegal in Massachusetts.**

5) A **Multiple listing** is a form of exclusive right to sell or exclusive office listing where the listing broker allows other brokers to share the listing. The commission is typically divided between the listing broker and the selling broker. Some listing agents do not compensate a buyer broker. The Multiple Listing Service is a part of the REALTOR® organization and listings are submitted through the local Board of REALTORS® M.L.S. system.

Termination of Agency

An agency may be terminated in a variety of ways:

1) **Completion of objective** - the property is sold.
2) **Expiration of time limit** - time passes beyond a certain time limit (for example, a sixty-day listing).
3) **Mutual consent** - Both seller and broker agree to cease.
4) **Revocation of either party** - The seller or broker unilaterally decides to terminate the agency without the mutual consent of the other party. This may result in damages due by one party to the other, depending on circumstances.
5) **Death of the party** - If either principal or agent dies, the agency is terminated.

6) **Destruction of subject** - If the property burns to the ground, the agency is terminated.
7) **Bankruptcy** - If either party is bankrupt, he loses his financial ability and the agency may be terminated.

Duties of an Agent

Under the Law of Agency the agent has a fiduciary relationship to his/her principal. A fiduciary relationship is one of trust and confidence. This basically means that the agent must act in the principal's best interest at all times.
The fiduciary responsibilities or duties of an agent are:

O - **Obedience**
L - **Loyalty**
D - **Disclosure**
C - **Confidentiality**
A - **Accountability**
R - **Reasonable Care and Diligence**

Duty of Obedience - An agent must obey the principal's instructions in all matters even if these instructions are not in the agent's best interest. However, this does not include instructions that may include a violation of the law such as misrepresentation in marketing and advertising or discrimination against a protected class of minorities.

Ex. Seller instructs the Broker to contact a neighbor who has expressed interest before any other showings.
Seller instructs the Broker to withdraw a counteroffer.

Duty of Loyalty - The broker as agent must act in the principal's best interest even when that is not in the best interest of the agent.
For example, a co-broke offer may be in the best interest of the seller as principal when a competing offer might result in a higher commission for the broker as agent if through the broker's office.
A Listing Broker owes Loyalty to the Seller.
A Buyer's Broker owes Loyalty to the Buyer.

Undisclosed Dual Agency is an excellent example of a violation of the Duty of Loyalty and in this case, to both Buyer and Seller.

Duty of Disclosure - (also known as **Duty of Notice**) an agent must keep the principal informed of any information that is in the principal's best interest. That agent must disclose any self interest such as being related to the buyer or having an equity position with the buyer. For example, a seller's agent must disclose any known financial information about the buyer, such as bad credit or willingness to make a higher offer. A buyer's agent must disclose known information about the seller such as the seller's being on the verge of foreclosure.

Duty of Confidentiality - Confidentiality is related to Loyalty and requires the Agent to keep confidential any information about the principal / client that should not be revealed to others.
Ex, Financial condition of client to customer.

Duty of Accountability - The broker as agent must account for all funds handled by him. This includes maintaining a separate account or accounts for deposits held and bringing those funds to the closing as called for in the purchase and sale agreement. Combining deposit monies with the agent's personal or business accounts is **co-mingling** of funds and is illegal. All funds held as an agent must be held separately in third party accounts known as escrow funds. In holding deposit funds the agent is known as an **escrow agent**, who is a third party holding monies for two other parties. In some areas a separate escrow agent is used but it is common for the real estate broker to act as escrow agent and to hold escrow funds.

Duty of Reasonable Care and Diligence - An agent should use a reasonable degree of care and skill in representing his or her principal. In the case of an agent representing a seller the agent should use reasonable care in making sure the listing information is accurate, that the property is marketed properly including adequate advertising, that the offer and purchase and sale agreement are properly executed and that all of the inspections, financing requirements and closing details are coordinated to insure that the closing takes place as agreed, all in the most professional manner and in the best interest of the seller.

The 4 D's - Decide, Disclose, Do and Document

One helpful way to review agency strategy is the 4 D's - Decide, Disclose, Do and Document.

1) Decide - Decide if you intend to represent the seller, the buyer or both.

2) Disclose - Disclose to the seller and the buyer what the agency options are (Seller Agency, Buyer Agency and Dual Agency) and what your agency relationship will be.

3) Do - Implement the Agency Obligations as required by Agency Law, Fiduciary Duties and Specific Agency Contract.

4) Document - Establish a file of all paperwork involved in agency relationships including Seller and Buyer Agency Contracts, Agency Disclosure Forms - Seller, Buyer and Dual and Sub-Agency rejections. It is also recommended that as part of the documentation plan that each office create a specific Office Agency Policy and Procedure Manual.

Massachusetts Agency Disclosure (254 C.M.R. 2.05)

One of the largest areas of complaint received by the Board of Registration of real estate brokers and salesmen involves agency. Many buyers are not aware that in most transactions the real estate agent is an agent for the seller and not for the buyer. It is possible for an agent to be a "buyer's broker" and to be hired by the buyer and then represent the buyer. This is not the case, however, in most transactions. The possibility of this type of misunderstanding is especially high in a co-broke situation where a broker or salesperson is showing a buyer many pieces of property through several listing offices. The buyer tends to identify with the sales associate and think of him as a "buyer's broker" when he is not.

The danger is also present that the broker or salesperson will fall into the same trap and forget who is the principal, and that his or her agency obligations are to the seller, and not the buyer.

Statements like these are often heard:

"How much do you think they will accept?" or
"I'll offer $190,000 but I'll come up to $200,000 if I have to."

These show the misunderstanding by the buyer of whom the broker represents.

Massachusetts is one of more than forty states that have some type of agency disclosure to attempt to clarify the agency misunderstanding.

The fundamentals of types of agency, their definitions and agency duties and responsibilities have been covered in Chapter 8 Real Estate Brokerage. This chapter should be reviewed if necessary for fundamentals.

In this section we will look at the updated Massachusetts Agency Disclosure Regulations 254 C.M.R. 2.05 effective July 2, 1993.

Amend 254 C.M.R. 2.05 as follows:

(15) Agency Disclosure. A real estate broker or real estate salesperson shall provide to a prospective purchaser or seller of real estate a notice developed and approved by the board which clearly discloses the relationship of the broker or salesperson with the prospective purchaser or seller of the real estate.

The notice approved by the Board shall be provided to a prospective purchaser or seller at the time of the first personal meeting between the prospective purchaser or seller and the broker or salesperson for the purpose of discussing a specific property where such broker or salesperson represents either the purchaser or seller exclusively.

Where the broker or salesperson has obtained the informed consent of both the purchaser and seller to represent both of them, such broker or salesperson must, at the time of obtaining the informed consent, provide written notice to the purchaser and seller informing them of the consensual dual agency representation and otherwise comply with the following requirements noted herein.

A broker or salesperson shall request a prospective purchaser or seller to sign and date such notice, provide the original to the prospective purchaser or seller and maintain a copy with their records for a period of three years from the date of the notice should the Board choose to inspect such.

If a prospective purchaser or seller declines to sign the notice the broker or salesperson shall make a notation indicating the date that the notice was given to the prospective purchaser or seller, and that the prospective purchaser or seller declined to sign it, and the reason, if any, given by the prospective purchaser or seller. The broker shall maintain such notice with his records in the manner noted herein.

Nothing herein shall require written notice to each prospective purchaser or seller who comes to an open house showing of real property provided, however, that the broker or salesperson by sign, poster, distributed listing literature or property description form conspicuously discloses their agency relationship. Where the listing literature or property description form is distributed at an open house, the written disclosure of the agency relationship therein shall be more conspicuous than any other written terms.

By way of this Amendment to the Agency Disclosure Regulation, real estate professionals have been told who must disclose, to whom they must disclose, what and when they must disclose and specifics on disclosure forms, record keeping and penalties.

Scope of the Agency Disclosure Regulation

The regulation applies to sales, both residential and commercial, but not to rentals, either residential or commercial. Disclosed Dual Agency is defined and is legal. A broker is a Dual Agent when he represents both the seller and the buyer in the same transaction. The Dual Agency must be disclosed to both seller and buyer. Undisclosed Dual Agency is illegal.

The Agency relationship including both seller agency, buyer agency or dual agency must be disclosed to all consumers. Subsequently that agency relationship is disclosed to a prospective buyer by means of the Agency Disclosure Form being discussed in this section.

Buyer vs. Seller Agency Disclosure

Real estate professionals (Brokers and Salespersons) are required to disclose their agency relationship with their principal (either Seller or Buyer). This agency must be disclosed to their prospective customer (either Buyer or Seller) at their first personal meeting to discuss a specific price of property. Ex.

1) How is the real estate market? - No Disclosure Required - General
2) Do you have any three bedroom capes? - No Disclosure Required - General
3) Could you tell me about the $160,000 Colonial in your Ad? or I would like an appointment to see the Colonial at 100 Main Street. Disclosure required- Specific

These questions are specific and require disclosure at the first personal meeting.

The Agency must be disclosed whenever the Agency is exclusive (either Seller or Buyer Agency) using a Board of Registration approved form (copy at the end of Chapter 12.)

The disclosure form must be signed by the consumer (Buyer or Seller) and the original given to the consumer (Buyer or Seller).

A broker with an exclusive listing with a Seller (client) to sell a parcel of property would be required to disclose the Seller Exclusive Agency relationship to the prospective buyer (consumer) at the first personal meeting to discuss and show the property.

A broker with an exclusive Buyer Agency agreement with a buyer (client) would be required to disclose the Buyer Exclusive Agency relationship to the Seller (Customer) or the Seller's Agent at the first personal meeting to discuss the subject property.

Note that the client - customer position changes when the Agency changes from Seller Agency to Buyer Agency. However, the requirement to disclose exclusive client agency to the customer at the first personal meeting to discuss a specific piece of property is the same.

Co-broke and Sub-agent Disclosure

A listing agent (Sellers Agency) must give a disclosure form to the Seller and to the Buyer (unless a subagent has already done so).

A Sub-agent (Co-broke) must give a disclosure form to the Seller (unless the listing broker has done so) and to the buyer.

A Buyer Agent must give a disclosure form to the Seller (through the Sellers listing Agent) and to the Buyer.

Dual Agency

Real estate Brokers or Salespersons must disclose a Dual Agency relationship in writing to both Seller and Buyer at the time that they obtain the informed consent of both the seller and the buyer.

Open House

Real estate Brokers and Salespersons do not have to provide an agency disclosure form or written notification of Dual Agency at an open house. However, they must conspicuously display their agency relationship at the open house.

Open house disclosure can include a sign or poster, distributed listing literature or property description form.

New Agency Disclosure Form

A copy of the new Agency Disclosure Form is included on the following page.

The front of the form explains agency and consumer rights and reminds the consumer to assume responsibility by asking questions about fee structure and encourages the consumer to seek the advise of a professional (such as lawyer or accountant) if necessary.

The broker or salesperson discloses his agency status identifying the agency relationship to either the seller or the buyer. The consumer signs and dates the form and keeps the original.

This form cannot be used for Disclosed Dual Agency. A separate form must be prepared.

The Broker or salesperson should have the consumer read both sides and must use the Board approved form. If the form is redone the type must be as large as the board approval form as a minimum and must retain as capitalized any letters capitalized in the Board approved form.

Record Keeping

An office principal must keep copies of all signed Agency Disclosure Forms or Disclosed Dual Agency Notifications for a period of three years to allow for Real Estate Board of Registration inspection. Original copies of Disclosure Forms must be given to the consumer.

Penalties

Penalties for non compliance with the Agency Disclosure Regulations can result in rescission of agents real estate license, loss of commission, damages, loss of Real Estate License, violation of M.G.L. c. 93A Consumer Protection Act and violation of the REALTOR® Code of Ethics.

Note

The new agency regulations and the complications of a changing seller and buyer agency environment will create many questions about Agency that will have to be worked out in the future.

Newly licensed real estate professionals should continue to take advantage of agency education provided by their office principals and their local and state REALTOR® Associations.

A copy of the form is as follows:

Massachusetts Board of Registration of Real Estate Brokers and Salespersons Mandatory Agency Disclosure — Agency Relationship

The purpose of this disclosure is to enable you to make informed choices before working with a real estate licensee. It must b provided at the first personal meeting that you have with an agent to discuss a specific property. THIS IS NOT A CONTRACT It is a disclosure notice for your information and protection. BE SURE TO READ THE DESCRIPTIONS OF TH DIFFERENT TYPES OF AGENCY REPRESENTATION ON THE OTHER SIDE OF THIS DISCLOSURE.

Consumer Information

1. Whether you are the buyer or the seller you can choose to have the advice, assistance and representation of your own agen Do not assume that a broker is acting on your behalf unless you have contracted with that broker to represent you.

2. All real estate licensees must, by law, present properties honestly and accurately.

3. If you are a seller you may authorize your listing agent to cooperate with agents from other firms to help sell you property. These cooperating agents may be subagents who work for the sellers' or buyers' agents.

4. If you are the buyer you have the option of working with sellers' or buyers' agents. This decision will depend on the typ of services you want from a real estate agent. A buyer should tell sellers' agents, including subagents, only what he/sl would tell the seller directly.

Consumer Responsibility

The duties of a real estate licensee do not relieve the consumer of the responsibility to protect his/her own interest. Consume with questions on whether and how real estate agents share fees should pose them to the agent. If you need advice for legal, ta insurance or other matters it is your responsibility to consult a professional in those areas.

ACKNOWLEDGEMENT

I have provided this disclosure form to _____. I will be assisting the abo

named consumer as a: (✓ check one) _____ Sellers' Agent _____ Buyers' Agent

_____   _____   _____ _____ , 19_____
(Signature of Real Estate Agent)   (License No.)   (Month)   (Day)   (Year)

I have read this agency disclosure form IN ITS ENTIRETY ON BOTH SIDES. I understand that this form is for agen disclosure AND NOT A CONTRACT. It was provided to me by the agent named above.

_____   _____ _____ , 19_____   Check here: _____ Buyer
(Signature of consumer)   (Month)   (Day)   (Year)   _____ Seller

_____ As a Consumer I recognize that I need not select any agency representation at this time. Therefore, I decline to sign th disclosure. Any additional reason for declining to sign:

_____

_____

Types of Agency Representation

Seller's Agent

When a seller engages the services of a listing broker that seller becomes the broker's client. This means the broker, and its subagents represent the seller. They owe the seller undivided loyalty, utmost care, disclosure, obedience to lawful instruction, confidentiality and accountability. They must put the seller's interest first and negotiate for the best price and terms for their client, the seller. (The seller may also authorize subagents to represent him/her in marketing its property to buyers).

Buyer's Agent

When a buyer engages the services of a broker then that buyer becomes the broker's client. This means the broker represents the buyer. The broker owes the buyer undivided loyalty, utmost care, disclosure, obedience to lawful instructions, confidentiality and accountability. The broker must put the buyer's interest first and negotiate for the best price and terms for their client, the buyer. (The buyer may also authorize subagents to represent him/her in locating property.)

Disclosed Dual Agent

A broker can work for both the buyer and the seller on the same property provided such broker obtains the informed consent of both parties. The broker is then considered a disclosed dual agent. This broker owes the seller and the buyer a duty to deal with them fairly and honestly. In this type of agency relationship the broker does not represent either the seller or buyer exclusively and they cannot expect the brokers undivided loyalty. Also, undisclosed dual agency is illegal.

Commissions

The first thing a broker must be able to demonstrate in order to collect a commission is that he or she was hired to sell the property. The broker must have had the listing to be entitled to a commission.

Tristram's Landing

Prior to a 1975 Massachusetts case known as the "Tristram's Landing" case, a broker earned a commission if a "ready, willing and able" buyer was produced. A closing or passing of papers was not necessary, although it was usual. The agent was referred to as the **"Procuring Cause"** which is defined as the one agent who is the active, efficient cause of a sale. Only one person can be a procuring cause.

The major change brought about by the 1975 "Tristram's Landing" case was that the court held that the rule for determining when a broker has earned his commission would have three parts unless the listing agreement sets forth a different rule.

The three requirements are:

1) The broker must produce a ready, willing and able buyer.
2) The buyer and seller must sign a contract to purchase.
3) A closing must occur, unless prevented by the wrongful conduct of the seller.

It must be noted that the listing agreement may set forth other terms, but in the absence of such other terms these three requirements apply.

The major impact on the brokerage profession is that in addition to producing a "ready, willing and able" buyer, a broker must also have a signed agreement and a closing must take place unless the transaction does not go forward due to the seller's wrongful conduct.

Commissions Negotiable

The commission earned for the sale of real property is determined by the agreement of the two parties, broker and principal (buyer or seller). The law does not specify what the commission will be; commissions are negotiable. For a selling agent, commissions are usually specified at the time of listing the property and are expressed as a percent of sell price (for example, "commission to be X percent of the selling price"). A broker often charges different rates, depending on the type of property listed. He may charge a certain percent of the sell price for new houses, a different percent for houses that are not new, and a third percent for land. Different brokers may have different rates even in the same area. It is important to remember that the commission rate or fixed fee is negotiable between the principal and broker. There are no set or fixed rates.

Within each office, the commission will be split according to the part a salesman played in putting the transaction together. The listing sales associate, selling sales associate and office commission split will vary from office to office. If the sale happened to be a co-broke, the commission is generally split between the two agencies prior to the salespeople receiving their shares.

Also, if the agency is a member of one of the national marketing companies/franchises, five to ten percent of an office's gross may have to be paid to the parent company. (See Math chapter dealing with commissions.)

There are no rules set as to the amount or share of a commission that a salesperson is to receive. This is a negotiable item and each office will have guidelines in this area. It is also important to note that a salesperson only has recourse to the employing agent for compensation, not the seller or buyer.

Also as stated earlier in this chapter, a Buyer Broker fee may be paid in full or in part from the Selling Broker's fee. The Buyer Broker fee may also be paid by the Buyer. This may be outside the transaction or out of the sale proceeds. All of these arrangements are subject to negotiation between the parties; Seller, Listing Broker, Buyer and Buyer Broker.

Capital Gains

The tax bill signed by the president on August 5, 1997 significantly changed capital gains implications for the home owner. Instead of a one time capital gain exemption of $125,000 after age 55 on the sale of your personal residence, married couples can exempt from capital gain tax up to $500,000 on each sale of a personal residence lived in for two of the last five years. A single person can exempt up to $250,000. Although the roll over provision to defer taxes by passing the gain on to a new and larger home have been eliminated, most people feel this new exemption is much better.

In addition to the larger exemption rates for capital gains the rate at which capital gains are taxed were reduced even though the time to qualify changed from twelve to eighteen months. For people in higher tax brackets the rate went from 28% to 20% and for others in lower brackets it went from 15% to 10%. These rates go down even further for property purchased after December 31, 2000 and held five years or more to 18% and 8%.

Other changes included the provision that some individuals could take up to $10,000 from an IRA to go towards the purchase of a first time home. As with any tax law, implications for individuals and circumstances to qualify vary greatly also the regulations can change. It is VERY important to discuss these options with your tax advisor or a professional in the field.

Broker vs. Salesperson

The real estate salesperson does not have a direct contractual relationship with the seller. The seller pays the broker and the broker pays the salesperson. In matters of handling deposit money, payment of commissions, or any dispute of those matters, the salesperson deals with the broker, not the principal (seller or buyer). A salesperson should give deposit money to the broker for disposition, not to the seller. A salesperson may not bill the seller for his fee. He must be compensated by the broker.

Realtor®

The term "REALTOR®" is a copyrighted and registered term reserved for those brokers and salespeople who have received their real estate licenses and who have joined the National Association of REALTORS®(NAR) and subscribe to the NAR Code of Ethics. In becoming a REALTOR®, the real estate professional joins a local board, The Massachusetts Association of REALTORS® and the NAR.

Consult the preface for more information and for the REALTOR® Code of Ethics.

Glossary Quiz

1) A type of listing where property is listed with one broker, owner retains the right to sell himself _____

2) That portion of contract law which affects the principal -agent relationship _____

3) One who is authorized to act for another _____

4) One who is in a position of trust and confidence _____

5) Mixing deposit money received as agent with personal or business funds _____

6) A listing agreement where the seller is to receive a specified amount and the broker retains anything over that amount _____

7) One who engages an agent to act in his behalf _____

8) One who is licensed and for consideration sells, rents, exchanges or negotiates options on real property _____

9) Contract between a seller and broker for the sale of real property for a commission _____

10) A type of listing where property is listed with one broker, owner does not retain the right to sell himself _____

Self Quiz A

1) Which of the following type of listing offers the Broker the best listing contract?
   A) Net Listing
   B) Open Listing
   C) Exclusive Right to Sell *could*
   D) Exclusive Agency *BE CO-LISTED*

2) Broker A(seller's agent) shows property listed with Broker B (seller's agent) through the Multiple Listing Service. Which of the following statements regarding Broker A's agency is correct?
   A) Broker A has a dual agency with Broker B and the Seller
   B) Broker A is the sub-agent of Broker B
   C) Broker A has no agency relationship with the Seller
   D) Broker A may not collect a fee from the Buyer even if the Seller is aware of such a fee.

3) In a transaction where we have a Seller, a Listing Broker and a Selling Broker as seller's agent selling on a co-broke arrangement, which of the following statements about the parties is not correct?
   A) The Listing Broker is the Principal, Selling Broker is the agent
   B) The Seller is the Principal, the Listing Broker is the agent
   C) The Listing Brokers is the agent, the Selling Broker is the sub-agent
   D) The Selling Broker has a fiduciary relationship with the Seller

4) The relationship of a Broker to a Seller is one of the following:
   A) Sub-agent
   B) General agent
   C) Universal agent
   D) Special agent

5) In a co-broke sale, the Selling Salesperson receives his/her commission from the:
   A) Listing Broker
   B) Bank Attorney
   C) Selling Broker
   D) Seller

6) A written listing agreement between a Seller and a Broker is an example of which of the following types of contract?
   A) Executed implied
   B) Executed bilateral
   C) Executory unilateral
   D) Executory bilateral

7) In Massachusetts, which of the following types of listings is illegal?
   A) Net Listing
   B) Open Listing
   C) Exclusive Listing
   D) Exclusive Right to Sell

8) In an open listing, the commission is due to the Broker who:
   A) First showed the property
   B) Brought the highest offer
   C) Provided a ready, willing and able buyer
   D) First listed the property

9) A salesperson's relationship to his/her Broker is that of:
   A) General Agent
   B) Special Agent
   C) Limited Agent
   D) No Agent

10) In which of the following relationships is there not an agency relationship?
   A) Seller and Broker
   B) Buyer and Seller
   C) Listing Broker and Selling Broker
   D) Broker and Salesperson

Self Quiz B

1) The head of a company managing a condominium complex would have the following type of agency:
   A) Limited agency
   B) Sub-agency
   C) Special agency
   D) General agency

2) In a co-broke where both offices represent the seller, which of the following statements is true:
   A) The Selling office has no agency relationship to the Seller
   B) The Selling office has an agency relationship to the Seller only
   C) The Selling office has a dual agency to the Seller and the Listing office
   D) The Selling office has an agency relationship to the Seller and to the Listing office

3) If a buyer cannot obtain financing by the required date
   A) The Salesperson should return the deposit
   B) The Salesperson should turn the deposit over to the Broker for disposition
   C) The Salesperson should hold the deposit in escrow until Buyer and Seller agree on its disposition
   D) The Salesperson should turn the deposit over to the Seller's Attorney for disposition

4) Which of the following statements regarding agency is true
   A) A Broker may not buy property listing with him
   B) A Broker may not represent both Buyer and Seller in the same transaction
   C) A Buyer Broker cannot Co-broker with a Seller's Broker
   D) A Broker may have a dual agency if all parties are informed

5) A broker hired to sell a house is which of the following
   A) General agent
   B) Special agent
   C) Sub-agent
   D) Universal agent

6) By putting deposit money in an escrow account the broker is demonstrating the agent's duty of:
   A) Care
   B) Obedience
   C) Accountability
   D) Loyalty

7) If the Seller has listed his property with one broker and retains the right to sell the property himself, the listing is:
   A) Exclusive office listing
   B) Exclusive right to sell
   C) Open Listing
   D) Net Listing

8) Which of the following is illegal in Massachusetts:
   A) Open Listing
   B) Net Listing
   C) Exclusive right to sell
   D) Exclusive office listing

9) Which of the following does not terminate an agency
   A) Death of the Seller
   B) Bankruptcy of the Broker
   C) Property burns to the ground
   D) Failure of the Broker to advertise

10) The real estate commission due is determined by:
   A) Massachusetts Association of REALTORS®
   B) Agreement of the Seller and Broker
   C) Real Estate Board of Registration
   D) Agreement of Selling and Listing Brokers

Answer Key

Glossary Quiz		Self Quiz A		Self Quiz B	
1)	Exclusive office listing	1)	C	1)	D
2)	Law of agency	2)	B	2)	D
3)	Agent	3)	A	3)	B
4)	Fiduciary	4)	D	4)	D
5)	Co-mingling of funds	5)	C	5)	B
6)	Net listing	6)	D	6)	C
7)	Principal	7)	A	7)	A
8)	Broker	8)	C	8)	B
9)	Listing	9)	A	9)	D
10)	Exclusive right to sell	10)	B	10)	B

9 Appraisal

The following terms and concepts will be covered in this chapter. They will also be found in the glossary at the back of the text.

Terms And Concepts

Accrued Depreciation
Anticipation
Appraisal
Appraisal Institute
Appraised Value
Appreciation
Assemblage
Assessed Value
Assessment Rate
Capitalization Rate
Certified Appraiser
Change
Comparative Market Analysis
Comparable
Condemnation
Conformity
Contribution
Cost
Cost Approach
Decreasing Return
Demand
Depreciation
Economic Obsolescence
Exchange
Fiduciary
FIRREA
Functional Obsolescence
Gross Income
Gross Rent Multiplier

Highest and Best Use
Income Approach
Increasing Return
Market Approach
Market Value
Massachusetts Association of
    Real Estate Appraisers
Member Appraisal Institute (MAI)
Net Income
Opinion of Value
Over improve
Plottage
Progression
Physical Deterioration
Rate of Return
Reconciliation
Regression
Replacement Cost
Reproduction Costs
Scarcity
Senior Residential Appraiser (SRA)
Square Foot Approach
Substitution
Supply and Demand
Tax Rate
Transferability
Unit-in Place
Useful Life
Utility
Value

Appraisal

An **Appraisal** is an estimate of market value. An appraiser does not determine, establish or set value; he/she estimates value. An appraisal is also considered somewhat subjective rather than objective since the final estimate is based in part on the appraiser's judgment. Knowledge of the market and a thorough understanding of appraisal concepts are tools necessary for accurate reports.

Appraisal is an area within the real estate profession that many people specialize in. In the past it was not necessary to have a license to perform appraisals. However, federal laws now require some form of license or certification in each state. Because of the savings and loan crisis of the 1980's and the expensive bailout of the industry, Congress passed the Financial Institution's

Reform, Recovery, and Enforcement Act of 1989 **(FIRREA)**. Investigations found that many of the losses sustained were directly related to poor appraisal skills and sometimes fraudulent appraisals. The law now requires that a real estate appraisal must be completed for any federally related transaction by a state licensed appraiser. Properties under $50,000 are exempt.

Although the federal government allows the states to set their own standards minimum requirements are detailed under FIRREA. To be licensed, an individual would have to complete 75 hours of classroom instruction, 2,000 hours of appraisal experience and pass a state exam. To receive a designation as a **Certified Appraiser** one would have to complete another 120 hours of classroom, at least two years of experience performing appraisals at least 50% of which must be nonresidential, and pass a state certification exam.

There are also professional designations and memberships appraisers can obtain at both the state and federal levels. In this state there is the **Massachusetts Association of Real Estate Appraisers** and nationally the largest is the **Appraisal Institute** which was founded by the merger of the American Institute of Real Estate Appraisers and the Society of Real Estate Appraisers in 1991. In each organization, the members are required to conform to strict codes of ethics similar in nature to the REALTOR® code of Ethics found at the beginning of this text.

Professional designations may be earned through these organizations by completing advanced course and experience requirements. As an example the Appraisal Institute awards a designation called **Senior Residential Appraiser (SRA)** which reflects experience in appraisals of one to four family units while the **Member Appraisal Institute (MAI)** designation indicates competence in all types of real estate appraisals.

While working as a real estate salesperson you would not be called upon for appraisals for loans or programs that were federally related unless you were also a licensed appraiser. This does not mean a knowledge of appraisal techniques is not necessary. Real estate professionals are from time to time asked to give "opinions of value" for a number of reasons. The most important is to set an appropriate price on a home to be marketed. Questions that you might encounter could include:

1)   I want to sell my house; what is it worth?

2)   Could we look at the income and expense figures on that six-family dwelling and see what the return of investment would be?

3)   What is the assessment and tax rate on that four-bedroom colonial?

These questions all involve appraisal issues and are typical of what a broker or salesperson may be asked. In order that these questions can be dealt with effectively, we shall look at some appraisal concepts and fundamentals.

Purpose

There are many situations where an individual would need an appraisal. To consider the different applications, one needs to understand the concept of **Market Value.**

Market Value can be defined as the highest price a buyer is willing to pay and the lowest price a seller is willing to accept as valued in monetary terms. This assumes a knowledgeable buyer and seller, that the property is on the market a reasonable amount of time, and that neither party is acting under any duress. The value of property is basically the worth of the property and may or may not be the same as its price. For example, a house may be worth $140,000, but for a variety of reasons a seller must sell quickly and accepts an offer $130,000.

Additionally, some individuals may confuse **cost** with **price** or **value**. The cost of a building, which includes land, construction materials and labor is not necessarily indicative of the market value. Even though the construction of a house may be of high quality, the selling price will only be as high as the market will bear. On the other hand, a conservatively built house in an exclusive area may sell well in excess of its cost.

Some reasons for an appraisal follow:

Sale of Property

As a real estate salesperson acting as a Seller's Agent this will be your most common use. As part of your fiduciary responsibility, you are to try to get the best price possible for the seller. If you overprice the property, it will remain on the market and may get a reputation as a problem property. If the asking price is low, the house will sell fast but you might have been able to do better for the seller. Many beginning salespeople find it difficult to estimate market value, especially in uncertain markets.

Loans

Banks will need an appraisal for financing purposes. Typically, a lending institution will loan up to 80 to 95 per cent of an appraised value, not the selling price, to insure that it's position is protected.

Insurance

In order for insurance companies to recommend an appropriate amount of coverage, it is important to first obtain an estimate of market value.

Real Estate Taxes

Cities and towns calculate real estate taxes based on the assessed value of a parcel of land. This assessed value is based on the market value of the property through appraisals. (See Math Chapter 19 for an in-depth treatment of real estate taxes.)

Condemnation

Is the process the government uses to take property by Eminent Domain. A fair price should be set on property taken, which helps avoid costly litigation.

Estate Settlement

Heirs will be interested in obtaining accurate value estimates to ensure an equitable distribution of assets in an estate and for purposes of inheritance tax resolution.

Business Acquisition

Market values of real estate will be required for accounting purposes on buildings and property acquired by a company. These needs would include values for the asset section of the balance sheet and/or for depreciation schedules.

Exchanges
Property values become particularly important in exchanges since, instead of an all-cash transaction, another piece of real estate will be used for all or part of the purchase price. Also under IRS code 1031, there may be the possibility of a tax-deferred exchange if certain conditions are met. Be sure to check with an accountant for further information in this area.

Value Elements

To create value in property, four conditions have to be met:
1) **Demand**
2) **Scarcity**
3) **Utility**
4) **Transferability**

Demand
Demand in this context represents the need or desire of potential buyers to own a piece of realty. To have true demand, the buyer must have the ability to pay.

Scarcity
Real estate is somewhat unique in the sense that it can't be reproduced. Even though a contractor may have many houses for sale, at some point this inventory runs out. This creates scarcity.

Utility
Another function property must fulfill before it can have value is to be used for some purpose. For example, a lot that can never be built on or put to use for any reason due to changes in environmental impact laws, would have little or no value.

Transferability
An individual should be able to transfer the property along with its "legal bundle of rights" without undue restrictions.

Environmental Influences to Value

Real estate is part of a world that is dynamic and ever-changing. The value of a piece of property will always be affected by forces we sometimes have little or no control over. The environment includes these categories:

1) **Physical**
2) **Social**
3) **Economic**
4) **Governmental**

Physical Forces
Many times we as individuals have little control over the physical characteristics that a parcel of realty takes on. The lay of the land, availability of water, weather conditions, or the ability to grow crops would fall into this category.

We could also include here the difficulty of getting utilities to a lot due to large rocks or other obstructions.

Social Forces

Social trends impact values not only in neighborhoods but in whole geographic locations at times. Changes in population growth, movements to more desirable locations, changes in age groups or social classes, and/or the size of the family unit will have an impact. One example of this would be the population shift from the city to the suburbs and then, to a certain degree, back to the city again.

Economic Forces

Trends in the economy would include job opportunities, growth rate of industries in a particular area, availability of financing, cost of living, real estate taxes, and the selling prices of homes as some examples.

Governmental Forces

The impact that governmental regulations have on real property values may be the force we have the most control over, by getting involved in the process. In any case, examples here might be zoning laws, building codes, moratoriums on certain kinds of construction and rent control.

Economic Variables to Value

All markets are affected by a number of different variables. Whether it be the stock market, futures market, or the money market, certain conditions or principles influence values. The real estate market is no different, and the following represents some of the variables with which a real estate professional should be familiar.

Supply and Demand

The law of supply and demand is similar to points raised in a previous section of this chapter. In general, though, this law is one of the most basic economic principles. Generally, if the quantity of a product is high, the price for that product will be low. Conversely, if the quantity of a product is low, the price it will command will be high.

This concept presents interesting reactions in the marketplace. Consider the position of manufacturers who see a product commanding a high price. The manufacturer would want to enter the market, thus increasing supply and ultimately lowering the overall selling prices. A good example of this is found in some areas where contractors have over built in the condominium market.

Highest and Best Use

This is one of the more interesting concepts in real estate. "Highest and best use" concerns itself with the fact that real estate is considered dynamic and ever-changing, always seeking its most profitable use.

A house worth $200,000 as a single-family residence may increase in value if a higher use as a commercially zoned office is possible.

Almost all of us know of areas of cities or towns that were once farm land and now are commercial or light industrial. There are also neighborhoods which years ago may not have been so desirable but are now in demand and vice versa.

These are examples of how land goes through cycles that represent its search for highest and best use.

Change

As mentioned previously, change is always occurring. Whether it be physical or economic, real estate will be advancing through its own stages of most profitable use. The important point to make here is that an individual involved in real estate sales should understand and try to anticipate these changes whenever possible. The importance of trying to foresee an appropriate use of a parcel of land cannot be overstated.

Anticipation

Value of property can increase or decrease based on benefits that may or may not be received in the future. People will look towards the enjoyment they would derive or income they could obtain by owning a particular piece of property as factors to help in evaluating the parcel in question.

Substitution

In order for a real estate professional to estimate values of properties effectively, the principle of substitution is of real importance. Potential home buyers usually do not purchase the first house seen. They shop around and get a feel for the market. When comparing houses to each other, it logically follows that when two homes are alike in the benefits offered, the buyer will choose the one that costs least. They will substitute the least expensive home for the one that costs more.

Plottage

This synergistic concept, also known as **assemblage**, increases the value of two contiguous lots by putting them together to form one large lot. For example, a number of small lots by themselves may have little value but, by putting them together you increase the frontage and total lot size which may in turn generate other options for development like a small mall or office building. The value of the whole is greater than the sum of its parts. (Plottage refers to the concept of combining lots, while assemblage refers to the process.)

Conformity

Properties located in neighborhoods where the homes are similar in nature tend to hold their values better than those houses that don't show a certain amount of continuity with the area. Many of us have heard the saying "buy the worst house on the street." This is usually true since the other homes will tend to increase the value of the "worst" house in the area. This is known as **Progression.** The converse would also be true if a large four- or five-bedroom home were built in a neighborhood of modest two- and three-bedroom houses. The value of the large home would be less here than it would be if built in an area of other like-type houses. This known as **Regression.**

Contribution

Most homeowners would like to think that any improvements made on their property will increase the value of that property by at least as much as the cost of the improvement. This is not always the case. As we have seen under our discussion on conformity, it is possible to over improve a piece of property. An example would be the owner of a house with an estimated value of $150,000. If the owner put an addition of a family room costing $20,000 on the house, one might assume a total house value of $170,000. This is not necessarily the case. Since other homes in the area were still selling for only $150,000, the house with the new addition may sell for only $160,000. The cost of the addition did not contribute an equal amount of value.

This condition is also known as the **Principle of Increasing or Decreasing Returns.** If, for every dollar invested in improvements gives you more than a dollar in value or return then you have an "**Increasing Return**" on your investment. Conversely, as in the over improvement case, when a dollar invested returns something less than a dollar in value you have what is considered a "**Decreasing Return**".

If your reason for improving real estate is done strictly for a return on investment basis than it is important to insure that you only spend those dollars that give you an increasing return. On the other hand, if you are a home owner and are adding a family room for personal use, striving for increasing returns may not be as important. In this case, even if you do not increase the value of your home an equal amount of investment, there is the intrinsic value you receive by using the space with your family. This is always hard to put a dollar value on since it is very subjective.

The Appraisal Process

In any decision making process there are a series of sequential steps that should be followed. While trying to estimate the market value of a piece of property you are in effect making a decision, the appraisal process is no exception. Even though each parcel of real estate is unique, the steps followed in an appraisal remain relatively the same. They are:

Define the Problem
The first step includes identification of the property not only by street address but, by its legal description (i.e. book and page number of the deed) which will give you direction in finding other information needed for a thorough appraisal. Also, clarify the reason for the appraisal to help understand the needs of your client and the final format the report should take.

Preliminary Analysis and Plan
Defining what type of property you will be evaluating causes emphasis on a certain appraisal method. There are three basic approaches to estimating value that are discussed in the next section of this chapter which include the 1) **Comparison**, 2) **Income** and 3) **Cost** approaches. This means different types of information may be needed and source locations should be identified. The neighborhood where the property is located should be evaluated in terms of zoning and/or changes that may be occurring to the area.

Data Selection, Collection and Analysis
In this step all necessary data is collected from the different sources identified. Care should be taken to compile only that information that relates to the problem to avoid confusion. Full legal description, compliance with zoning and building codes, permits for any specialized usage as in a business, economic conditions in the community, alternative uses of the subject property, rights of way (whether dominant or servient), future trends or construction that might affect the

area, and any amenities or encumbrances on the subject property are some examples of the types of information to be collected.

Additionally, depending on which appraisal methods are to be used, information relative to competitive properties, construction costs, and the capitalization rate for the investment and other data would be necessary.

Land Value Estimate

Based on a "highest and best use analysis", zoning laws, and values of other similar parcels of property recently sold, the value of the land alone is estimated. Some appraisal reports require separate figures for land versus improvements to the land.

Application of the Three Approaches

Appraisers should use as many of the three approaches as possible in estimating value. It is understood that one or two of the three may not be applicable or accurate information may not be available for all three. But, even for a single family home which would clearly use the "comparative market analysis" as a basis for estimating value, one could benefit from trying the other approaches to validate your choice in the report.

Typically, emphasis is placed on the comparative market analysis for residential, cost approach for younger commercial buildings, and the income approach for investment in businesses or larger(five or six units and above) rental properties. This doesn't mean you can't apply each method to other types of property. For instance, you should try the income approach or a "gross rent multiplier" (explained in the next section) on a single family home for contrast.

Reconciliation of Value Estimates

The appraiser's skills are tested during the reconciliation. If the estimate included all three approaches that varied significantly, which one would be the appropriate one to report. Since an average is not taken, the answer lies in the type of property being evaluated. As mentioned above, each kind of property is usually more closely associated with a particular approach. Comparing the value of the most appropriate method with the others is what the reconciliation is all about. "Why do the differences exist and should this vary the value in any way?" is the one of the questions that should be asked in this step.

Final Report of Value Estimate

In this last step the appraiser puts the final value estimate into report form. This may be a special form or a letter with support information depending on the purpose of the report. Information that should be detailed includes the date of value estimate, special contributing factors of value, comparative properties used, unique licensing conditions if any, reason for the report, sources for construction estimates, any plot plans used, source of information on environmental conditions, a justification of your analysis, and your credentials are some of the items that should be part of the report.

Three Approaches to Value

There are three basic approaches to value:
1) **Market or Comparison Approach**
2) **Income Approach**
3) **Cost Approach**

Market Approach

The market approach is the type used most often in residential real estate appraisal. It involves comparing the property to be appraised with other properties that have sold recently in the same or similar areas. In other words, we are going to perform a market analysis of "like" types of properties in "like" types of neighborhoods. Since no two properties are exactly alike, it will be the appraiser's job to make adjustments up or down on the **Comparable** values to match the subject property. For instance, if one of the comparable properties has an extra half-bath that the subject property does not have, an amount would be subtracted from the selling price to reflect this fact.

To show what a market analysis would look like, it's best to have an example. Let's assume you are to list a home for sale and the seller wants to know what the fair market value might be in order to set a selling price. The simplified chart that follows indicates value. You will notice some differences in the properties. In "Comp #1", everything is almost the same, except it has a one car garage and has the oldest selling date. "Comp #2" only has seven rooms but an extra half-bath and the newest construction, while the third one has the largest lot.

	Subject Property	Comparable 1	Comparable 2	Comparable 3
Selling Price	?	$145,000	$148,000	$150,000
Date Sold	Current Date	1/3/96	3/16/96	4/2/96
Total Rooms	8	8	7	8
Bedrooms	4	4	4	4
Baths	2	2	2 1/2	2
Lot Size	16,000 sq.ft.	16,225 sq. ft.	14,000 sq. ft.	18,000 sq. ft.
Garage	2 car	1 car	2 car	2 car
Age	12 years	14 years	8 years	15 years
Proximity to Subject		2 blocks	3 blocks	1/2 miles
Condition	Very Good	Equal	Fair	Equal

Based on the information gathered, the value of the house would certainly be in the high $140,000 range, depending on the current market. An asking price may be a little higher, but a seller should expect the possibility of settling for a sell price lower than what they ask.

This form has been simplified for clarity and, as a professional, you can expect to find different methods or forms depending on the reason for the appraisal and where you work.

Often times a full appraisal is not required, and an **"opinion of value"** by the broker or salesperson is sufficient. This is commonly called a **comparative market analysis** or **CMA.**

Income Approach

This approach is used when dealing with investment or income properties or businesses. Since the value of an investment is dictated by its future stream of income, it stands to reason the more income generated, the higher the value.

When investing, we would all like to capitalize on an opportunity as best as possible, thus the term **capitalization rate**. This rate represents the return we desire on our invested funds, and in the Math chapter entitled "Return on Investment" there is a detailed explanation and problems to try. Basically though, there are three factors:

1) **Market Value - the worth of the property**
2) **Net Income - gross or total income minus expenses.**
3) **Capitalization rate**

Based on previous experience or research, an appraiser should know what the capitalization rate should be for this particular type of property or business. The next step in valuing the property would be an analysis of accounting records to find the net income. Once we know these two factors, the value can be estimated by a simple division problem.

The formula is:

$$\text{Value} = \frac{\text{Net Income}}{\text{Capitalization Rate}}$$

Example: A six-family house generates income of $700 per apartment per month. The expenses are:

Real Estate Taxes	$3,600
Insurance	1,800
Utilities	1,200
Maintenance and Repairs	1,400
Miscellaneous	400

The appraiser has reviewed similar properties and found that an appropriate capitalization rate is 12 percent. What would he or she estimate the value to be?

Solution:

Gross Income

(Total Income) = $700 per unit x 6 units x 12 months = $50,400

Expenses:

Real Estate Taxes	$3,600
Insurance	1,800
Utilities	1,200
Maintenance and Repairs	1,400
Miscellaneous	400
Total Expenses	- 8,400
Net Income: (Gross Income less Expenses)	$42,000

$$\frac{\text{Net Income}}{\text{Capitalization Rate}} = \text{Value} \quad \text{therefore} \; ; \quad \frac{42,000}{.12} = \$350,000$$

Note: Appraisers also use what is called a **Gross Rent Multiplier (GRM)** to come up with a quick estimate or "ball park" figure of value. To use this method the appraiser would have to know the average relationship that gross incomes on properties have to past selling prices. For instance, when dealing with residential property, the multiplier is based on monthly gross income, so if a multi-unit building sold for $280,000 that had a total gross monthly income of $3,200 the GRM would be 87.5

$$\frac{\$280,000}{\$3,200} = 87.5$$

If other sales in the area generated approximately the same GRM, it would be safe to use for estimates. When appraisers look at a building that has gross monthly income of $2,000 they could multiply that amount by the 87.5 **GRM** and come up with a value of $175,000 for the property.

The Gross Rent Multiplier may also be expressed in annual terms. Assume a 6 unit apartment building renting at $800/ month and a typical Annual Gross Rent Multiplier of 7. What is the indicated value?

6 x $800 per month equals $4,800 per month gross rent x 12 months equals $57,600 per year gross rent. $57,600 annual gross rent times an annual GRM of 7 equals $57,600 x 7 or $403,200 indicated value.

Cost Approach

This method is best used on properties that can't be evaluated by the other two approaches or as a check on estimates derived at in other ways.

In using this approach, an appraiser would start with the **reproduction cost** (the cost of an exact duplicate) or the **replacement cost** (the cost of a similar but not an exact duplicate) of the building, then subtract an amount for depreciation of the building and add this figure to the value of the land. The final total would represent the estimate of market value.

To estimate replacement cost, the **unit-in-place** method is sometimes used, which sums the cost of each component or "unit" of the structure. The cost of the foundation would be added to the doors, etc., to come up with the total cost if the building were to be replaced.

Another, more simplified method is the **square-foot approach.** Appraisers and contractors who are good at their jobs could estimate the cost of replacing a garage 20 feet wide by 40 feet long with a 14 foot ceiling and four-foot concrete slab foundation very easily. Based on their knowledge, they would know the cost would be, let's say, $35.00 per square foot for this type of structure, so replacement cost would be $28,000 (20 feet × 40 feet = 800 sq. ft. × $35.00)

There are also other methods of estimating replacement cost and all of them are fairly accurate. The area that represents more difficulty for the appraiser is the estimate for **depreciation.** This value is to be subtracted from the replacement cost before you can add in the land value. It can at times be very subjective by nature. Depreciation may be of three types:

1) **Physical Deterioration** - the building is literally wearing out from use.
2) **Functional Obsolescence** - the property is out of date or cannot be used for its intended purpose as in the case of an older warehouse whose ceilings are too low to accommodate present-day storage requirements.
3) **Economic Obsolescence** - factors external to the property such as a deteriorating neighborhood or recently discovered toxic waste problem.

It should be pointed out here that not all decreases in value due to depreciation are incurable. Depreciation is considered curable when the cost of rectifying the defect gives an acceptable return on the investment.

The appraiser may use one or more of these categories to come to a value for deprecation.

Glossary Quiz

1) An estimate of value _____

2) Comparison of value to net income, used by an appraiser in estimating value of income property or net income divided by value _____

3) Appraisal technique that uses current replacement cost less depreciation to estimate value _____

4) External factors such as neighborhood and community deterioration that lessens the value of property _____

5) Lessening of value because property is outmoded or out of date _____

6) Total revenue from rents and other sources _____

7) Appraisal technique that divides net income of property (gross in come less expenses) by a capitalization rate to estimate value

_____

8) Appraisal technique that compares subject property with similar properties that have sold recently to estimate value

_____

9) Gross income (total revenue) less expenses

_____

10) Reduction in value because property is wearing out

_____

Self-Quiz A

1) In order for property to have value, it must meet four conditions. These conditions are demand, scarcity, utility and:
   A) Contribution
   B) Progression
   C) Transferability
   D) Change

2) Economic obsolescence is concerned with:
   A) Over improvement of a piece of property
   B) Factors external to the property
   C) Net income minus expenses
   D) Zoning laws and building code

3) The value of a piece of property is most closely associated with the:
   A) Selling price of the property
   B) Worth of the property
   C) Value placed on the property by an appraiser
   D) Assessed value as indicated by a city or town

4) An appraiser using the income approach to estimate the value of a business found the following information. The statements showed that the business earned $28,000 from sales and another $16,000 from services. Expenses included: Merchandise - $19,000, Salaries - $5,000, and rent - $6,000. Using an 8% capitalization rate, what value would the appraiser place on this investment?
   A) $500,000
   B) $350,000
   C) $200,000
   D) $175,000

5) An appraiser:
   A) Estimates value
   B) Establishes value
   C) Sets market conditions
   D) Does not use a capitalization rate

6) In estimating value, deprecation may be affected by:
A) Distress situation of seller
B) Physical deterioration
C) High capitalization rate
D) Real estate taxes

7) Appraisal of residential property most often employs:
A) Income approach
B) Cost approach
C) Market approach
D) Depreciation

8) A home buyer will typically look at a number of houses before making a buying decision. When comparing two houses, the purchaser will choose the one that costs less if all other things are equal. This is an example of the:
A) Substitution principle
B) Market approach to value
C) Utility principle
D) Contribution principle

9) "Economic Forces" might include:
A) Growth rate of industry in a particular area
B) Governmental policies
C) Estate settlement
D) Availability of water

10) All of the following are reasons for an appraisal **EXCEPT:**
A) Real estate taxes
B) Business acquisitions
C) Conformity
D) To sell property

Self Quiz B

1) Economic variables to value include all of the following except:
A) Substitution
B) Change
C) Insurance
D) Anticipation

2) Buying the worst house on the street because the value of the neighborhood will tend to bring up your value is an example of:
A) Progression
B) Change
C) Anticipation
D) Substitution

3) In appraising property the appraiser:
A) Calculates Value
B) Estimates Value
C) Determines Value
D) Sets Value

4)   All of the following are types of depreciation except:
   A)   Functional Obsolescence
   B)   Economic Obsolescence
   C)   Age
   D)   Poor Physical Condition

5)   If an appraiser multiplies the 3,000 sq. ft. in a house times $100 per sq. ft. to arrive at a value of $300,000, he is using:
   A)   Cost Approach
   B)   Income Approach
   C)   Comparative Market Analysis
   D)   Substitution Approach

6)   Net Income on a four family is determined by:
   A)   Totaling all four rental incomes
   B)   Subtracting vacancy amounts from gross income
   C)   Subtracting total expenses from gross income
   D)   Subtracting principal, interest and taxes from total rent

7)   The Capitalization approach in appraising is associated with:
   A)   Income Approach
   B)   Market Approach
   C)   Cost Approach
   D)   Profitability Approach

8)   Estimating value via the capitalization approach is most common is appraising:
   A)   Single Family Residence
   B)   New Housing Construction
   C)   Multi-Family Residences
   D)   Land Subdivisions

9)   An office building without air conditioning today is an example of:
   A)   Economic Obsolescence
   B)   Physical Deterioration
   C)   Age Depreciation
   D)   Functional Obsolescence

10) Multiplying total annual rent of $24,000 times a constant of 12 to arrive at a value of $288,000 is an example of:
   A)   Estimating Value via the Capitalization Method
   B)   Estimating Value via a gross rent multiplier
   C)   Estimating Value via the Income Approach
   D)   Estimating Value via a net Income Multiplier

Use the following annual income statement for Questions 11, 12 and 13

Rents:

Apt. #1	$7,200	
Apt. #2	7,200	
Apt. #3	8,400	
Total Rent:		$22,800
Washer and dryer Income	$1,200	
Vending Machine Income	600	
Sub-total:		1,800
Gross Income:		$24,600

Expenses:

Taxes	$3,000	
Heat	2,000	
Utilities	600	
Misc. Expense	1,000	
Total Expense:		6,600
Net Income:		$18,000

11) Using a capitalization rate of .12 the value would be:
   A) $273,600
   B) $295,200
   C) $150,000
   D) $205,000

12) Using a gross rent multiplier of 10 the value would be:
   A) $228,000
   B) $246,000
   C) $180,000
   D) $66,000

13) Using a gross income multiplier of 14 the value would be:
   A) $344,400
   B) $319,200
   C) $228,000
   D) $128,571

14) If a builder paid $24,000 for a lot and plans to build a 40' X 60' ranch which will cost $100 per sq. ft., what must he sell it for to realize a 15% return on his investment?

15) Given rents of $24,000 and expenses of $10,000 two appraisers use capitalization rates of .12 and .14, how much of a difference between their two appraisals?

Answer Key

Glossary Quiz		Self Quiz A		Self Quiz B	
1)	Appraisal	1)	C	1)	C
2)	Capitalization Rate	2)	B	2)	A
3)	Cost Approach	3)	B	3)	B
4)	Economic Obsolescence	4)	D	4)	C
5)	Functional Obsolescence	5)	A	5)	A
6)	Gross Income	6)	B	6)	C
7)	Income Approach	7)	C	7)	A
8)	Market Approach	8)	A	8)	C
9)	Net Income	9)	A	9)	D
10)	Physical Deterioration	10)	C	10)	B
				11)	C
				12)	A
				13)	A
				14)	$303,600
				15)	$16,667

10 Mass. Consumer Protection / Environmental Laws & Regulations

The following terms and concepts will be covered in this chapter. They will also be found in the glossary at the back of the text

Terms And Concepts

Asbestos

Caveat Emptor

Demand Letter

Department of Public Health (DPH)

Lead Paint Notification Form

Letter of Compliance

Letter of Interim Control

Mass Consumer Protection Act - MGL c. 93A

Mass Environmental Code - Title 5

Mass Lead Paint Law - MGL c. 111

Mass Smoke Detector Regulation

M.G.L. c. 21E

Radon

Rivers Protection Act

Smoke Detector

Triple Damages

UFFI

"Underwood" Case

"Urman" Case

Underground Storage Tanks

Wetlands Protection Act

Mass. Consumer Protection Law - M.G.L. c. 93A

Until recent consumer protection legislation, the buyer's position in a real estate transaction was described by the phrase **caveat emptor,** "let the buyer beware." During this time, the buyer had to ask a question to receive information. If the buyer didn't ask the right questions, he did not get the right answers. There generally was no legal pressure on the broker or seller to disclose any problems.

This situation has dramatically changed with the passage of the Massachusetts Consumer Protection Act. Massachusetts General Law c.93A is directed at all persons engaged in business and regulates their actions and practices in dealing with consumers; therefore, 93A Consumer Protection Act.

We will discuss 93A as it pertains to the real estate brokerage profession specifically.

The major change because of 93A is that real estate brokers and salespersons are required to disclose to the buyer anything that might affect the buyer's decision to purchase the property. Therefore, any problems must be disclosed to the buyer.

Under this concept, you are now legally responsible to disclose known defects to the buyer.

This new consumer protection law has opened up an extremely large area of legal exposure for real estate professionals. It also puts the broker and salesperson in a very difficult position of consumer disclosure to the customer while at the same time you have a fiduciary responsibility to your principal.

Demand Letter. 93A calls for a 30-day demand letter to be sent to the individual against whom the action is taken. This letter must be sent 30 days prior to any court action. The letter must outline the specifics of the complaint, the parties involved, the damages incurred and the requested relief, including the amount of money being sought. The individual receiving the demand has 30 days to respond and possibly make an offer of settlement.

If the settlement offer is rejected and later found by the court to be reasonable, the damages may be limited to the offered amount.

If the court later finds that the broker willfully and knowingly misrepresented or withheld information, the court may award not less than two times, but not more than three times the damages sought plus plaintiff's attorney's fees and costs.

If a broker wrongfully fails to respond to a claim letter, the court may find a basis for awarding treble damages.

In summary, the major changes brought about by MGL c. 93A for the real estate professional are:

1)   Full disclosure to the buyer of everything you know.
2)   Thirty-day demand letter.
3)   Up to triple damages plus attorney's fees and costs if action is found to be willful and knowledgeable.

"Underwood vs. Risman"

In a 1993 decision the Supreme Judicial Court reversed a decision in a case known as "Underwood vs. Risman" or the "Underwood Case" that substantially changes the application of M.G.L. c. 93A against Real Estate professionals for what they "should have known".

In "Underwood vs. Risman", Risman, the owner of a two family house, in Medford, rented an apartment to a couple, "Underwood", who at the time had no children. Risman then sold the two family to a third party. The Underwoods subsequently had a child, requested a lead paint inspection and the new owner deleaded. The deleading was performed illegally by the owner, not a licensed deleader as required by law. The child tested positive for lead suffering permanent neurological damage. The Underwoods sued the new owner and settled. The Underwoods also sued Risman claiming under 93A that Risman "knew or should have known" lead paint was present and warned them.

The lower court found for the Underwoods and ordered a judgment of $605,000 damages. Along with triple damages plus interest and attorney's fees, the judgment amounted to $2.2 million.

In reversing this decision the Supreme Judicial Court held that real estate professionals can only be held accountable for disclosing what they knew not what they "should have known."

This decision is a major one for any one in the real estate profession. After years of defending against legal claims that a real estate broker or salesperson "should have known", and therefore is responsible, the courts have held that the responsibility is to disclose anything "known" but not what someone alleges they "should have known".

The court decision did leave the door of responsibility open for things a real estate professional did not know but had "reason to know" and we will have to see how this develops in the courts. This ruling has an effect on both the M.G.L. c. 93A Consumer Protection Law and the M.G.L. c. 111 Lead Paint Law.

"Urman vs. South Boston Savings"

The Urmans bought a house from the South Boston Savings Bank who had foreclosed on the prior owner. They subsequently discovered the neighborhood elementary school had been closed due to ground contamination of hazardous chemicals from a nearby business.

The judge dismissed the claim stating the Urmans had not shown they had any illness caused by the contamination nor that the South Boston Savings was aware of the contamination.

The larger significance of this case is that the judge ruled that a complainant must show objective damages and not subjective distress alone.

Mass Lead Paint Law M.G.L. c. 111

Note: This section on lead paint shows the progression of the law before and after the 1984 amendment and is done chronologically.

In dealing with the subject of lead paint in Massachusetts real estate brokerage, we will look at the historical use of lead paint, the development of the current Massachusetts Lead Paint Law, and lastly the real estate broker and salesperson's responsibilities in matters concerning lead paint.

Historical Use of Lead Paint. It was only in recent years that the danger of lead poisoning, and therefore the dangers of using lead-based paint, has been understood. From the late 1600s until 1978 when it became illegal, lead was used in the manufacture of much interior and exterior paint, as well as some clear varnishes and stains. Therefore, you cannot assume that older natural wood finishes do not contain lead because they were not painted. On the other hand, not all older paints were lead-based. Some used other bases and therefore, not all old paint had a lead base. The only prudent approach is to recognize the high risk of lead paint in older finishes, and have it tested.

From the 1950's onward, the use of lead in paint decreased as its dangers became better known; but it was 1978 when the use of lead officially became illegal. One continuing concern is that store inventories and even paint stored in an individual's basement still present the risk of lead paint, where cans of paint manufactured before 1978 may have been stored and used currently.

Massachusetts Lead Paint Law. The law governing the use of lead paint in this state is Massachusetts General Law c. 111, specifically Sections 190 to 199, which deal with lead poisoning prevention and control.

This law was passed in 1971 and deals with lead poisoning from any source. We will deal with lead paint and its effect on those of us in the real estate profession.

The current law was originally passed in 1971 and was amended in 1987. The lead paint law is very complex. Detailed study and legal advice is highly recommended in any matters regarding lead paint. In this text, we will highlight some major provisions only. This material should not be considered complete and certainly not acted upon until such legal counsel is obtained. The lead paint law recognizes that very small amounts of lead in the human body can cause various medical problems. This risk is not limited to children, but the risk is greater for children.

The lead paint law requires that any property where a child under six resides must be deleaded. When property transfers ownership, the new owner assumes responsibility.

The 1971 lead paint law as amended in 1987, states that the owners of all property occupied by a child under six years of age shall delead.

This deleading shall include the covering or removing of all lead paint up to a height of five feet. The height was raised from four feet to five feet by the 1987 amendment and there is a "grandfather" provision for those who deleaded to the four-foot height prior to the 1987 amendment. The surfaces to be deleaded are referred to as "chewable, accessible surfaces," and the details of what surfaces must be deleaded is beyond the scope of this text and requires further study. The disclosure provisions of the current lead paint law has a considerable impact on real estate brokers and salespersons, and will be covered shortly.

In addition to these disclosure provisions, there are a number of additional items in the amendment:

Lead Paint Licenses. As of July 1, 1990, only licensed persons are authorized to inspect for lead paint or to delead. (see 1994 amendments in this chapter.)

Financing. No lending institution may discriminate in approving a mortgage due to the presence of lead paint. Banks are also exempt from liability if lead paint is present.

Fair Housing/Discrimination. A seller or property owner may not discriminate in the sale or rental of property because of children under six and the presence of lead paint or the need to delead.

Tax Credit. A $1500 tax credit per dwelling unit is allowed for deleading with a five-year tax carry-forward provision.

Lead Paint Disclosure Requirements. The disclosure provisions of the 1987 amendment to M.G.L. c. 111 place considerable responsibility on those of us in the real estate brokerage profession.

Effective July 1, 1988, all prospective purchasers of residential property constructed prior to 1978 must be notified by way of a disclosure form, called the "Department of Public Health Property Transfer Notification" form.

These forms can be obtained from the Massachusetts Department of Public Health or your local REALTOR® Board. This disclosure is also required by sellers where no real estate broker is involved.

This disclosure form goes into considerable detail about the dangers of lead paint, the Massachusetts Lead Paint Law, deleading procedures, the buyer's right to a lead paint inspection, and the buyer's options if lead paint is found as a result of lead inspection.

The real estate agent must verbally explain the potential presence of lead paint and its dangers, as well as the availability of inspections for dangerous levels of lead paint.

MGL c.111 - 1994 Amendment

On January 4, 1994, the Massachusetts Legislature passed a major change to the Massachusetts Lead Paint Law. The changes were numerous, far reaching and the entire amendment should be reviewed with legal advice for interpretation.

However, some of the major provisions that affect the real estate professional include:

1) **Grandfathering** - any letter of compliance that had been previously issued under earlier standards would be honored in the

future (ex. earlier 4 ft. height requirements vs. current 5 ft. height requirement)

2) **Exemptions** - The new amendment exempts rooming houses providing no child under age six resides there, eliminates applicability to lead content in soil or water and limits applicability to property built prior to 1978.

3) **Letter of Interim Control** - allows a property owner to clean up major hazards, such as peeling and chipping paint, and obtain a "Letter of Interim Control." This would give the property owner one year to delead with a possible second year under certain circumstances.

4) **Short Term Rentals** - exempts vacation rentals of 31 days or less as long as paint is not chipping or peeling.

5) **Encapsulation** - Orders the Department of Public Health (DPH) to approve encapsulants which are a liquid coating over lead paint which seals the lead and prevents exposure.

6) **Owner Deleading** - authorizes the DPH to approve certain deleading to be performed by the property owner, or the owner's agent, without the use of a licensed deleader. Such work includes removal of doors, windows and woodwork as long as no sanding or scraping takes place.

7) **Tenant Disclosure** - requires property owners to give tenants or prospective tenants a lead paint information package prepared by the DPH regarding the dangers of lead paint and the requirements of the Lead Paint Law.

8) **90 Day Window** - gives a new owner 90 days after purchasing property to obtain a "Letter of Compliance" that the property meets the requirements of the Lead Paint Law or a "Letter of Interim Control" that there is no peeling or chipping paint and the owner will proceed to delead and obtain the "Letter of Compliance" within one year.

9) **Tax Credit** - increases the maximum tax credit for abating or containing lead paint from $1,000 to $1,500 per unit and includes window replacement which was not previously included. Thus a three family owner can receive a tax credit on his state income tax return for the first $4,500 cost of lead paint work including window replacement.

We repeat that these are only some of the highlights of a very complicated Lead Paint Law. Legal advice should be obtained for any matter regarding the interpretation and application of the Lead Paint Statute.

Federal Lead Paint Law Title X (Sect. 1018)

The most recent development in control of lead paint is the TITLE X (SECT. 1018) Real Estate Lead-Based Paint Disclosure Regulations from the Federal government. The following is a summary from the Massachusetts Association of Realtors®:

Section 1018 of Title X of the Residential Lead-Based Paint Hazard Reduction Act regulates disclosure of lead-based paint in sales and lease transactions involving properties built before 1978. In cases where a seller or lessor utilizes the services of a real estate agent, the agent has the responsibility to inform the seller/lessor of their obligations under the Act and to ensure compliance. The basic requirements of Section 1018 are that:

1. Sellers and lessors of most residential properties built before 1978 must disclose the presence of known lead-based paint and/or lead-based paint hazards in the housing;

2. Sellers and lessors must provide purchasers and lessees with copies of any available records or reports pertaining to the presence of lead-based paint and/or lead-based paint hazards;

3. Sellers and lessors must provide purchasers and lessees with a federally approved lead hazard information pamphlet;

4. Sellers must provide purchasers with a period of up to 10 days prior to becoming obligated under the purchase contract during which the purchaser may conduct a risk assessment or inspection for the presence of lead-based paint and/or lead-based paint hazards. The purchaser may agree to waive that testing opportunity;

5. Sales and lease contracts must include specified disclosure and acknowledgment language.

For further information you may contact the National Lead Information Clearinghouse toll free at 1-800-424-LEAD.

Lead Paint Notification and Certification Requirements

The combined result of the Massachusetts Lead Paint Law c. 111 and the Federal Lead Paint Law Title X is that there is a required Notification Form for all Buyers of residential property which explains the law, the dangers of lead paint and the procedures to be followed. There is a separate Certification Form for the Seller, Buyer and Real Estate Agent, if any. to sign.

In addition, all tenants must be given a Tenant Notification Form and a Certification Form for the Landlord, Tenant and Real Estate Agent, if any, to sign.

Tenant Notification and Certification Forms are required for all tenancies not just at the time of sale or of rental to a new tenant.

One major new provision is that the owner must state what lead paint data they have, if any, and make it available to all buyers and tenants.

The Massachusetts Department of Public Health or the local Board of Health can provide additional details.

Title 5 of the Massachusetts Environmental Code (310 CMR 15.00 and 314 CMR 5.00)

Note: Title 5 is new legislation and under constant review and change. Please check for current status of the law at the time you are studying this section. The following is a short summary of the law for an overview.

Revisions to title 5 of the Massachusetts Environmental Code include changes in 310 CMR 15.00 and 314 CMR 5.00 and are commonly referred to as "Title 5". These changes have an effective date of March 31, 1995 and constitute major new standards for installation of new sewage disposal systems and inspection and upgrade of existing systems.

These "systems" include cesspools which are defined as an underground pit which hold sewerage until it decomposes and is absorbed by the ground and "septic tanks" which are holding tanks that allow sewage to breakdown into gases, liquids and solids before discharge into an underground leaching bed. A septic tank is generally considered of a higher quality than a cesspool. Be careful not to represent a cesspool as a septic tank.

The "Title 5" information in this text is at best a summary of the new provisions and a general guide for the real estate professional. Detailed requirements and procedures should be obtained from your local REALTOR® Board, the Massachusetts Association of Realtors or independent legal counsel.

In general terms, Title 5 requires that any application for a permit to build a new sewage disposal system must include an evaluation from a Department of Environmental Protection (DEP) evaluator approving the plan. Furthermore an existing system must be inspected:

A) At time of transfer of title - Sale of Property.
B) At time of expansion of or change in use of a system - Local Building Permit to add bedrooms or baths.
C) Every three years in a condominium if a shared system.
D) At time of division of ownership combining of systems
   ex: converting to condominiums or removing one septic tank out of four being used in an apartment complex
E) By July 1, 1996 for large systems(10,000 gal. per day outflow or larger) - repeat once ever 3 years.
F) At any time if ordered by local Board of Health

New System Siting

The siting of new systems is more restrictive than in the past and the actual "Title 5" regulations should be referred to for specifics. They establish standards for the minimum setback requirements for a septic tank or soil absorption system (leaching field) from surface water supplies and their tributaries (reservoirs, lakes, ponds, rivers, streams), private wells and elevation of systems and leaching fields above high ground water levels.

There are grandfathering provisions for phasing in the new requirement on building lots depending on their status as:
A) Pending Applications
B) Isolated lots and lots within approved subdivisions.
C) Contiguous lots not within approved subdivisions.

The grandfathering standards are designed to soften the impact of the transition to the new standards.

Transfers and Title 5

The most frequent involvement in Title 5 for the real estate professional will involve the inspection requirement at the time of transfer of ownership.

A septic system must be inspected within two years prior to the transfer of ownership (three if pumped annually). If the inspection is too old it will have to be updated or repeated. If the weather prevents inspection prior to sale, the inspection must be completed as soon as possible but no more than six months following the transfer of ownership. In this situation buyers and lending institutions will most likely require a holdback at the time of sale to cover repairs or replacement if the subsequent inspection shows a damaged or failed system.

The problem will be determining how much should be held back and getting the buyer, seller and bank to agree.

If the inspection shows a system that is below standards then the local Board of Health can establish upgrade approvals to improve the system. However, there are limits that the D.E.P. will not allow a Board of health upgrade to exceed.

Variances may be issued by the Board of Health for some conditions, but not for others.

It should be noted that the "Title V" requirements are minimum standards and a local community may set a higher standard with more restrictive regulations.

Another consideration is the newly established role of a DEP approved "inspector". The DEP will be establishing a training program and "approving" Septic Systems Inspectors. Who will they be, what education and background will they require, what training will they require, what errors and omissions insurance protection will they require are all matters to be determined.

This interaction between the seller, the buyer, the lending institution, the DEP, the DEP inspectors, the local Building Inspector and the local Board of Health is all new territory that the real estate agent will need to become and stay informed about as we all implement these new Title 5 requirements.

The DEP has established a "Title V" hotline at 1-800-266-1122 that can be helpful as a resource for answering questions regarding "Title V".

Asbestos

Asbestos is a naturally occurring material which is heat resistant. It is commonly used in building materials such as ceiling and floor tiles, insulation, pipe covering and outdoor shingles. Scientists and public health officials have determined that exposure to asbestos that is in an unsafe condition may increase a person's risk of developing lung cancer and asbestosis, a fabrotic scarring of the lung. The use of asbestos has been generally prohibited since 1978. However, even if a building was constructed after 1978, it may still contain asbestos since older building materials may have been used in the construction. While experts recommend that asbestos in good condition and in an area that is not likely to be disturbed be left alone, in certain situations the removal of asbestos - containing products is a health necessity. Numerous local, state and federal authorities regulate the use, storage, transport and removal of asbestos.

For any demolition, handling, renovation or disposal involving asbestos - containing materials which are friable or containing 1 percent or more asbestos, the building owner or contractor must contact the Massachusetts Department of Environmental Protection (DEP) 20 days prior to performing the work. (see 310 CMR 7.00)

Under state sanitary code, if asbestos is to be removed, an owner must submit an asbestos removal plan which must be approved by the local board of health prior to the commencement process.

Special asbestos disposal requirements also apply. Asbestos may only be disposed of in Massachusetts municipal landfills that have been approved by the local board of health or in two commercial landfills located in Chicopee, MA. Special transport requirements are also required by federal regulation. Additional requirements regarding the treatment of asbestos exist. Consult legal counsel to ensure complete compliance with all local, state and federal requirements.

(Material from the Massachusetts Association of REALTORS® Legal Issues Summary on Asbestos has been used for this unit.)

Urea Formaldehyde Foam Insulation (UFFI)

Urea Formaldehyde Foam Insulation (UFFI) is a home insulation pumped into the walls and ceiling. Formaldehyde in the insulation reacts with heat and humidity in the air, allowing formaldehyde gas to be released. Formaldehyde can cause symptoms such as breathing difficulties, headaches, nausea, nosebleeds, eye and ear irritation and dizziness. Some scientists suspect formaldehyde of being a carcinogen. This type of insulation, popular in the 1970's, was banned in 1979. In 1986, M.G.L. c 255, section 12I was passed into law mandating property sellers and landlords to determine whether UFFI is in their dwelling. (It is not sufficient to say "to the best of my knowledge") If UFFI is present, the seller must disclose this information to the buyer or tenant. This statute does not mandate that the seller or landlord remove UFFI if found in the dwelling.

Regulations require that disclosure be made prior to the seller's accepting a deposit from the buyer, receiving a written offer to purchase from the buyer, executing a written purchase and sale agreement or accepting the purchase price from the buyer, whichever occurs first.

(Material from the Massachusetts Association of REALTORS® Legal Issues Summary on UFFI has been used for this unit.)

Radon

Radon is a radioactive cancer causing gas. It is formed by the natural breakdown of uranium in soil, rock and water and typically finds its way into homes through cracks and other holes in the foundation. Radon has been found in all styles of construction, new and old homes and in all areas of the country. The EPA and the Surgeon General have recommended radon testing in all homes.

Radon levels can be reduced by sealing foundation cracks and by a system of venting air showing high radon readings.

Radon does not get eliminated entirely. According to the EPA, radon occurs naturally in the outside air at a level of 0.4 pCi/L (picocuries per liter) and the average indoor radon level is 1.3 pCi/l. The EPA recommends fixing homes with levels of 4 pCi/L and notes that some risk exists even below 4 pCi/L and can be improved.

There are radon tests that can be purchased at the local hardware store or you can hire a professional radon tester. Before conducting a radon test you should learn the details of properly testing for radon including long term vs. short term testing, test location within the house and how to prepare the house before and during the actual test.

From a brokerage point of view there is no current legislation that mandates radon testing. It is optional. The broker or salesperson is governed by the laws of disclosure and if radon information that the buyer should be made aware of is known by the broker or salesperson, it should be disclosed.

One practical concern for the real estate professional is the timing of the results of a radon test. Often the radon test is done at or after the home inspection. The canister testing for radon is mailed to a laboratory and the test results are available one, two or more days later. The home inspection date in the purchase and sale agreement must not expire before the test results are available. You could be in a situation where the home inspection is done near the deadline in the Purchase and Sale Agreement and if the turnaround time for obtaining the radon test results from the lab extends beyond the P&S inspection date, you could find the radon levels too high, but the time for reacting to this has expired. Make sure the home inspection date in the P&S covers the radon test result return date; if it doesn't, get it extended.

Underground Storage Tanks (UST)

Many parcels of residential and commercial property have underground storage tanks for storing heating oil. As these tanks age they often corrode and develop leaks. Such leakage can result in significant damage to the environment as well as significant liability to the property owner.

The cost to the property owner to remove and dispose of contaminated soil can be extremely high. Oil tank leaks can go undetected for long periods of time and the resulting contamination can extend far beyond the immediate tank area. Another concern is that insurance policies often times contain a " pollution exclusion" clause resulting in additional owner liability exposure.

In many instances, liability may include prior owners in the chain of title even if there was no known leak at the time of sale.

The safest course of action if you have an underground storage tank is to have it removed, whether it is leaking or not, and have the soil tested. If there is a leak, you can fix the situation before it gets worse and if there is no leakage, you will now have soil tests to demonstrate that. This is also excellent protection against a future claim that any contamination was caused while you owned the property.

Eliminate Doubt - Take It Out

The Massachusetts Department of Public Safety (DPS) regulates the installation, maintenance and removal of underground tanks. The agency relies primarily upon the local fire departments to ensure that this work is done in accordance with the law. For tank removals, local fire officials issue the necessary permits, determine when conditions are safe for excavation and respond to emergencies or public safety hazards. They also ensure that measurements are made for contamination when the tanks are removed.

When tanks are found to be leaking, additional work is usually needed to determine the extent of the problem and whether cleanup will be required. Contamination should be reported to the local fire department and in some instances to the Massachusetts Department of Environmental Protection (DEP).

State law does not require the removal of a residential underground tank if it is not leaking, but there may be local requirements in your community. Check with your fire department or health board.

MGL Chapter 21E

Massachusetts General Law Chapter 21E (MGL c 21E), known as the state superfund law, was enacted in 1983 and rewritten in 1993 to expand the private sector's role in cleanup activities.

Chapter 21E gives the Department of Environmental Protection (DEP) the task of ensuring permanent cleanup of oil and hazardous material releases, determining who is legally responsible for them and requiring those parties to do the work or reimburse the Commonwealth for cleanup costs.

To assist in this program, a new state license has been created; Licensed Site Professional (LSP). An LSP is an environmental expert licensed by an independent Board of Registration who is trained in hazardous material contamination and cleanup and is utilized to manage cleanup operations.

Massachusetts Smoke Detector Law

Massachusetts law requires that a smoke detector certificate be present at every closing of residential real estate.

This means that before a transfer of residential property takes place, the local city or town fire department inspects the property, tests the smoke detectors to verify that they are the correct type, in good working order and in the proper location. The fire department then issues an inspection certificate which is brought to the closing. The responsibility and cost to install the smoke detectors and obtain the certificate is the seller's.

To determine the exact number and required location of smoke detectors, it is recommended that the seller or broker call the local fire department and ask them specifically where they want the detectors installed prior to the installation. Otherwise you would run the risk of installing detectors and then, at the time of inspection, having the fire department require that you move them.

March 1998 changes to the state building code have created new requirements for smoke detectors. All new construction plus substantial renovation to existing buildings may now require hard wired smoke detectors in each bedroom and/or hard wired smoke and heat detectors with battery back-up in common areas of multiple unit dwellings. (substantial renovation is to be determined by the local building inspector or fire department)

Note: Please check with the local building inspector or Fire Department to verify that the subject property is in compliance.

The fee for the inspection certificate is determined by the local fire department and is paid by the seller. By this procedure, every piece of property when changing owners, is required to install smoke detectors if it does not already have them, and to certify that they are in good working order. In this manner, the residential housing stock in Massachusetts contains a steadily growing percentage of living units where the occupants are protected with smoke detectors.

Wetlands Protection Act

The Massachusetts Wetlands Protection Act (WPA), MGL c. 131, s 40, implemented by 310 CMR 10.00, sets forth a public review and decision making process by which certain designated environmentally sensitive areas are to be regulated by local conservation commissions and the Massachusetts Department of Environmental Protection (DEP) in order to ensure maximum environmental protection for environmentally sensitive areas.

The following areas are subject to protection under the WPA: any a) bank, b) freshwater wetland, c) coastal wetland, d) beach, e) dune, f) flat, g) marsh or h) swamp that borders on the ocean, any estuary, creek, river, stream, pond or lake. Also included is land under any of the above listed water bodies, land subject to tidal action, land subject to coastal storm flowage and land subject to flooding. In certain circumstances, this protected area may include an additional radius of 100 feet from the protected area (the so - called "Buffer Zone").

Any activity proposed or undertaken within an area listed above that will remove, fill, dredge or alter that is subject to regulation under the WPA and requires the filing of a Notice of Intent (NOI). In addition, activities located within 100 feet of one of the protected areas, which in the opinion of the local Conservation Commission, will alter the protected area are subject to regulation under the WPA.

Once it is determined that the WPA applies to the applicants project, the applicant must submit a Notice of Intent (NOI) to the local conservation commission. The WPA statute and regulation proscribes a process and timetable which a project applicant and the local conservation commission must adhere to.

In reviewing the NOI, the local conservation commission will determine whether the proposed project will have a significant adverse impact on one or more of the interests identified in the WPA.

The 8 interests identified in the WPA are:

1)   protection of public and private water supply
2)   protection of ground water supply
3)   flood control
4)   storm damage protection
5)   prevention of pollution
6)   protection of land containing shellfish
7)   protection of fisheries
8)   protection of wildlife habitat

If determined that the proposed project will effect one or more of these values, the local conservation commission will issue an Order of Conditions specifying the necessary changes to the project to minimize such adverse impacts.

(Material from the Massachusetts Association of REALTORS® Legal Issues Summary on the Wetlands Protection Act has been used for this unit.)

Rivers Protection Act

The Massachusetts Rivers Protection Act (Rivers Act), effective August 7, 1996 is an expansion of the Wetlands Protection Act to address the protection of rivers. Prior to August 7, 1996, the WPA only applied to resource areas ("environmentally sensitive areas" including a buffer zone of up to 100 feet from the resource area. The Rivers Act added a new resource area called the "riverfront area" to the list of areas protected under the WPA. The riverfront area extends 200 feet (25 feet in municipalities with large populations and in densely developed areas) on each side of perennial rivers and streams throughout the Commonwealth.

The Rivers Act defines a river as " any naturally flowing body of water that empties into any ocean, lake or other river and which flows throughout the year."

The Rivers Act creates no new procedural requirements different from those under the WPA. As with the WPA, the Rivers Act is administered primarily through the local conservation commission.

(Material from the Massachusetts Association of REALTORS® Legal Issues Summary on the Rivers Protection Act has been used for this unit.)

Self-Quiz A

1) M.G.L. c.93A requires the broker or salesperson to:
    A) Answer only questions asked by the buyer
    B) Disclose all positive information under Fiduciary Rule to seller
    C) Disclose all known information, good or bad, to the buyer
    D) Refer all questions to the seller and seller's attorney

2) Under M.G.L. c.93A, if a broker is found to have willfully misrepresented something to a buyer the maximum penalty is:
    A) $1,000 fine
    B) 30-day license suspension
    C) $5,000 fine
    D) Triple damages plus attorney's fees

3) Which of the following is true?
    A) All manufacture of lead paint has been illegal since 1978
    B) All paint made before 1950 contains lead
    C) All natural wood surfaces do not contain lead
    D) All apartments must be de-leaded

4) M.G.L. c.111 Lead Paint Law requires:
   A) Deleading if children under 5 are residents
   B) Deleading if children under 6 are residents
   C) Deleading to a height of six feet
   D) Painting over lead paint if child under 6 is a resident

5) Under the M.G.L. c.111 Lead Paint Law, which of the following is not true? Real Estate agents must:
   A) Warn buyers of the lead paint danger in all housing built prior to 1978
   B) Have buyers sign a lead paint notifications form before signing a Purchase and Sale Agreement
   C) Inform buyers of the availability of lead paint inspections
   D) Refuse to rent to families with children if lead paint is present

6) Massachusetts smoke detector requirements at time of passing papers are:
   A) Hard-wired detectors in all dwellings
   B) Battery-operated detectors in all dwellings
   C) Smoke Detector Certificate issued by local Fire Department
   D) Either battery-operated or hard-wired detectors in all dwellings units.

7) As of January 1, 1990, brokers will be required to have buyers sign an Agency Disclosure Form:
   A) Before showing any property
   B) Before signing a Purchase and Sale Agreement
   C) At the time of passing of papers
   D) Before the broker can financially qualify the buyer

8) Caveat Emptor means:
   A) Qualify the buyer
   B) Passing of papers
   C) Let the buyer beware
   D) Consumer protection

9) A Massachusetts real estate salesperson must:
   A) Disclose lead paint danger in an old house
   B) Have Lead Paint Disclosure Form signed for new construction
   C) Have buyer sign Agency Disclosure form after 1/1/90 before qualifying a buyer
   D) Have all those attending an open house sign an Agency Disclosure Form after 1/1/90

10) The Massachusetts Consumer Protection Act is known as:
    A) M.G.L. c.151B
    B) M.G.L. c.93A
    C) M.G.L. c.111
    D) M.G.L. c.183A

Answer Key

Self-Quiz A

1) C
2) D
3) A
4) B
5) D
6) C
7) A
8) C
9) A
10) B

11 Fair Housing / ADA

The following terms and concepts will be covered in this chapter. They will also be found in the glossary at the back of the text.

Terms And Concepts

Americans with Disabilities Act
Blockbusting
Federal Civil Rights Act 1866
Federal Fair Housing Act 1968 (Title VIII)
Massachusetts Fair Housing - M.G. L. c.151B
M.C.A.D. - Massachusetts Commission Against Discrimination
Protected Class
Redlining
Steering

This chapter will familiarize you with the fundamentals of Fair Housing Regulations, both federal and state and the Americans with Disabilities Act.

The area of Fair Housing is extremely sensitive and in a continuing state of change. Thus, even more than in other units in this text, the material covered should be utilized for general references only. For specific status and legal impact of any of the items covered in this chapter, legal advice is recommended from personal, business, local REALTORS® boards or Massachusetts Association of REALTORS® legal counsel.

The sequence of coverage in this chapter will be as follows:

A) Federal Civil Rights Act - 1866

B) Federal Fair Housing Act - 1968 and 1988 Amendments

C) Massachusetts General Law c.151B

D) Americans with Disabilities Act

Federal Civil Rights Act - 1866

The Federal civil Rights Act of 1866 made all discrimination based on race illegal. The detailed language of the Act, as it relates to real estate, states specifically that:

"All citizens of the United States shall have the same right, in every State and Territory, as is enjoyed by white citizens thereof to inherit, purchase, lease, sell, hold and convey real and personal property."

In a relatively modern case, a judgment by the United States Supreme court on June 17, 1968, reinforced and clarified the 1866 law by holding in a case known as Jones vs. Mayer that "all racial discrimination, private as well as public, in the sale or rental of property" is prohibited.

Current discrimination issues are rarely enforced via the Federal Civil Rights Act of 1866. The Federal Civil Rights Act of 1968 and Massachusetts Fair Housing Legislation (which will be covered further on in this chapter), offer more effective legislation and penalties in resolving discrimination matters. Although they will be utilized to a far greater degree, it should be noted that the Federal Civil Rights Act of 1968 and the Massachusetts Fair Housing Act have a number of exemptions where these laws will not apply.

In any area of racial discrimination, although these current federal and state laws may offer an exemption, the Federal Civil Rights Act of 1866 does apply, due to the overall violation of discrimination based on race. There are no exemptions under the 1866 Federal Civil Rights Act.

Federal Fair Housing Act - 1968 (Title VIII)

The current federal legislation used to regulate discrimination in housing is Title VIII of the Fair Housing Act of 1968. The law went far beyond the Civil Rights Act of 1866 which covered discrimination based solely on race. The Fair Housing Amendment Act of 1988, effective March 12, 1989, substantially revised the Federal Fair Housing Law, and these amendments are included in this chapter.

Protected Classes
The Fair Housing Act of 1968 prohibits discrimination based on race, color, religion, national origin or sex. These are referred to as **"Protected Classes."**

The March 12, 1989 amendment expands the protected class to include the handicapped and families with children. ("Handicapped" is defined in the amendment to include any person who has a physical or mental impairment which substantially limits one or more major life activities, a record of having such a impairment or being regarded as having such an impairment.)

Prohibited Practices
The Fair Housing Act of 1968 prohibits the following practices:
1. Refusal to sell, rent or otherwise deal with any person
2. Discrimination against any person in establishing terms or conditions for the sale or rental of housing
3. Discrimination in any advertising for the sale or rental of a dwelling.
4. Denying that housing is available when it is
5. **Blockbusting** - attempting to influence any individual to sell or rent with threats that persons of a particular protected class status are entering the neighborhood
6. **Steering** - showing members of a protected class property in neighborhoods made up predominantly of the same minority background while not showing comparable properties in other neighborhoods

New Construction
New Residential Construction, for March 13, 1991 occupancy, of four-family or larger must be handicapped-accessible, including:
1. Hallway and doorway design
2. Lowered light switches and thermostats
3. Raised electrical outlets
4. Bathrooms and kitchen design

(These design requirements apply to ground-floor units and upper floors of buildings with elevators.)

Discrimination in Financing

It is illegal for any bank or other lending institution to vary the terms and conditions of a loan because of a loan applicant's protected class status. For example, a bank may not require a larger down payment or higher interest rate because of the applicant's race.

Redlining - In this illegal practice, a lending institution decides to exclude a geographic section of a city or an entire city for any lending activity. The name **"redlining"** comes about from the thought that the lending institution had drawn a red line around that area and declared it off limits. This practice often resulted in intended or "de facto" discrimination, in that poorer communities with high minority populations were often targets of such redlining.

Discrimination in Providing Brokerage Services

It is illegal to deny access or vary terms and conditions for access to any multiple listing service, broker's service or any other facility related to the sale or rental of housing.

Discrimination in Appraisal Reports

It is illegal for an appraiser to assign a value to a piece of property because of the impact on the area of any of the protected classes. Thus, an appraiser cannot state that a downward adjustment of $10,000 is being made because the house is in a minority neighborhood.

Housing Not Covered by the Fair Housing Act of 1968

The following categories of housing are not covered by the Federal Fair Housing Act of 1968 and are referred to as exempt:

1. **Single Family** - Sale or rental of a single family house by a private owner-occupant is exempt. (The single-family exemption for the private owner-occupant is limited to one sale in any 24-month period. The exemption would also not apply if the owner was considered to be in the business of selling property, which is defined as one who participated as a principal in three or more transactions in a 12-month period.)
2. **Multi-Family** - rental of units in an owner-occupied two-three- or four unit building.
3. **Religious Organization** - sale or rental of property owned by a religious organization as long as limited to noncommercial purposes and membership in the religion is not based on race, color or national origin.
4. **Private Club** - sale or rental of property owned by a private club to members only, as long as it is not for commercial purposes.

Note: In order to use these exemptions, an individual may not use a real estate agent and may not use discriminatory advertising.

Enforcement of the Fair Housing Act of 1968

A violation of the Federal Fair Housing Act may be reported through three separate channels:

1. Department of Housing and Urban Development (H.U.D.), Washington , D.C.
2. Department of Housing and Urban Development (H.U.D.), Regional Office

3.   United State District Court

If a complaint is taken to U.S. District Court, the court may issue an injunction or restraining order, award damages and assess fines as follows:
A) $10,000 - First Offense
B) $25,000 - Second Offense within five years
C) $50,000 - Third offense within seven years

(Note: These civil penalties are available under HUD's administrative processing; different relief is available if a court action is elected. See summary of federal and state fair housing laws for additional remedies.)
The law also provides for criminal prosecution and penalties for anyone who attempts to coerce, intimidate, threaten or interfere with a person in the exercise of his rights under the law.

Federal Fair Housing Amendments of 1988
The Federal Fair Housing Act of 1968 has been changed significantly via the Fair Housing Amendments of 1988. These amendments became effective on March 12, 1989, and are included in this chapter.

Massachusetts Fair Housing - Massachusetts General Law Chapter 151 B

The Massachusetts Fair Housing Law, known as Massachusetts General Law c.151B, covers many of the same areas as the Federal Fair Housing Law. However, there are differences and these differences should be studied very carefully, especially as both laws are amended from time to time. The Federal Fair Housing Law was changed in 1988 with the changes effective March 1989.
In studying Massachusetts Fair Housing Law, we will study three separate categories of protected classes, each with its own prohibited practices and major exemptions. Then we will study the enforcement and/or remedy available in the event of any violation.

Massachusetts Protected Class #1
Those protected in Class #1 are those discriminated against because of race, color, religion, national origin, ancestry, sex, age (excluding minors), marital status, veteran history, handicap or sexual orientation.

Prohibited Practice - Class #1. The prohibited practices are the same as those found under the Federal Fair Housing Act 1968 (Title VIII)

Major Exemptions - Class #1. There are certain exemptions to those protected in the Class #1 as follows:
1.   Leasing of a unit in an owner - occupied two-family.
2.   State-aided or federally aided elderly development, age exemption only.
3.   Elderly retirement community with 10 acres or more and a minimum age requirement of 55 years, age exemption only.

Massachusetts Protected Class #2- Public/Rental Assistance

Those protected under class #2 are those discriminated against because they are public-assistance or rental- assistance recipients.

The details in this class are very easy to digest. It is a prohibited practice in Class #2 to discriminate in furnishing all credit, services, or in renting accommodations, and there are no exemptions.

In addition, to discriminate because of any requirement of such public assistance, rental assistance or housing subsidy program is also prohibited.

Massachusetts Protected Class #3 - Children

Those protected under Class #3 are those discriminated against because they have children.

The prohibited practice is to refuse to rent, sell or otherwise deny housing.

Major Exemptions to Protected Class #3 - Children. There are certain exemptions to those protected under Class #3 as follows:

1. Dwellings with three units or less, one of which is occupied by an elderly or infirm person for whom the presence of children would be a hardship.

2. Temporary leasing/subleasing by owner/principal occupant for one year or less.

3. Leasing of unit in an owner-occupied two-family house.

4. Private housing developments of 100 or more units in which the number of children residing in the development equals 50% of the number of units; children may be restricted to specific units.

One of the most common complaints the Massachusetts Commission Against Discrimination receives involves the mistaken impression by owners and real estate agents that they may not rent to families with children if lead paint is present. This is discrimination and is illegal. The applicant cannot be denied because of children. If the children are under six, the landlord must de-lead. (Note: In order to use any of these exemptions, an individual may not use a real estate agent and may not use discriminatory advertising.)

"Reasonable Modifications"

When dealing with the handicapped in matters of housing, it is considered discriminatory to refuse to make **"Reasonable Modifications"** to accommodate the handicap.

Such modifications are to be at the expense of the tenant in private housing of less than 10 units and at the expense of the owner in publicly assisted housing or any multiple housing consisting of 10 or more units. Ex. wheelchair ramps, wide doorways, grab bars or raised numbers to assist the blind. Owners able to show "undue hardship" would be exempt.

It is also discriminatory to refuse to make reasonable accommodations in Rules, Policies, Procedures or Services in renting to those with a handicap. Ex. allowing a seeing eye dog or a reserved parking space near the door.

There are new guidelines for residential construction of multi-family dwellings of three or more units to accommodate the handicapped.

The details and implementation of these matters are complex and should be referred to office management and/or legal counsel specializing in discrimination law and regulation.

Massachusetts Fair Housing Enforcement/Remedy

The enforcement or remedy available under M.G.L. c. 151B for any violation of all prohibited practices and protected classes is as follows:

1. File complaint with the Massachusetts Commission Against Discrimination (M.C.A.D)

2. Civil action may be filed in the appropriate Superior, Probate or Housing court. (90-day waiting period for M.C. A. D. investigation)

3. Injunctive relief may be obtained, including temporary restraining orders enjoining the sale or rental of property pending final determination.

4. $2,000 limit on damages is available.
5. For licensed real estate brokers and salespersons, Massachusetts law calls for a 60-day license suspension for the first finding of discrimination and a 90-day suspension for a second finding of discrimination within a two-year period.

Summary of Federal and State Fair Housing Laws

The following summary of federal and state Fair Housing laws has been prepared by the Massachusetts Commission Against Discrimination. This summary includes the changes to the Federal Fair Housing Law effective March 1989. The cooperation of the M.C.A.D. in the preparation of the material in this chapter is acknowledged and appreciated.

Massachusetts Commission Against Discrimination: Summary of Federal and State Fair Housing Laws

Law	Civil Rights Act of 1866
Protected Classes	Race
Prohibited Practices	All discriminatory practices prohibited
Major Exemptions	There are no exemptions - all properties are covered
Enforcement Mechanisms/Remedies	File civil action in appropriate court; unlimited damages.
Law	Title VIII of the Civil Rights Act of 1968, as amended

Protected Classes	Race, color, national origin, sex, religion, handicap, familial status (Children)
Prohibited Practices	- Refusal to sell or rent - Discriminate in terms, conditions, or privileges of sale or rental - False representation of availability - Discriminatory advertising - Blockbusting - Steering, failure to show all available properties - Discrimination in brokerage services - discrimination in mortgage lending - Interfering with, coercing, threatening, or intimidating in the exercise of rights under the Act
Regarding Handicap	- Refusal to permit, at the handicapped person's expense, reasonable modifications of existing premises failure to design and construct certain multi-family dwellings (intended for first occupancy after 3/13/91) so as to be handicapped-accessible
Major Exemptions	Single-family houses sold or rented by owner only if without use of broker and without discriminatory advertising. Rooms/units in owner-occupied dwellings of four units or less. Additional exemptions that apply to familial status discrimination only. - state or federally -aided elderly developments - Housing intended and operated for occupancy by at least one person 55 years or older per unit - Housing intended for and solely occupied by persons 62 years or older Additional exemptions that apply to handicap discrimination: - Persons whose tenancy would constitute a direct threat to the health or safety of others - Persons whose tenancy would result in substantial physical damage to the property

Enforcement Mechanisms/Remedies

File complaint with U.S. Department of Housing and Urban Development, which can result in either a hearing before an Administrative Law Judge (ALJ) or civil action in U.S. District Court; or file civil action directly in the U.S. District or State Court.

The ALJ can award actual damages and injunctive relief, in addition to ordering civil penalties of up to $10,000 for the first violation; $25,000 for the second and $50,000 for the third. Actual damages, punitive damages, and injunctive relief are available in a civil action.

Law	Massachusetts General Laws, Chapter 151 B
Protected Classes	Race, color, national origin, ancestry, sex, religion, handicap, age (excluding minors), marital status, veteran history public assistance/rental assistance, or sexual orientation
Prohibited Practices	- Refusal to sell or rent - Discrimination in terms, conditions, or privileges of sale or rental - False representation of availability - Discriminatory advertising - Blockbusting - Sexual harassment of tenants - retaliation because a person exercises a protected right - Inquiring about or recording protected class status. (except in cases of children or public assistance recipients)
Regarding Children	- refusal to rent to families with children because of the presence of lead paint in the unit. As per MGL c. 111.
Regarding Handicap	- refusal to permit, at the handicapped person's expense, reasonable modification of existing premises (costs for reasonable modifications for publicly assisted housing of ten units or more and privately own housing of ten contiguous or more shall be paid by the owner) - failure to design and construct certain multi-family dwellings intended for first occupancy after 3/13/91 so as to be handicapped accessible
Regarding rental assistance	refusal to rent because of requirements of assistance program
Major Exemptions	Two-family owner-occupied dwellings done without the use of a broker and without discriminatory advertising (In the case of discrimination on the basis of public assistance or rental assistance recipients, there are no exemptions. All types of properties are covered, including two-family owner-occupied dwellings.) Additional exemptions that apply to age discrimination only: - state or federally-aided elderly developments - elderly retirement communities of 10 acres or more with a minimum age requirement of 55 years

Additional exemptions that apply to children discrimination only:
- dwellings of three units or less, one of which is occupied by an elderly or infirm person for whom the presence of children would be a hardship

- temporary renting of one's principal place of residence for one year or less

Note - these exemptions do not apply to persons whose business includes engaging in residential real estate related transactions.

Enforcement Mechanisms/Remedies

File complaint with the Massachusetts Commission Against Discrimination (MCAD). Ninety days after filing with MCAD, complainant may bring civil action in Superior, Probate or Housing Court.

Injunction relief, including temporary restraining orders enjoining sale or rental of property, pending final determination, may be obtained. $2,000 limit on damages at M.C.A.D.

Automatic license suspension for 60 days upon finding of discrimination against a licensed broker or salesperson at hearing (M.G.L., c.112).

For additional information contact MCAD at:

One Ashburton Place
Boston, MA 02108
(617) 727-3990

Americans With Disabilities Act

The Americans with Disabilities Act (ADA) has several sections or "Titles" dealing with discrimination against those with disabilities or "handicapped" as follows:

Title 1 - Employment
Title ll - Public Services operated by State and Local Government
Title lll - Public Accommodation & Services operated by Private Entities
Title lV - Telecommunication
Title V - Miscellaneous
Those of us in the real estate profession are mostly affected by Title lll.

Title lll prohibits discrimination based on disability in public accommodations. Private entities covered by Title lll include places of lodging, establishments serving food or drink, places of exhibition or entertainment, places of public gathering, sales or rental establishments, service establishments, stations used for specified public transportation, places of public display or collection, places of recreation, places of education, social service center establishments and places of exercise or recreation. Title lll also covers commercial facilities (such as warehouses, factories and office buildings), private transportation services, and licensing and testing practices.

Title lll is of concern in matters of brokerage when we are dealing with the sale, rental, construction or renovation of commercial property.

The ADA does not generally address matters in the sale or rental of private residential property.

Once again, the details and implementation of these matters are complex and should be referred to office management and/or legal counsel specializing in discrimination law and regulation.

Further information can be obtained by contacting the ADA Technical Assistance Center at 1-800-949-4232.

SELF QUIZ A

1) The Federal Civil Rights Act of 1866 prohibits discrimination based on:
   A) Race or religion
   B) Race, religion or national origin
   C) Race only
   D) Race, religion or sexual preference

2) The Federal Fair Housing Act of 1968 (Title VIII) protects which of the following classes?
   A) Race, religion and wheelchair handicap
   B) Race or public/rental assistance
   C) Sex or sexual preference
   D) Race, religion or marital status

3) Massachusetts Fair Housing Law does not protect which of the following classes?
   A) Marital status in agent rented owner occupied two family
   B) Blind or hearing impaired in a four family
   C) Public/rental assistance in a three family
   D) Wheelchair handicap in a two family owner occupied

4) Under the Federal Fair Housing Act of 1968 (Title VIII) all of the following would be prohibited except:
   A) Refusal to rent to an unmarried couple
   B) Requiring an extra security deposit because of a tenant's religion
   C) A Bank "redlining" a neighborhood due to racial population
   D) Showing a buyer property in a specific neighborhood because of the buyer's race or religion

5) The Federal Fair Housing Act of 1968 prohibits discrimination on the basis of :
   A) Marital status
   B) Public assistance
   C) Sex
   D) Veteran Status

6) Which of the following is not prohibited by the Federal Fair Housing Act of 1968 (Title VIII)?
   A) Refusal of tenancy based on poor credit history
   B) Redlining
   C) Steering
   D) Blockbusting

7) Under the Fair Housing Act the fine for the first offense can be as high as:
   A) $1,000
   B) $5,000
   C) $10,000
   D) $50,000

8) The Massachusetts Fair Housing Law is known as:
   A) M.G.L. c.93A
   B) M.G.L. c.111
   C) M.G.L. c.183A
   D) M.G.L. c.151B

9) Under the Massachusetts Fair Housing Law, which of the following statements is true?
   A) Owner-occupied two-family residents are exempt in all rental matters
   B) Owner-occupied three-family does not have to rent to a family with children if one tenant is 62 or older
   C) There are no exemptions in matters dealing with public/rental assistance recipients
   D) A non-owner-occupied two-family must pay for renovations for a wheelchair handicap tenant

10) A bank denies a mortgage application because the property is located in a neighborhood with a high minority population. This is an example of:
   A) Blockbusting
   B) Steering
   C) Legal refusal
   D) Redlining

Self Quiz B

1) The Federal Civil Rights Act of 1866 deals with
   A) Racial and Religious Discrimination in matters of housing
   B) Racial discrimination if found in housing matters
   C) All Racial Discrimination in any area
   D) All Discrimination if it concerns housing

2) The Federal Fair Housing Act (Title VIII) includes the following protected classes
   A) Color, Religion and Marital Status
   B) Race, Religion and Handicapped
   C) Race, National Origin and Rental Assistance
   D) Religion, Sex and Veterans Status

3) The Massachusetts Housing Law, M.G.L.c. 151B does not include the following protected classes
   A) Religion and Sexual Orientation
   B) Marital Status and Veterans History
   C) Public/Rental Assistance and Handicapped
   D) Race and Credit History

4) Under the Federal Fair Housing Act (Title VIII) all of the following would be illegal except
   A) Refusing to rent to two people because they are gay
   B) Refusing to rent to a couple because they had children
   C) Showing a minority couple only houses in a minority neighborhood
   D) Refusing to rent to a tenant because he was in a wheelchair

5) The Federal Fair Housing Act would find which of the following illegal:
   A) Rental of apartment in an owner occupied six family
   B) Rental of an owner occupied two family to lesbians
   C) Rental of an owner occupied two family to a family on a housing assistance program
   D) Requiring an extra security deposit because of a tenants national origin

6) Massachusetts Fair Housing would find each of the following illegal except:
   A) Refusing tenant an apartment in a federally funded elderly apartment complex because the applicant was too young
   B) Refusing to rent to blind tenant because she had a guide dog
   C) Refusing to rent to a housing subsidy program tenant because the program requires a one year lease
   D) Refusing to rent to an unmarried couple on religious grounds.

7) Violations of the Federal Fair Housing Act (Title VIII) may be reported to:
   A) H.U.D. in Washington or U.S. District Court
   B) H.U.D. or the Local Housing Authority
   C) H.U.D. in Washington or County Housing Court
   D) Local Housing Authority

8) A complaint filed with the Massachusetts Commission against Discrimination may result in the following except:
   A) 60 Day Suspension for real estate license holders if found guilty
   B) civil Action in Superior Court
   C) Restraining Order Against a Landlord
   D) $10,000 fine if found guilty

9) Refusing to loan money in a minority neighborhood is called:
   A) Redlining
   B) Steering
   C) Blockbusting
   D) Discrimination

10) Which of the following statements is true regarding discrimination and real estate agents
   A) An Agent may rent an owner occupied two family and exclude children
   B) An Agent may rent a single family home and exclude public assistance recipients, but may not advertise such
   C) An Agent may rent legally exempt discriminatory situations, but may not advertise them
   D) A Real Estate Agent may never become involved in any discriminatory rentals

---

Answer Key

Self Quiz A

1) C
2) A
3) D
4) A
5) C
6) A
7) C
8) D
9) C
10) D

Self Quiz B

1) C
2) B
3) D
4) A
5) D
6) A
7) A
8) D
9) A
10) D

12 Massachusetts License Law

The Massachusetts Board of Registration of Real Estate Brokers and Salesmen has prepared a pamphlet containing the major points of the Massachusetts laws that should be known by candidates for the real estate license examination. A copy of this pamphlet is included in the latter part of this chapter.

In order to assist the student in review of the laws, the first part of the chapter contains an outline of the state pamphlet. The outline groups together information about licensing laws in a more logical sequence and in a somewhat more readable fashion.

The outline is only a summary; therefore, the laws contained in the state's pamphlet should be reviewed for full treatment. You will also find practice questions at the end of the chapter.

Massachusetts License Law Outline

I. **Duties and Powers of the Real Estate Board of Registration**

    A) The governor shall appoint the board with advice and consent of council.

    B) The board shall have five members.

        1) The members will be citizens of the commonwealth
        2) Three members must have been actively engaged in the field of real estate full time for at least seven years and they must also hold a broker's license
        3) The other two members of the board shall be representatives of the public
        4) The governor will designate the chairperson
        5) Term of office is five years and members are eligible for re-appointment

    C) The board will hold at least four regular meetings each year.

        1) A quorum, or legal meeting, requires a minimum of three board members
        2) If the chairperson is absent the most senior member will take charge
        3) A written record shall be kept of all meetings and of any business transacted which shall be open to the public

    D) The board may make rules or bylaws, that are consistent with other laws, that they feel are necessary in the performance of their duties.

E)   The board, or its designee, shall conduct examinations for licensure.

    1)   Exams shall be prepared by the board or a designated independent testing service to determine competence of an applicant to transact the business of a broker or salesperson

    2)   Exams will be held a minimum of six times per year for broker and eight times per year for salesperson

    3)   There will be no limits on applicants on any given test date

    4)   The applicant shall show a fair understanding of the principles of real estate practice, real estate agreements, principal/agents relationship, rudimentary economic principles, and real estate appraisal

    5)   The salesperson's exam shall be on the same general subject matter as the broker's exam, but more elementary

F)   The board is empowered to conduct investigations and hearings which are appropriate and necessary to administer and enforce these laws.

    1)   The board may require by summons the testimony of witnesses

    2)   The board may require by summons any books, papers or records for review in connection with an investigation or hearing

G)   The board may, and upon the receipt of a verified complaint in writing from an aggrieved person, investigate the action of any broker or salesperson or any person who attempts to act as such in the commonwealth. When a license has been suspended or revoked it shall be delivered to the board within seven days of receipt of notice. The board may suspend, revoke, or refuse to renew a license when the board has found as a fact that the licensee has:

    1)   Knowingly made any substantial misrepresentation or use advertising that is false or misleading

    2)   Acted in dual capacity of broker and undisclosed principal in the same transaction

    3)   Acted for more than one party in a transaction without the knowledge and consent of all parties

    4)   Failed, within a reasonable time, to account for or remit any monies that belong to others which have come into the broker's or salesperson's possession

    5)   Paid a commission or fee to any person who is required by law to be licensed and is not

    6)   Accepted, given or charged any undisclosed commission, rebate or profit

    7)   Induced any party to a contract or lease on real estate to break the same for personal gain of licensee

    8)   Commingled money or other property of the principal with that of the licensee

    9)   Failed to give both the buyer and seller a copy of the purchase and sale agreement

    10)   committed any act expressly prohibited in any section of the Massachusetts Real Estate License Laws

11) Solicited for sale or lease, or listed for sale or lease, residential property on the grounds of an alleged change in value due to the presence or prospective entry of persons of another race, economic level, religion or ethnic origin (this includes distributing material or making statements designed to induce a residential property owner to sell or lease his property due to such change in the neighborhood)

12) Accepted from a potential seller a net listing, which is an agreement where the licensee shall keep as a fee any monies received from the sale of property in excess of the amount the seller wishes to receive

13) Failed to comply with the requirements as set forth for the Promotional Sales of Out-of-Sate Property (see section CMR 6.00 in Real Estate License Laws and Section III, Paragraph I of this summary)

14) Obtained license by false or fraudulent representation

15) Failed to notify Board of any change of business address

16) Failing to fully disclose to the parties in a transaction for any interest in real property, in writing, that they or any kin have a financial interest

17) As a broker, failing to disclose that you are a prospective purchaser of interest in real estate from someone who has approached the broker to act as their agent in the sale of the property

18) Failure to provide Board approved notice to the buyer and seller at the first personal meeting to discuss a specific property that discloses the relationship of the brokers or salespersons and the principals
(See also 254 CMR 3.00 #13, the Disclosure Form in the reference pages following the Massachusetts License Law and Chapter 10 in the text)

19) Practiced while impaired by drugs, alcohol or other reason

20) Practiced while license was expired, revoked, suspended or otherwise not valid (possible fine)

21) Discriminated in providing services on the basis of age, marital status, gender, sexual preference, race, religion, socioeconomic status or disability

22) Assumed duties in an area for which he or she did not have adequate preparation or competence

23) Failure to comply with all the laws of the Commonwealth, the United States or any other state in which he or she is licensed

24) Failure to report to the Board within thirty days a conviction of any misdemeanor or felony under the law of the Commonwealth, the United States or of any other jurisdiction which if committed in Massachusetts would be considered a crime

25) Fraudulently certifying that the continuing education requirement (see 254 CMR 5.00, #3) had be satisfied (the Board may suspend until requirements fulfilled)

H) Upon notification of a final finding from the Massachusetts Commission on Discrimination that a licensed broker or salesperson has violated Chapter 151B (see Chapter 11 for discrimination laws) in the course of their duties, the board will suspend the individual's license for sixty days. If the licensee has been found guilty of a violation of Chapter 151B within the two previous years, the board shall suspend the license for a period of ninety days. If section I.G.11.(from above) has been violated, there shall be a fine of not less than $1,000 or more than $2,500, or by imprisonment for not more than six months, or both. (Note: A person whose license has been suspended or revoked may also be liable for punishment under other laws of the commonwealth.)

I) The board may reconsider any decision it has made and reinstate or reissue any license suspended or revoked.

J) Board decisions will be by a majority vote, in writing, signed and sent to each interested party. No license may be revoked, suspended, or not renewed unless there is a hearing. A ten-day written notice with reasons for the hearing is required. The applicant or licensee has the right to appear before the board, be represented by counsel, cross-examine witnesses, and produce evidence.

K) Any person whose license is suspended, revoked, or not renewed has the right to appeal. The appeal will be made to a superior court in the county where he lives or has his business, or in Suffolk County. The appeal has to be filed within twenty days of a finding by the board. The appeal does not act as a "stay" against suspension, revocation or refusal to renew. No costs shall be allowed against the board unless gross negligence, bad faith, or malice can be proven.

II. Licensing Requirements

A) Any person will need a broker's license if he or she receives or expects to receive a fee, commission, or other consideration while acting on behalf of another person, and performs or attempts to perform any of the following:
   1) Sell, exchange, purchase, rent or lease, negotiate, make offers, list real estate to sell, or deal in options on real estate
   2) Any person who advertises or represents himself as a person or leasing real estate
   3) Any person who assists or directs in the procuring of prospects for the sale or lease (apartment searching is included) of real estate
   4) Any person who assists in the negotiation or completion of any agreement which may or may not result in a sale, exchange, purchase, lease, or renting or any real estate

B) A "Salesperson's" license is required by any person who performs any acts listed in the previous section (II.A.). The difference between a broker and a salesperson lies in the fact that a salesperson **cannot complete** any of the transactions listed. The salesperson must have the broker he or she works for complete the sale, exchange, purchase or lease. The broker may delegate this activity to the salesperson; however, the broker retains full responsibility. The term "Active Association" describes the relationship between a salesperson and his or her broker.

C) A corporation, Limited Liability Company (LLC), society, association, Limited Liability Partnership (LLP) or partnership may be issued a broker's license. The license can only be issued when at least one of the officers or partners acting as a representative of the organization has a broker's license in his/her own name. If the designated officer's or partner's license is suspended, revoked or unrenewed, the organization's license will also be surrendered unless there is another officer or partner with a broker's license to be designated. In the case of death, disability, or severance of a sole-designated officer or partner, an organization may continue with a broker's license for a period of one year from the date of the loss of the licensed officer or partner. The organization may also designate a new individual for the position if he or she is properly licensed. All designated officers or partners and their relationship to the organization shall be made known to the board. No unlicensed person may act as a broker or salesperson for a licensed organization. In addition to conforming to all other sections of the license law, the organization shall pay a fee as determined by the Board and post a bond. No corporation, LLC, society, association, LLP or partnership is eligible for a salesperson's license.

A Limited Liability Company (LLC) or a Limited Liability Partnership (LLP) shall maintain professional liability insurance in accordance with 254 CMR 2.00, #12. (See license law at the end of this chapter)

D) A non-resident individual (or non-resident corporation for broker's license) may receive a broker or salesperson's license in the commonwealth. The individual must:
1) Conform to all sections of the license law
2) File with the board a power of attorney appointing the chair as the individual's true and lawful attorney
3) The board may exempt from written examination any broker or salesperson licensed in another state if a similar exemption is given to licensed individuals from the commonwealth applying for a license in said state. A non-resident licensee will not be required to have a usual place of business in the commonwealth if one is maintained within the state where they reside

E)   In order to be eligible for a license in the commonwealth, an applicant must do the following:

1) To obtain a broker or salesperson's license, the applicant must take and pass a written exam given by the board (see Section I.E. in this outline). An attorney of the commonwealth is exempt from the exam but must still obtain the license.

2) Applicants for a salesperson's license must complete a course approved by the board prior to the exam. The course shall contain a minimum of 24 classroom hours of instruction. (Exempt from this course would be an individual who has taken a course in "real property" at an accredited law school in the state.) Certification is valid for two years.

3) Applicants for a broker's license must, prior to the exam, provide proof that the individual has been actively engaged with a real estate broker for at least one year. The "apprenticeship" will include a minimum of 25 hours per week as a salesperson under the supervision of a broker. The apprenticeship must have occurred within two years of taking the broker's exam. An applicant for the broker's license shall also take another course in real estate with a minimum of 30 classroom hours.

4) Unless the applicant is an attorney of the state or applying for a license as a non-resident, there is a one-year residency requirement for the broker's license.

5) An applicant for a broker's license shall post a bond in the sum of $5,000 through a surety company authorized to do business in the state. The bond shall be payable to the commonwealth for the benefit of any aggrieved persons. The applicant must also show good moral character as evidenced by the recommendations of three unrelated, reputable people who live or work in the Commonwealth who will certify that the applicant has a reputation for honesty and fair dealings and that a license be granted to the individual.

6) In the event of the death of a broker who is the sole proprietor of the real estate business, his or her legal representative or designated individual approved by the board, may be issued a license. In this situation, a bond must also be posted. The license is valid for only one year from the date of death of the broker, and is non-renewable.

7) Applicants for a broker or salesperson's license must be at least eighteen years of age.

8) Payment of prescribed fees. Any person who fails the exam may retake the exam if license exam course certification is still valid and upon payment of prescribed fees.

F)   An individual's license has a two-year term being renewed on the licensee's birthday. In order to have the renewal date on the applicant's birthday, your first license will be valid for the number of months between issuance of the first license and whenever your next birthday occurs, plus two years.

All fees are reviewed annually but are currently listed in Massachusetts License Law Section 87ZZ at the end of this chapter. Consult application information in the "Real Estate Candidate Handbook" provided by your instructor for exact test fees.

G) After January 1, 1999 all applicants for renewal of a brokers or salespersons license shall satisfactorily complete courses or programs approved by the board. This "continuing education" requirement shall have been completed not more than twenty-four months prior to license renewal. The courses or programs shall be no less than twelve hours except the law provides that after January 1, 2001 the minimum may go down to six.

A minimum of six hours shall come from the following areas: fair housing, equal employment opportunity, accessibility for the disabled, agency law, environmental issues in real estate, zoning and building codes, real estate appraisal and financing, property tax assessments and valuation, and Board regulations. The Board will certify the curriculums.

At the time of renewal that applicant will certify that the requirements have been met in accordance with Board procedure. If at the time of renewal the education requirement has not been met the applicant may be granted "inactive status". The inactive status will remain in effect until the applicant demonstrates completion of the requirement. An inactive broker may not practice but, may receive a referral fee from a licensed active real estate broker.

Each authorized school shall maintain records of salespersons or brokers for a minimum of three years of completion of the continuing education.

H) There are situations where an individual does not need a license to sell or otherwise deal in real estate. The following is a list of those people who are exempt from the license law:

1) Any person who acts for himself as owner, lessor, lessee or tenant

2) Any person who is the regular employee of the owner, lessor, lessee or tenant, if the acts are performed in the regular course of the management of the real estate or investment

3) Any person seeking to acquire or lease real estate for his or her own use or his regular employee acting on behalf of said person, if it is part of his/her regular duties

4) Any person trying to negotiate or obtain a loan on real estate for himself or his employees, if it is part of their regular duties

5) A salaried managing agent or his/her regular employees, if it is part of his/her normal duties while working for the owner

6) A licensed auctioneer

7) A person buying or selling any stocks, bonds, or beneficial interest in a trust

8) A public officer performing his or her official duties

9) A person who has power of attorney from the owner of real estate to act on his behalf
10) An attorney acting on behalf of his or her client
11) A receiver, trustee in a bankruptcy, executor, administrator, guardian, or conservator in the official course of their duties
12) A person selling real estate by court order
13) A trustee or his regular employees, if it is a normal part of their duties
14) Banks, credit unions, and insurance companies or their regular employees, if it is within their normal course of duty - this includes real estate owned or leased

III. Laws and Statutes

There are many other laws and statutes that the broker and salesperson must abide by. The following is an outline of some of the miscellaneous laws with which each licensee should be familiar.

A) Licensees are prohibited from placing "blind ads." These are ads that do not disclose the fact that you are a licensed broker. Brokers must advertise "affirmatively" and include the brokers name in the advertisement. Also:
1) Individuals with a salesperson's license cannot place their own ads
2) There shall be **no** discriminatory advertising

B) An individual with a salesperson's license **must** work for a broker and can have the status of an independent contractor or a regular employee. In addition:
1) A salesperson can only work for one broker at a time
2) A salesperson can only seek his or her fee or commission from the broker with whom he/she works. In other words, a salesperson cannot sue the seller or buyer, but he/she can sue the broker
3) Any broker who has a salesperson working for him/her shall be responsible for any violations of the license law
4) No person shall recover any fees for acts performed as a broker or salesperson unless he/she has said license
5) In a co-broke situation the second agent can be acting as a sub-agent of the listing agent or a buyers broker (see Ch. 8)
6) Any broker who is employed by another broker cannot hire a salesperson to work for him/her
7) A salesperson shall promptly notify the Board of any change of business address

C) **Commissions are negotiable**. Any commission, fee, or other consideration is by agreement between the parties, namely the seller or buyer and the broker.

D) It is necessary that the broker or salesperson makes sure that the principals in a transaction understand with whom the licensee's responsibility lies. Although the payment of a fee usually follows the agency relationship, this is not essential. Payment of a fee does not establish an agency relationship. To avoid a conflict of interest and confusion the Mass Agency Disclosure Law has been implemented (see Ch. 8). The buyer has the right to hire a broker to work for him or herself. It is also important to remember that if the licensee or any relatives of the licensee has any interest in the real estate being purchased, sold, or leased, this fact must also be made known to all parties in writing. (See chapter 8 for more on agency disclosure.)

E)   Any offers received by a broker or salesperson shall be **immediately conveyed** to the owner of the real estate, and all parties to a transaction shall receive copies of any contracts.

F)   Any salesperson or broker employed by another broker shall immediately turn over any deposits to the employing broker. Unless agreed to in writing, the broker shall place these funds in a fiduciary bank account (escrow account) immediately. This escrow account, set up to handle funds of clients, may be an interest-bearing account. The broker will be required to ensure that the amount on deposit and interest are turned over to the appropriate persons, according to the contract's terms. The broker shall keep accurate records of all escrow accounts, including where the monies came from, date deposited, check number, date withdrawn, and any other information concerning the transaction. The board has the right to inspect these records.

G)   All licensed brokers shall maintain a business address. If a broker is employed by another broker, the employing broker's business address shall be the address of record. In addition:
     1)   If there is more than one broker at an address, the contractual relationship shall be forwarded to the board
     2)   Licensed resident brokers shall display their licenses in a conspicuous place on the premises of the business
     3)   No individual may hold a broker's and salesperson's license at the same time
     4)   If a person is to sell real estate under a trade name, a certified copy of the business certificate from the city or town shall be forwarded to the board
     5)   A licensed salesperson must work for a licensed broker, and cannot be self-employed
     6)   Employing brokers shall notify the board of all brokers and salespersons working for them. The notification shall include name, address, license number, and beginning date of employment. An employing broker shall also notify the board of any termination's of licenses

H)   It is illegal for a broker or salesperson to advise against the use of an attorney in any real estate transaction.

I)   Promotional sales of an interest in real property that is part of a land development located in another state shall be registered with the Board. "Real Property" shall include land, building, fixtures, condominiums, cooperatives and time sharing intervals or an interest in any of the above. Promotional advertising shall include any advertising material offered through any means of communication in the Commonwealth.

No interest in real property in a development which is part of a promotion shall be offered in the commonwealth without a Massachusetts licensed broker who will notify the Board within seven days of accepting such a client. The broker on behalf of the owner/developer shall file an application with the board along with prescribed fees. The application, along with any supporting documents shall be sworn to under oath and reviewed by the broker for accuracy and that any promotional materials reasonably portray the facts of the development.

the Board retains the right to inspect the development and the cost of such inspection shall be paid for by the developer. Any reports issued by the Board shall be kept on file for the time the development is registered plus one year by both the Board and the developer.

Once the Board registers an out of state property development for promotional sales in the Commonwealth, this fact shall be included in all future advertisements in a form approved by the Board.

J) A written "Notice to Prospective Tenants" shall be given by the real estate broker at the time of the first personal meeting to the prospective tenant. This notice shall disclose that whether the tenant will pay a fee for such service, the amount of the fee, when and how it is to be paid and if the fee or a portion of the fee is payable even if the tenancy is not created.

The notice including the salespersons or brokers name and license number, the prospective tenants name, and the date the notice was given must be signed by both parties. If the tenant refuses to sign, that fact must be noted on the form by the salesperson or broker. A copy of the notice shall be kept on file for at least three years from date and files shall be available to the board for inspection.

Brokers shall maintain all listings and documents pertaining to the availability of apartments at the time it was advertised for a period of at least three years from the date the apartment was rented.

Brokers shall maintain a copy of any check, money order or receipts for any fees or payments made by prospective or actual tenants for a period of three years. Brokers shall also maintain a copy of any check issued on an escrow account which they control for at least three years from date of issuance.

Unless a prospective tenant agrees in writing, a real estate broker cannot charge a fee if a tenancy has not been created.

K) To provide instruction in real estate for the license preparation or continuing education classes a school has to be authorized by the Board. Application, with the appropriate fee, is to be made to the board which approves the suitability of the location of the classes.

Each location, which the Board may limit, has to be authorized separately and the certification is to be renewed every two years.

Each school shall designate one individual as "authorized agent" who will be responsible for:
a. Maintaining records of students names, attendance, dates of completion and curriculum for at least two years
b. Verify only those students who have successfully completed any program or course with the appropriate hours receive Board approved certified forms or certificates of completion
c. Notify the board within seven days of any changes to address, phone number or the authorized agent of the school
d. Having only qualified instructors teach

The Board may suspend, revoke or refuse to renew any school authorization if the school does not adhere to the regulations including:
a. Fail to maintain records as required
b. Fail to provide appropriate notice to the board of any changes to address, phone number or authorized agent
c. Fail to provide Board with any requested information
d. Fail to use the exact name of the school in ads, postings or any medium of communication
e. Fail to have a qualified/authorized instructor teaching the appropriate curriculum
f. Obtained school authorization through fraud or misrepresentation
g. Discriminate against any individual on the basis of age, marital status, gender, sexual preference, race, religion, socioeconomic status or disability
h. Fail to provide student with appropriate certification of completion
i. Provide certification of completion of any curriculum to someone who has not done so
j. Combining any part of the salesperson, broker, continuing ed or instructor classes into one offering
k. Fail to offer Board approved curriculum

To become a Board Qualified Instructor and teach in an approved school an individual must:
a. Hold a current brokers license issued by the Board
b. Have a minimum of two years work experience as a real estate broker involving at least 25 hours per week
c. Have co-taught or audited the curriculum in an authorized school
d. Have a minimum of 30 hours of instruction at an instructor training school approved by the Board
e. The Board may issue an "authorization to act as an instructor" to anyone who has completed the above requirements or the equivalent as determined by the Board
f. An instructor may employ specialists to teach particular portions of the salesperson or broker curriculum who do not need to obtain authorization from the Board but not for the whole course

Self Quiz A

1) Which of the following statements is not true?
   A) Real Estate Brokers must maintain a $10,000 bond.
   B) Real Estate Brokers must display their licenses at their place of business.
   C) Real Estate licenses must be renewed every two years.
   D) Real Estate Brokers must place deposit monies in an escrow account.

2) A broker sold a parcel of real estate and received a 6% commission on a selling price of $160,000. The broker's accountant, who is not licensed to sell real estate, referred the seller to the broker. The broker gave the accountant a $100.00 finder's fee.
   A) This act is permitted due to the immaterial amount of the finder's fee.
   B) Would have been permissible if the seller had been informed.
   C) The broker may be subject to a fine not to exceed the total commission.
   D) The broker may be subject to a suspension or revocation of license.

3) A salesperson may work for:
   A) Another salesperson
   B) An attorney even though they do not hold a real estate license.
   C) An unlicensed owner of a 300-unit apartment complex for rentals only as long as payment is by commission.
   D) A broker/owner of a real estate firm.

4) A broker contracted for a listing in which the seller would be satisfied as long as he received $120,000 in proceeds from the sale. The broker was allowed to keep anything he could obtain over the amount as his fee.
   A) This is an example of an illegal net listing.
   B) This situation is not covered under Massachusetts License Law
   C) Fees contracted in this manner are permissible if all parties agree.
   D) This is legal as long as the fee is not more than ten percent of the selling price.

5) A salesperson may advertise real estate in his own name if:
   A) The ad states he is a salesperson.
   B) The ad states the name and location of the real estate office.
   C) The real estate is owned by the salesperson.
   D) Written permission is obtained by the seller.

6) An individual must be licensed in order to:
   A) Work for an owner/developer on salary while selling condos.
   B) List property for sale in hope of receiving a commission.
   C) Sell his or her own home.
   D) Sell the home of another who has given power of attorney for that reason.

7) A deposit received by a salesperson should be:
   A) Deposited in the salesperson's escrow account.
   B) Held by the salesperson until passing of papers.
   C) Turned over to the broker
   D) Turned over to the seller

8) Jones is a developer and hires White on a $500 per week salary to sell his homes. White sells a house to Conor who paid a $2,000 fee to Ryan for helping with negotiations and contracts. A broker's license is required by:
   A) Conor
   B) Ryan
   C) Jones
   D) White

9) An ad was placed in the local newspaper by a real estate broker describing a piece of property along with a phone number to call but nothing else. Which of the following best describes this ad?
   A) An ad for leads.
   B) An information ad
   C) A broker ad
   D) A blind ad

10) A broker has presented an offer to the seller for $142,000. While the seller is considering the offer, the broker receives a second offer for $139,000. The broker should:
   A) Present the second offer to the seller to consider.
   B) Hold the second offer until the seller decides on the first offer.
   C) Reject the offer because a higher offer has been made.
   D) Refuse to accept the offer until the time limit has run out on the first one.

Self-Quiz B

1) The classroom instruction requirement for a real estate license in Massachusetts is:
   A) Mandatory for attorneys.
   B) 30 hours for the broker's license.
   C) 30 hours for the salesperson's license.
   D) Only required for brokers form out of state.

2) A license to sell real estate is required by:
   A) A person dealing in options on real estate for a fee.
   B) A licensed auctioneer.
   C) A public officer performing official duties.
   D) A person selling real estate even though by court order.

3) A salesperson who did not receive his or her commission on the sale of a piece of property may:
   A) Sue the seller for the total amount of the commission plus damages.
   B) Immediately place a lien on the property.
   C) Sue the broker he or she works for.
   D) Withdraw an amount equal to the commission from his or her escrow account.

4) Which of the following individuals are **NOT** required to take and pass an exam for licensure as a broker to sell real estate in Massachusetts?
   A) An individual with a broker's license from another state which requires a broker from Massachusetts to take and pass its exam.
   B) A person who assists others in finding apartments for a fee.
   C) The legal representative of a deceased sole proprietor of a real estate business as approved by the Board for a period of one year.
   D) An individual who has taken and passed a course in "real property" at an accredited law school in the state.

5) A secretary in a real estate office who does not have a real estate license may:
   A) Type purchase and sale agreements.
   B) Give customers prices and other information over the phone.
   C) Earn a commission for showing an apartment owned by the broker.
   D) Accept property listings over the phone.

6) The Real estate Board of Registration:
   A) May limit the amount of applicants who can take the exam.
   B) Allows a broker to continue business during an appeal process for a suspended license.
   C) May not have an official meeting if the chairperson is absent.
   D) Allows the licensee to appeal decisions of the Board to the Suffolk County Superior Court.

7) The Board of Registration in proceeding with a complaint:
   A) Must have a unanimous vote to enforce a decision
   B) Must give ten days' written notice to the broker or salesperson
   C) May commence investigations based on an oral complaint.
   D) May not summons any books, papers or records connected with the he hearing due to the privacy of client's information.

8) Which of the following statements concerning the Board of Registration is accurate?
   A) Members of the Board are not eligible for reappointment.
   B) The Board shall have two members who are representatives of the public.
   C) The Board shall have at least six members.
   D) The Board shall have four members who have been actively engaged in the he field of real estate for at least five years.

9) A commission may **NOT** be split with:
   A) A broker who was not part of the transaction but referred the client.
   B) A salesperson by an employing broker.
   C) A broker from another real estate firm.
   D) An attorney without a broker's license.

10) A broker:
   A) Who is employed by another broker cannot hire a salesperson to work for him or herself.
   B) Cannot be held accountable for the actions of a salesperson working for him or herself.
   C) Does not have to disclose that he is the principal in a transaction.
   D) May use his or her bond to pay legal expenses in a hearing.

Self-Quiz C

1) A nonresident of the state:
   A) May not obtain a broker's license.
   B) Must have an in-state place of business to obtain a license
   C) Must file a power of attorney with the Chairman of the Board.
   D) May only promote out-of-state land within the Commonwealth.

2) A corporation:
   A) May hold a salesperson's license.
   B) With a valid real estate license may allow all corporate officers to sell real estate without obtaining licenses as individuals.
   C) Must have at least one officer with a valid broker's license as an individual.
   D) Must have at least two officers with broker's licenses as individuals in the event one leaves or is terminated.

3) Commissions:
   A) Are negotiated between the principal (seller/buyer) and the broker.
   B) Are fixed according to market conditions.
   C) can be split with family members without disclosure.
   D) are based on geographic locations.

4) As of January 1, 1990, full disclosure of agency/principal relationship must be made to prospective buyers. This requires:
   A) A letter of intent to the buyer at the closing.
   B) A notice to a prospective buyer prior to the showing of property.
   C) A sign at the business location of the broker or salesperson.
   D) A notice to a prospective buyer inquiring about current market conditions.

5) The costs of any investigation of out-of-state land sales in the commonwealth of Massachusetts shall be paid by the:
   A) Broker
   B) Board of Registration
   C) Individuals purchasing the property
   D) Owner or developer of the property

6) Which of the following statements would be considered **false** with respect to the sale of out-of-state land within the Commonwealth?
   A) The broker must supply the Board with a price list for each specific lot to be sold.
   B) The Board may recommend that a land court prohibit the sale of the property within the Commonwealth.
   C) A copy of the Board's report must be given to each buyer prior to the signing of a purchase and sale agreement.
   D) All property located in another state that is part of a promotional offering in the commonwealth shall be done through a Massachusetts licensed broker.

7) An apartment rental service:
   A) Shall show all apartment listings to all applicants regardless of what has been set forth in the contract between them.
   B) Will verify availability of a unit with the landlord within no more than eight days prior to providing a listing to a customer.
   C) May keep any monies in excess of thirty dollars if they have shown at least three apartments to the client.
   D) May advertise by simply stating number of rooms, range of rents, or special features even if they do not have a specific listing in order to obtain prospects.

8) Each listing provided by an apartment listing service shall include all of the following **except:**
   A) Whether or not pets are permitted.
   B) The floor location.
   C) Whether or not there may be an option to purchase.
   D) Whether or not elevator service is available.

9) It is **not** a violation of the license law to:
   A) Sell property without a license as an employee of a bank if it is in the regular course of the individual's duties.
   B) Advise a client against the use of his or her attorney if the bank is using its attorney.
   C) Withhold information concerning a property's condition if expressly told to do so by the principal.
   D) Help to negotiate a loan to be secured by real estate for a fee without a license.

10) If a licensed individual has been found guilty of a violation of Massachusetts General Law c.151B for a second time within the previous two years, the Board shall suspend the license for:
   A) 60 days
   B) 30 days
   C) 45 days
   D) 90 days

Self-Quiz D

1) Which of the following statements concerning deposit monies is true?
   A) Deposits must be held by the listing broker.
   B) Deposits may not be held by the seller.
   C) If the broker holds the deposit it must be in an escrow account.
   D) Either the broker or selling salesperson may hold the deposit.

2) An agency which is a partnership:
   A) May hold a broker's or salesperson's license
   B) May hold a broker's license, but not a salesperson's license.
   C) May hold a salesperson's, but not a broker's license.
   D) May not hold either a broker's or salesperson's license.

3) A salesperson may work for:
   A) Another salesperson or broker.
   B) A developer as long as payment is by commission.
   C) Licensed broker only.
   D) no more than two brokers at the same time.

4) In Massachusetts an attorney:
   A) May not receive a co-broke referral.
   B) Does not require a license to receive a co-broker fee.
   C) Does not require a bond to be licensed.
   D) May obtain a license without taking the real estate exam.

5) A broker may co-broke with:
   A) A salesperson from another office.
   B) Any attorney who has passed the Mass. Bar Exam.
   C) Anyone producing a ready, willing and able buyer.
   D) Another broker only.

6) The Agency Disclosure Law requires the real estate licensee to present the prospective buyer with an agency disclosure form:
   A) Prior to signing of the Purchase and Sale Agreement.
   B) Prior to signing of the offer.
   C) Prior to any discussion with the sales associate about the subject property.
   D) At first meeting with the sales associate to be qualified.

7) When a Massachusetts Broker is selling out-of-state land in Massachusetts, which of the following is not true:
   A) A Massachusetts broker must be used for all out-of-state sales.
   B) a copy of the Board of Registrations report on the development must be given to each buyer before a P&S is signed.
   C) The Board of Registration may require an on-site inspection of the development at the developer's expense.
   D) If the designated Mass. Broker ceases to represent the development, the developer must cease marketing in Massachusetts.

8) In regards to an apartment listing service, which of the following is true?
   A) An apartment listing service does not require a broker's license.
   B) An apartment listing service may provide addresses only without a license.
   C) Must verify apartment availability within 8 days of providing the address to a tenant.
   D) The listing service must refund all monies over $100 if the customer fails to find an apartment.

9) A broker may lose his/her license for which of the following?
   A) Acting as a disclosed principal in a real estate transaction.
   B) Acting as a dual agent if disclosed
   C) Acting as a buyer's agent
   D) Acting as an undisclosed buyer's and seller's agent.

10) If a friend refers a listing to a broker who then receives a commission for selling the property, the broker should.
   A) Co-broker with the friend.
   B) Give a referral fee to the friend.
   C) Buy a gift for the friend.
   D) Thank the friend.

Answer Key

	Self Quiz A	Self Quiz B	Self Quiz C	Self Quiz D
1)	A	B	C	C
2)	D	A	C	B
3)	D	C	A	C
4)	A	C	B	D
5)	C	A	D	D
6)	B	D	B	C
7)	C	B	B	A
8)	B	B	C	C
9)	D	D	A	D
10)	A	A	D	D

Massachusetts
Real Estate
License Law and
Regulation

PRODUCED BY THE MASSACHUSETTS BOARD OF REGISTRATION OF REAL ESTATE
BROKERS AND SALESMEN

May 1, 1998

BOARD ADDRESS:

BOARD OF REGISTRATION OF
REAL ESTATE BROKERS AND SALESPEOPLE
100 CAMBRIDGE STREET - ROOM 1313
BOSTON, MASSACHUSETTS 02202

PHONE:

(617) 727-2373

BOARD MEMBERS

ANNE BLACKHAM, CHAIRPERSON
FRED KOED
ALFRED R. RAZZABONI
RICHARD BARRY
G. HOWARD HAYES

EXECUTIVE DIRECTOR
BOARD OF REGISTRATION OF
REAL ESTATE

JOSEPH AUTILIO

DIRECTOR
DIVISION OF REGISTRATION

WILLIAM WOOD

CHCKLST\REGCOVR.DOC

Massachusetts License Law   12-21

M.G.L. CH. 13

sec. 54. Board of Registration of Real Estate Brokers and Salesmen; Appointment; term; re appointment; Filling of Vacancies.

There shall be a board of registration of real estate brokers and salesmen, in this section and in sections fifty-five to fifty-seven, inclusive called the board, to be appointed by the governor, with the advice and consent of the council, consisting of five members, citizens of the commonwealth, three of whom shall be actively engaged in the real estate business as a full-time occupation for at least seven years prior to their appointment and who shall be licensed real estate brokers, and two of whom shall be representatives of the public. The governor shall designate the chairman. As the term of office of a member of the board expires, his successor shall be appointed by the governor, with like advice and consent, to serve for five years. Each member shall be eligible for re appointment and shall serve until the qualification of his successor. The governor may also, with like advice and consent, fill any vacancy of the board for the unexpired portion of the term.

sec. 55. Same Subject; Meetings.

The board shall hold at least four meetings each year and may hold special meetings as required. Time, place and notice of all meeting shall be as required by rules or by-laws made by the board. A quorum shall consist of three members. In case of vacancy in the office or the absence of the chairman the senior member shall perform the duties of the chairman. A written record which shall be open to public inspection shall be kept of all meetings and of the business transacted thereat.

sec. 56. Same Subject; Rules or Bylaws; Seal; Annual Report.

The board may make such rules or by-laws, not inconsistent with the law, as it may deem necessary in the performance of its duties. The board shall have a seal. The board shall annually render to the governor and the general court a report of its proceedings, which shall include an itemized statement of all receipts and expenses of the board for the year.

sec. 57. Same Subject; Compensation and expenses; Employment of Secretary and Clerical and Technical assistants and Compensation thereof.

Each member of the board shall serve without compensation, but shall be paid by the commonwealth the expenses necessarily incurred by him in the discharge of his official duties. The board may, subject to chapter thirty-one, employ a secretary and such other clerical and technical assistants as may be necessary to discharge its official duties, shall establish their duties, and, subject to the provisions of sections forty-five to fifty, inclusive, of chapter thirty, shall fix their compensation which shall be paid by the commonwealth. The commonwealth shall provide the board with adequate office space and shall pay the expenses of the board in the performance of its duties.

M.G.L. CH. 112

sec. 87PP. Definitions

For the purposes of sections eighty-seven PP to eighty-seven DDD, inclusive, the following words and phrases, unless the context otherwise requires, shall have the following meanings:-

"Board", the board of registration of real estate brokers and salesmen.

"Non-resident", shall include and deemed to apply to an individual whose principal place of abode is without the commonwealth and to corporation, society, association or partnership, organized, formed or existing under the laws of another state and which does not maintain a usual place of business within the commonwealth.

"Real estate broker", hereinafter referred as broker, any person who for another person and a fee, commission or other valuable consideration, or with the intention or with the expectation of upon the promise of receiving or collecting a fee, commission or other valuable consideration, does any of the following:- sell, exchange, purchases, rents or leases, or negotiates, or offers, attempts or agrees to negotiate the sale, exchange, purchase, rental or leasing of any real estate, or lists or offers, attempts or agrees to list any real estate , or buys or offers to buy, sells or offers to sell or otherwise deals in options on real estate, or advertises or holds himself out as engaged in the business of selling, exchanging, purchasing, renting or leasing real estate, or assists or directs in the procuring of prospects or the negotiation or completion of any agreement or transaction which results or is intended to result in the sale, exchange, purchase, leasing or renting of any real estate.

"Real estate salesman", hereinafter referred to as salesman, an individual who performs any act or engages in any transaction included in the foregoing definition of a broker, except the completion of the negotiation of any agreement or transaction which results or is intended to result in the sale, exchange, purchase, renting or leasing of any real estate.

sec. 87QQ. Sections 87PP to 87DDD Not to be Applicable to Certain Persons.

The provisions of sections eighty-seven RR to eighty-seven DDD, inclusive, shall not apply to the following:- any person whom, acting for himself as owner, lessor, leasee, tenant or mortgagee, shall perform any of the aforesaid acts of a broker or salesman with reference to real estate owned or leased or rented by or to him; the regular employees of any person aforesaid, with respect to such real estate, if such acts are performed in the regular course of, or as an incident to, the management of such real estate and the investment therein; any person, while acting for himself, who seeks to acquire, lease or rent real estate for his own use or investment or his regular employees acting in behalf of such person in the regular course of their employment; a person acting for himself in negotiating a loan secured or to be secured by a mortgage or other encumbrance upon real estate, of his regular employees acting therein in behalf of such person in the regular course of their employment; a managing agent while acting under a contract with the owner of the real estate or the regular employees of such agent acting in his behalf in the regular course of their employment; a person acting as a licensed auctioneer; a person buying selling or otherwise dealing in stock, bond or other security or certificate of beneficial interest in any trust; a public officer or employee while performing his official duties; a person acting as attorney in fact under a duly executed power of attorney from an owner of real estate authorizing the final consummation by performance of any contract for the sale, leasing or exchange of real estate; the services rendered to a client by an attorney at law in the performance of his duties as such; a receiver, trustee in bankruptcy, executor, administrator, guardian or conservator, while acting as such: a person selling real estate under order of any court; a trustee acting under a written instrument of trust, or deed or declaration of trust, or will, or his regular employees, acting in the course of their employment; a bank as defined in section one of chapter one hundred and sixty-seven or organized under the laws of the United States or an insurance company lawfully engaged in business in the commonwealth, or the regular employees of such bank or insurance company acting in the course of their employment, when such bank or insurance company is acting in any aforementioned capacity of fiduciary or is acting for itself in negotiating a loan secured or to be secured by a mortgage or other encumbrance upon real estate or is acting for itself with reference to real estate owned, mortgaged, leased or rented, by or to it or which it seeks to acquire, lease or rent for its own use; a credit union organized under chapter one hundred and seventy-one or the regular employees thereof acting in the course of their employment.

sec. 87RR. *License to Engage in Business as Broker or Salesman; Relationship Between Salesman and Broker, Recovery of Fees.*

Except as otherwise provided, no person shall engage in the business of or act as a broker or salesman directly or indirectly, either temporarily or as an incident to any other transaction, or otherwise, unless he is licensed.

No salesman may conduct or operate his own real estate business nor act except as the representative of a real estate broker who shall be responsible for the salesman and who must approve the negotiation and completion by the salesman of any transaction or agreement which results or is intended to result in the sale, exchange, purchase, renting or leasing of any real estate or in a loan secured or to be secured by mortgage or other encumbrance upon real estate. No salesman shall be affiliated with more than one broker at the same time nor shall any salesman be entitled to any fee, commission or other valuable consideration or solicit or accept the same from any person except his licensed broker in connection with any such agreement or transaction. A salesman may be affiliated with a broker either as an employee or as an independent contractor but shall be under such supervision of said broker as to ensure compliance with this section and said broker shall be responsible with the salesman for any violation of section eighty-seven AAA committed by said salesman.

Except as otherwise provided no person shall recover in any suit or action in the courts of the commonwealth for compensation for services as a broker performed within the commonwealth unless he was a duly licensed broker at the time such services were performed; provided, however, that nothing contained herein shall be construed as affecting the right of a licensed salesman to recover in a suit or action against a broker on any contract or agreement with said broker.

sec. 87SS. *Requirements for Issuance of License; Compliance with sec. 87SS to 87DDD; Classroom Instruction; Written Examinations.*

No license to engage as a broker or salesman shall be issued to any applicant unless he has complied with all the pertinent provisions of this section and sections eighty-seven II to eighty-seven DDD, inclusive, and if the applicant is an individual, unless he shall have satisfactorily passed a written examination conducted by the board or an independent testing service designated by the board, and, in the case of an application for broker's license by an individual resident of the commonwealth, unless he shall have had his principal place of abode within the commonwealth for one year next prior to the issuance of such license; provided, however, that any applicant who is an attorney at law of the commonwealth shall not be required to take such examination or to have had such principal place of abode for such period.

Every individual applicant for a license as a salesman who is required to take an examination therefor shall, as a prerequisite to taking such examination, submit proof satisfactory to the board that the has completed courses in real estate subjects approved by the board, such courses to total twenty-four classroom hours of instruction; provided, however, that applicants having successfully completed a course in real property while enrolled in an accredited law school in the commonwealth may also take such examination. Every individual applicant for a license as a broker who is required to take an examination therefor shall, as a prerequisite to taking such examination, submit proof satisfactory to the board that he has been actively associated with a real estate broker for a period of one year as a real estate salesman and that he has completed additional courses in real estate subjects approved by the board, such courses to total thirty classroom hours of instruction.

Such examination shall be prepared by the board or the designated independent testing service to enable the board to determine the competence of the applicant to transact the business of a broker or a salesman. The board or its designated independent testing service shall conduct such examinations at least six times in each calendar year for broker's examinations and at least eight times in each calendar year for salesman's examinations. There shall be no limit placed on the number of applicants who may take the examinations on any examination date. In determining competence the board shall require proof that the applicant has a fair understanding of the principles of real estate practice, real estate agreements and principal and agent relations, of the rudimentary principles of the economics and appraising of real estate, and of the provisions of sections eighty-seven PP to eighty-seven DDD, inclusive. The examination for a salesman's license shall be based upon the same general subject matter as for a broker's license, but shall be more elementary in character.

The board may make, and from time to time alter, amend or repeal rules and regulations for the conduct of such examinations not inconsistent herewith.'

s 87TT. Requirements for Issuance of License; Application for License; Issuance; Bond by Applicant for Broker's License; Temporary License upon Death of Broker.

Applications for licenses, signed and sworn to by the applicant, shall be made on forms furnished by the board and shall be accompanied by the prescribed fee for examination. The fee for the issuance of the license shall be payable upon receipt of notice of passing the examination. Each applicant shall furnish evidence of good moral character. If an application for a broker's license is made by a corporation, society, association or partnership, evidence of the good moral character of all the officers and directors, or holders of similar positions, or of all the partners, as the case may be, shall also be furnished. No license shall be issued unless evidence of good moral character, as required by this section is found.

No license shall be issued unless the application has been on file with the board at least ten days. No broker's license shall be issued to any individual under eighteen years of age.

No broker's license shall be issued or renewed until the applicant gives to the board a bond in the form approved by said board in the sum of five thousand dollars, executed by the applicant and by a surety company authorized to do business within the commonwealth, or by the applicant and by two good and sufficient sureties approved by the board. Said bond shall be payable to the commonwealth, for the benefit of any person aggrieved, and shall be conditioned upon the faithful accounting by the broker for all funds entrusted to him in his capacity as such. Any person so aggrieved may bring suit on the bond in his own name; provided, however, that the aggregate liability of the surety to all such persons shall, in no event, exceed the sum of such bond. The board may revoke the license of any broker whenever the bond filed by him ceases to be in full force and effect.

In the event of the death of a licensed broker who is the sole proprietor of a real estate business, the board shall, upon application by his legal representative, issue, without examination, a temporary license to such legal representative, or to an individual designated by him and approved by the board, upon filing of a bond as aforesaid and the payment of the prescribed fee, which shall authorize such temporary licensee to continue to transact said business for a period not to exceed one year from the date of death subject to all other provisions of sections eighty-seven PP to eighty-seven DDD applicable to a licensed broker except that such temporary license shall not be renewed.

sec. 87UU. Issuance of Broker's License to Corporation, etc.; Effect; No Salesman's License to Be Issued to Corporation, etc.

An application for a broker's license by a corporation, society, association or partnership shall designate at least one of its officers of partners as its representative for the purpose of obtaining its said license, and each such officer or partner so designated shall apply to the board for a broker's license in his own name at the same time unless he is already as licensed broker.

No broker's license shall be issued to a corporation, society, association or partnership unless an officer or partner so designated has been issued a broker's license as an individual. when the officer or partner so designated has been issued a broker's license as an individual and the corporation, society, association or partnership has complied with all pertinent requirements for the issuance of a broker's license to it, the board shall, for a fee, as determined annually by the commissioner of administration under the provisions of section three B of chapter seven, paid in advance to the board, issue to it a broker's license which shall also bear the name of each designated officer or partner to whom a broker's license as an individual has been issued, and each such designated officer or partner shall be entitled to perform all the acts of a broker as agent or officer of such corporation, society, association or partnership, but shall not so act on his own behalf so long as he continues to be a designated officer or partner, unless the written consent thereto of such corporation, society, association or partnership is filed with the board. The license of a corporation, society, association or partnership shall cease unless at least one such designated officer or partner, as the case may be, is a licensed broker. If any designated officer or partner shall be refused a license or renewal, or if his license is revoked or suspended, or if he ceases to be connected with or to act in behalf of such corporation, society, association or partnership, it shall have the right to designate another officer or partner in his place who shall apply for a broker's license as an individual, unless he is already a licensed broker. Upon the death or disability of a sole designated officer or partner, who has been licensed, or upon the severance of his connection with the corporation, society, association or partnership, the corporation, society, association or the surviving partner or partners or successor partnership of the licensed partnership, if any, acting by another officer or partner, as the case may be, may continue to transact business and to exercise all rights of a broker subject to such regulations as may be made by the board, for a period not to exceed one year from such death, disability or severance as if its license were in full force and effect, subject to the suspension or revocation of such privilege for any cause which would be grounds for the suspension or revocation of a license; provided, that it shall proceed with due diligence to qualify for the issuance of a new license; and provided, further, that the corporation, society, association or the surviving partner or partners or successor partnership, as the case may be, shall maintain in effect during said period a bond as prescribed in section eighty-seven TT as if a broker's license had been issued and was in effect for such period.

Except as otherwise provided, nothing in this section shall permit any other individual connected with any corporation, society, association or partnership, to which a license has been issued, to act as a broker or salesman on its behalf or otherwise without first obtaining a license so to act, and nothing in this section shall be construed as preventing any such other individual who is a licensed broker or salesman from acting as such on its behalf, if so authorized by it.

No salesman's license shall be issued to a corporation, society, association or partnership.

sec. 87VV. Unlicensed Salesman Not to Be Affiliated with Broker; Certain Acts of Licensed Salesman Prohibited; Notice of Change of Business Addressee.

No salesman who is not licensed shall be affiliated with a broker. A licensed salesman affiliated with a licensed broker shall not act as salesman for any other licensed broker while so affiliated, nor accept any valuable consideration for the performance of any act a s a real estate salesman from any person except the broker with whom he is affiliated. A licensed salesman shall promptly give written notice to the board of any change of his business address, and failure to give such notice shall be grounds for the revocation of such license.

sec. 87WW. Licensing of Non-Resident as Broker or Salesman; Appointment of Chairman of Board to Receive Service of Process.

A non-resident may be licensed as a broker and a non-resident individual may be licensed as a salesman upon conforming to all pertinent provisions of sections eighty-seven PP to eighty-seven DDD, inclusive; provided, that the board may exempt from the written examination prescribed in section eighty-seven SS a broker or salesman duly licensed in any other state of the United States under the laws of which a similar exemption is extended to licensed brokers and salesmen of the commonwealth. Such non-resident licensee shall not be required to maintain a usual place of business within the commonwealth; provided, that such non-resident broker shall maintain a usual place of business within such other state in which he is so licensed.

No license shall be issued to such non-resident until he shall have filed with the chairman of the board a power of attorney constituting and appointing said chairman and his successor his true and lawful attorney, upon whom all lawful processes in any action or legal proceeding against him may be served, and therein shall agree that any lawful process against him which may be served upon his said attorney shall be of the same force and validity as if served on said non-resident, and that the authority thereof shall continue in force irrevocably as long as any liability of said non-resident remains outstanding in the commonwealth. Service of such process shall be made by leaving duplicate copies thereof in the hands or office of the chairman, and the chairman shall forthwith send one of said copies by mail, postage prepaid, addressed to the defendant at his last address as appearing on the records of the board. One of the duplicates of such process, certified by the chairman as having been served upon him, shall be deemed sufficient evidence of such service, and service upon such attorney shall be deemed service upon the principal.

sec. 87XX. Issuance of License; Form; Term; Renewal; Board to Keep Record and Provide for Publication of Lists of Licensed Brokers and Salesmen.

The board shall issue a license to an applicant who has complied with all pertinent requirements which shall entitle him to act as a broker or a salesman, as the case may be; provided, however, that a license issued to a corporation, society, association or partnership shall not authorize any unlicensed individual connected therewith to act as broker or salesman except as expressly provided in section eighty-seven UU. Such license shall be in such form as the board may determine, shall set forth the name and address of the licensee, shall specify the nature of the license, whether for a broker or salesman, the date of issuance, and shall bear a facsimile of the seal of the board. Except as otherwise provided in section eighty-seven UU in the case of a license issued to a corporation, society, association or partnership, a license shall be valid for a period of two years from the date of issue unless sooner suspended or revoked and shall be valid for a period of two years from the date of issue unless sooner suspended or revoked and shall be renewed by the board biennially thereafter, without examination, upon payment of the fee prescribed in section eighty-seven ZZ; provided, that the application for renewal is made not later than one year from the expiration of the license, and the applicant, if an individual, or, if a corporation, society, association or partnership, each officer and director or holder of similar position or each partner, of whom evidence of good moral character is required in connection with the application for an original license in section eighty-seven TT, has not been found to be disqualified because of lack of good moral character, or for any ground set forth in sections eighty-seven PP to eighty-seven DDD, inclusive; and, provided, further, that the license of a corporation, society, association or partnership shall be renewed only upon the renewal of the individual license of at least one of its designated officers or partners as the case may be. No fee shall be required of a corporation, society, association or partnership for the renewal of its license. Applications for renewals of licenses shall be signed and sworn to by the applicant and shall be made on forms furnished by the board. Such application forms shall be mailed by the board to each broker and salesman registered with the board, together with notice of the expiration of his license, not less than thirty days prior to such expiration. Renewal licensed shall be in such form as the board may determine. Notwithstanding the foregoing, the license originally issued to an individual shall be valid until the anniversary of the licensee's date of birth next occurring more than twenty-four months after the date of issuance. The board shall keep a record of all licensed brokers and salesmen which shall be open to inspection by the public and shall, from time to time, cause to be printed a new or revised publication containing an alphabetical list of such brokers and salesmen, together with their addresses, accompanied by such other information relative to the enforcement of the provisions of this chapter as it may deem of interest to the public.

sec. 87XX½. Continuing Education

Any person holding a real estate broker or salesman license, which is subject to renewal on or after January First, nineteen hundred and ninety-nine, shall, within twenty-four months prior to each renewal, satisfactorily complete courses or programs of instruction approved by the board; provided, that for licenses renewed on or before December thirty-first, two thousand, the attendance at such courses or programs of instruction shall be equal to a total of twelve hours; and provided, further, that for licenses renewed on or after January first, two thousand and one, such number shall be no less than six hours but no more than twelve hours as determined by the board. The curriculum contained in such courses or programs shall contain at least six hours of instruction concerning or related to compliance with laws and regulations selected from any of the following subjects: fair housing; equal employment opportunity; accessibility for the disabled; agency law; environmental issues in real estate; zoning and building codes; real estate appraisal and financing; property tax assessments and valuation; and real estate board regulations. The board shall certify in advance the curriculum forming the basis of such courses and programs which satisfy the provisions of this section.

Every person who is subject to the provisions of this section shall furnish, in a form satisfactory to the board, written certification that the required courses or programs were successfully completed. Upon such completion of approved courses or programs, the licensee shall be deemed to have met the continuing education requirements of this section for license renewal. Every person who fails to furnish, in a form satisfactory to the board, written certification that the required courses or programs were completed shall be granted inactive status by the board upon renewal of his license in accordance with section eighty-seven XX.

Any person failing to meet requirements imposed upon him by this section or who has submitted to the board a false or fraudulent certification of compliance therewith, shall, after a hearing thereon, which hearing may be waived by such person, be subject to the suspension of his license until such time as such person shall have demonstrated to the satisfaction of the board that he has complied with all of the requirements of this section as well as with all other laws, rules and regulations applicable to such licensing.

The provisions of this section shall not apply to any person licensed by the board under the provisions of section eighty-seven SS who is not required to take an examination to be licensed; provided, however, that any out-of-state licensee who receives reciprocity from the board to practice in the commonwealth shall demonstrate to the board compliance with a continuing education program in such licensee's home state.

The provisions of this section shall not apply to any person licensed by the board who has been granted inactive status by the board. A person licensed by the board and whose license is inactive may not engage in the business of, or act as, a real estate broker or salesman, as defined in section eighty-seven PP, except that he may assist with or direct the procuring of prospects and may receive referral fees for such procurement activities. A person licensed by the board whose license is inactive shall be considered unlicensed for the purposes of section eighty-seven RR. Engaging in the business of, or acting as, a real estate broker or salesman while a license is inactive, except as otherwise provided in this section, may be grounds for the revocation of such license. A person licensed by the board and whose license is inactive shall renew such license in accordance with section eighty-seven XX while such license is inactive. A person licensed by the board and whose license is inactive may apply to the board to reactivate such license, upon demonstration of completion of the continuing education requirement for the renewal period immediately preceding the application for reactivation of such license and compliance with all then acceptable requirements for licensure.

The board shall perform such duties and functions necessary to carry out the provisions of this section and shall promulgate rules and regulations pertaining to the development and administration of an inactive license designation. Such rules and regulations shall include, but not be limited to, developing procedures for the granting of inactive status, the reactivation of licenses, renewal fees and notification of licensees of continuing education requirements prior to license reactivation.

The board of registration of real estate brokers and salesmen, created pursuant to sections eighty-seven PP through eighty-seven DDD, inclusive, of chapter one hundred and twelve of the General Laws, shall promulgate rules and regulations to implement the provisions of this act within one hundred and eighty days after its effective date.

sec. 87YY. Licensed Resident Broker to Maintain Usual Place of Business; Display of License Therein; Notice of Change of Business Location.

A licensed resident broker shall maintain a usual place of business in the commonwealth and shall display conspicuously therein or in any branch thereof his license or a certified copy thereof. He shall promptly give written notice to the board of any change of business location, and the board shall issue a new license for such new location for the unexpired term of such license. failure to give such notice shall be grounds for the revocation of such license.

sec. 87ZZ. Fees.

Fees, as determined annually by the commissioner of administration under the provision of section three B of chapter seven, shall be paid by individuals in advance for the following:-

[From and after July 1, 1985, paragraph (a) shall read as follows:]

(a) For each examination for a broker's license, fifteen dollars; for each examination for a salesman's license, eight dollars; provided, however, that a veteran holding an honorable discharge or a blind person shall not be required to pay any examination fee; and provided, further, in the event the examination is conducted by an independent testing service designated by the board under authority of section eight-seven Ss, in addition to the above fee, each individual shall pay to the testing service a fee, approved by the board, covering the actual cost of giving the examination.

(b) Issuance and renewal of a broker's license; provided, however, that a blind person or a veteran suffering from paraplegia, as defined in section six B of chapter one hundred and fifteen, shall not be required to pay such fee.

(c) Issuance and renewal of a salesman's license; provided, however, that a blind person or a veteran suffering from paraplegia, as defined in section six B of chapter one hundred and fifteen, shall not be required to pay such fee.

(d) The applicable fee for the issuance of a license shall be adjusted by the board on the basis of each month during which the license originally issued would be valid unless revoked or suspended and, for this purpose, any part of a month shall be considered as a full month.

sec. 87AAA. Suspension, Revocation or Refusal of Renewal of License; Grounds; Reinstatement; Other Punishment.

The Board may, and upon the verified complaint in writing of a aggrieved person shall, investigate the action of any broker or salesman or any person who attempts to act in such capacity within the commonwealth, and, in addition to any grounds hereinbefore enumerated, may suspend, revoke or refuse to renew any license which it has found to have been obtained by false or fraudulent representation. The board may suspend, revoke or refuse to renew any license, when the board has found as a fact that the licensee, in performing or attempting to perform any act authorized by his license, has (a) knowingly made any substantial misrepresentation; (b) acted in the dual capacity of broker and undisclosed principal in the same transaction; (c) acted for more than one party to a transaction, without the knowledge and consent of all the parties for whom he acts; (d) failed, within a reasonable time, to account for or remit any moneys belonging to others which have come into his possession as a broker or salesman; (e) paid commissions or fees to or divided the same with any person, who, being required to be licensed as a broker or salesman in this or any other state, is not so licensed; (f) accepted, given or charged, any undisclosed commission, rebate or profit on expenditures for a principal; (g) induced any party to a contract or lease relating to real estate to break the same when such action is effected for the personal gain of the licenses; (h) commingled the money or other property of his principal with his own; (i) failed to give to both the buyer and seller a copy of the purchase and sale agreement; or (j) committed any act expressly prohibited in sections eighty-seven RR to eighty-seven CCC, inclusive; (k) affirmatively solicited for sale, lease, or the listing for sale or lease, of residential property on the grounds of alleged change of value due to the presence or the prospective entry into the neighborhood of a person or persons of another race, economic level, religion or ethnic origin or distributes, or causes to be distributed, material or makes statements designated to induce a residential property owner to sell or lease his property due to such change in the neighborhood; or (l) accepted from a prospective seller a net listing, an agreement to sell real estate for a stated price which authorized the broker to keep as commission any amount of money received from the sale of said real estate in excess of the stated price. The board shall, after notice by the Massachusetts commission against discrimination that said commission has made a finding, which finding has become final, that a licensed broker or salesman committed an unlawful practice in violation of chapter one hundred and fifty-one B arising out of or in the course of his occupation as a licensed broker or salesman, shall suspend forthwith the license of said broker or salesman for a period of sixty days and, if the said commission finds that said violation by such licensed broker or salesman occurred within two years of the date of a prior violation of said chapter one hundred and fifty-one B, which finding has been final, it shall so notify the board, and the board shall forthwith suspend the license of such broker or salesman for a period of ninety days. Whoever violates the provisions of clause (k) shall be punished by a fine of not less than one thousand nor more than twenty-five hundred dollars, or by imprisonment for not more than six months, or both.

No broker shall engage in a sale in the commonwealth of real property located in a land development in another state which is the subject of promotional advertising in the commonwealth unless the owner or developer of such land has submitted to the board full particulars regarding such land and the proposed terms of sale thereof and has deposited with the board such sum as it shall determine, to pay the expense of the investigation hereinafter prescribed. Any broker acting for such owner or developer and his salesmen, shall comply with such rules, regulations, restrictions and conditions pertaining thereto as the board in its discretion may impose. The board shall investigate such matters and all reasonable expenses incurred by the board in such investigation shall be borne by the owner or developer of the property involved. No broker or salesman shall in any manner refer to the board of registration of real estate brokers and salesmen or to any member or employee thereof, in selling, offering for sale, or advertising or otherwise promoting the sale, mortgage or lease of any such property, nor make any representation whatsoever that such property has been inspected or approved or otherwise passed upon by said board or by any official, department or employee of the commonwealth. The board may suspend, revoke or refuse to renew any license when it has found that the licensee has failed to comply with the requirements of this paragraph or any part thereof.

The board may also suspend, revoke or refuse to renew any license when it has found that the licensee has been convicted of a criminal offense by a court of competent jurisdiction of this or any other state which demonstrates his lack of good moral character to act as a broker or salesman as the case may be.

The board may reconsider any decision made by it and may reinstate any license which has been suspended and reissue any license which has been revoked.

Any person whose license is suspended or revoked shall also be liable to such other punishment as may be provided by law.

sec. 87BBB. Enforcement by Board; Hearings and Matters Related thereto; Decisions; Appeal; Costs; Appeal Not to Stay Refusal, etc.

A. The board is hereby empowered to conduct such investigations and hearings and to take such action as may be appropriate and necessary to administer and enforce the provisions of sections eighty-seven PP to eighty-even CCC, inclusive, and to report the violation of any provision of said sections to the proper prosecuting officers. The board may require by summons the attendance and testimony of witnesses and the production of books and papers. Witnesses at hearings shall be duly sworn. Any member, or agent of the board designated for such purpose, may administer oaths, examine witnesses and receive evidence. The board may take testimony by deposition as in civil actions in the superior court. In case of the failure or refusal of a witness to appear and testify or to produce books and papers as required, the superior court for the county in which the investigation is carried on, or for the county in which the witness resides or has his principal place of business, upon application by the board, shall have jurisdiction to issue to such witness an order requiring such witness to appear before the board, there to produce books and papers, if so ordered, or to give testimony concerning the matter under investigation or in questions. Witnesses summoned before the board shall be paid the same fees and mileage paid to witnesses in civil cases in the courts.

B. Decisions of the board shall be by at least a majority thereof and shall be in writing, signed by the members making the same, and shall contain a statement of the reasons therefore including determination of each issue of fact or law necessary thereto, and shall be sent to each interested party. No renewal of a license shall be refused, and no license shall be suspended or revoked, except after a hearing, of which at least ten days' written notice, including a statement of the grounds and a copy of the complaint or charges, if any, which the board proposes to consider, shall be given to the applicant for renewal or the licensee, who shall have the right to appear personally and by counsel at such hearing and to cross-examine witnesses and to produce evidence. In the case of a decision refusing to grant an original license, such a hearing shall be held, if, within ten days of the receipt of the decision the applicant files a written request with the board for such a hearing. The board shall fix the time and place of all hearings.

C. Any person aggrieved by a decision of the board refusing to grant or renew, or suspending or revoking, a license after a hearing, may appeal to the superior court sitting in equity for the county wherein he resides or has his principal place of business, or to said court sitting in equity for the county of Suffolk; provided, that such appeal shall be filed in such court within twenty days following receipt of notification by the board of such decision. the court shall hear all pertinent evidence and determine the fact, and upon the facts as so determined, annul such decision if found to exceed the authority of the board, or make such decree or decision as justice and equity may require. The foregoing remedy shall be exclusive, but the parties shall have all rights of appeal and exception as in other equity cases.

Costs shall not be allowed against the board unless it shall appear to the court that the board acted with gross negligence or in bad faith or with malice in making the decision appealed from. Costs shall not be allowed against the party appealing from the decision of the board unless it shall appear to the court that said party acted in bad faith or with malice in making the appeal to the court.

Such appeal from a decision of the board refusing renewal of or suspending or revoking a license shall not operate as a stay of such refusal, suspension or revocation pending the final determination of such appeal.

sec. 87CCC. Penalty.

Whoever, without being licensed as required by section eighty-seven RR, acts as a broker or salesman or advertises that he is a broker or salesman shall be punished by a fine of not more than five hundred dollars.

sec. 87DDD. Section 61-65 Not to Apply to Board, etc.

The provisions of section sixty-one to sixty-five, inclusive, shall not apply to the board, to the registration or licensing of real estate brokers or salesmen, or to any real estate broker or salesman or to any person acting as such.

sec. 87DDD 1/2. Charging of Fees for Locating Dwelling Accommodations for Prospective Tenants: License Required.

No person shall engage in the business of finding dwelling accommodations for prospective tenants for a fee unless such person is a licensed broker or salesman as defines in section eighty-seven PP of chapter 112.

254 CMR 1.00: *Reserved*

254 CMR 2.00: **Licensure.**

(1) Purpose. 254 CMR 2.00 sets forth the application procedures, examination, experience, good moral character requirements for licensure.

(2) Applications. Applications for licenses shall be made on forms furnished by the Board and shall be accompanied by the prescribed fee.

(3) Examinations. No broker or salesperson license shall be issued to any individual unless such individual satisfactorily passes a written examination conducted by the Board or its agent. Prior to taking the examination applicants must submit certification to the Board that the required education has been completed. This certification shall be valid for a period not to exceed 24 months following the date on which the education was completed. Any applicant who is an attorney at law in good standing of this Commonwealth shall not be required to take such examination.

(4) Re-Examination. An individual who fails to pass the written examination for a real estate broker or salesperson may be re-examined by paying the prescribed fee.

(5) License Fees. An individual who has been notified of passing the examination for real estate broker or salesperson must pay the prescribed fee within 30 days from the date of notification. If the required fee is not paid within the specified time period the individual shall be required to be re-examined and pay the prescribed fee for such examination. This requirement may be waived by the Board upon showing of good cause.

(6) Experience Requirement for License as a Broker. A salesperson seeking licensure as a real estate broker must:

(a) Be employed or affiliated with a licensed real estate broker in performing those activities as defined (for licensed salespeople) in M.G.L.c. 112, § 87PP for at least one year. The Board shall determine the form and manner to verify such employment or affiliation.

(b) Be employed or affiliated with such licensed real estate broker for a minimum of twenty-five hours per calendar week under the supervision of such broker.

(c) Obtain licensure as a real estate broker within two years of the date that such employment or affiliation as a real estate salesperson is terminated.

(7) Moral Character. Each individual seeking a license as a broker or salesperson shall furnish evidence of good moral character. Applications for a license shall be accompanied by the recommendations of three reputable citizens, not related to the applicant, who reside in or have their place of business in the Commonwealth. Each recommendation shall certify that the individual bears a good reputation for honesty and fair dealing and shall recommend that a license be granted to such individual.

(8) Personal Appearance. Applicants may be required to appear at the office of the Board for an interview.

(9) Qualification Reports. The Board may require each individual seeking a license to submit a report from an independent source pertaining to the individual's previous occupation or any other information which is material to the qualification of such individual for a license.

(10) Surety Bonds. No broker's license shall issue or be renewed until such broker gives the Board the bond required by M.G.L. c. 112, § 87TT.

(11) Business Entities. No licensee may engage in the business of real estate brokering in a corporation, limited liability company (LLC), partnership, limited liability partnership (LLP), association or society unless the entity is licensed by the Board.

No broker's license shall issue to a corporation, LLC, partnership, LLP, association or society unless an officer in such corporation, society or association or partner in a partnership is a licensed broker in the Commonwealth and designated as the broker of record for the entity. The broker of record must be currently licensed at all times, otherwise the license of the entity shall cease. The broker of record shall be in responsible charge of the business entity and personally responsible for the acts of the entity and its employees and agents.

(12) LLC, LLP Insurance. An LLC and LLP must maintain professional liability insurance which meets the following minimum standards:

(a) The insurance shall cover negligence, wrongful acts, errors and omissions and insure the LLC and it officers or the LLP and its partners as required by M.G.L. c. 156C, §. 65 and M.G.L. c. 108A, §. 45(8)(a).

(b) The insurance shall be in an amount for each claim of at least $50,000 multiplied by the number of individual licensees employed by, or officers of, the LLC, and in an aggregate amount of at least $150,000 multiplied by the number of individual licensees who are employed by, or officers of, the LLC.

(c) The insurance shall be in an amount for each claim of at least $50,000 multiplied by the number of individual licensees employed by, or partners of, the LLP, and in an aggregate amount of at least $150,000 multiplied by the number of individual licensees who are employed by, or partners of, the LLP.

(d) The requirements of 254 CMR 2.00(12) shall be satisfied if the LLC or LLP maintains insurance sufficient to provide coverage at a level of at least $300,000 for each claim with an aggregate top limit of liability for all claims, during any one year, of at least $1,000,000; and

(e) The insurance required by 254 CMR 2.00(12) may provide that it does not apply to any dishonest, fraudulent, criminal, or malicious act or omission of the insured LLC, or any officer or employee thereof, or the LLP, or any partner or employee thereof.

(f) Cancellation or any other interruption in required insurance coverage shall require the LLC or LLP to immediately cease the practice of real estate brokering until such time as the LLC or LLP is in compliance with 254 CMR 2.00(12).

(g) An LLC or LLP must notify the Board within 5 business days, if the LLC or LLP insurance coverage is canceled or otherwise interrupted. Failure to provide required notice to the Board will subject the LLC and its officers or the LLP and its partners who are licensed by the Board to disciplinary action pursuant to M.G.L. c. 112, § 87AAA.

(h) An LLC or LLP may be required to provide verification of compliance with 254 CMR 2.00(12), satisfactory to the Board, when it seeks initial licensure, the renewal of such license and at any other time at the request of the Board.

(13) **Reciprocal Licensure.** The Board may issue a real estate salesperson or brokers license to individuals licensed in other states or jurisdictions without requiring the satisfaction of the education and examination requirements where such other state or jurisdiction has laws similar to the Commonwealth governing the practice of real estate brokering and extends the same privilege to licensed Massachusetts real estate brokers and salespersons. Applicants for reciprocal licensure shall apply on the form provided by the Board and pay the prescribed fee.

(14) **License Renewal.** No license may be renewed later than one year following the expiration of such license nor may any broker or salesperson practice when such license has expired. Any license renewal sought after license expiration but prior to the end of the one year grace period must be on the form provided by the Board and verify to the Board's satisfaction completion of continuing education as required by M.G.L. c. 112, § 87XX 1/2, and be accompanied by the prescribed fee.

254 CMR 3.00: **Professional Standards of Practice** - violation of any of the provisions of 254 CMR 3.00 may result in the suspension, revocation or discipline of a license.

(1) **Address Reporting.** Each broker and salesperson shall provide to the Board written notice of their current business and residential address at all times.

(2) **Broker Employee.** A broker who is employed by or affiliated with another broker shall not employ or have affiliated with him/her any salespersons within the business entity.

(3) **Business Name.** Any broker operating under a business or trade name (doing business as) shall provide the Board with written notice of such name.

(4) **Display of License.** Each broker and salesperson shall display a copy of their license in a conspicuous location that is readily observable to the general public.

(5) **Single License Requirement.** No broker shall also be licensed as a salesperson nor shall any salesperson be licensed as a broker.

(6) **Salespersons Cannot Be Self-Employed.** A licensed salesperson must be engaged by a licensed broker and a licensed salesperson shall not conduct his own real estate business.

(7) **Notification to Board of Affiliation.** Brokers shall furnish the Board with the names, addresses and license numbers of all brokers and salespeople engaged by them at the commencement of such association or affiliation and shall further notify the Board of the termination of such relationship at the time such relationship is terminated.

(8) **Sharing of Fees.** No fee, commission or other valuable consideration shall be paid to or shared by an owner's managing agent or its employees as the result of the sale of real estate for the owner unless such agent and its employees are licensed brokers or salespersons, except as provided for in M.G.L.c. 112, § 87QQ.

(9) <u>Advertising.</u> A broker shall not advertise in any way that is false or misleading.

(a) <u>Broker Identification</u>. No broker may advertise real property to purchase, sell, rent, mortgage or exchange through classified advertisement or otherwise unless he/she affirmatively discloses that he/she is a real estate broker. No broker shall insert advertisements in any advertising publication or other means where only a post office box number, telephone, facsimile, electronic mail number or street address appears. All advertisements shall include the name of the real estate broker.

(b) <u>Salespersons Prohibited From Advertising.</u> Salespeople are prohibited from advertising the purchase, sale, rental or exchange of any real property under their own name.

(c) <u>Discriminatory Advertising Prohibited.</u> No broker shall advertise to purchase, sell, rent, mortgage or exchange any real property in any manner that indicates directly or indirectly unlawful discrimination against any individual or group.

(10) <u>Client Funds:</u>

(a) <u>Escrow Accounts</u>. Unless otherwise agreed to in writing by the parties in transactions involving the sale, purchase, renting or exchange of real property, all money of whatever kind and nature paid over to a real estate broker to be held during the pendency of a transaction shall be immediately deposited in a bank escrow account and such broker shall be responsible for such money until the transaction is either consummated or terminated, at which time a proper account and distribution of such money shall be made. An escrow account is an account where the broker deposits and maintains the money of other parties in a real estate transaction and such broker has no claim to such money. An escrow account may be interest or non-interest bearing but where it is interest bearing the broker must make a proper account of such interest at either the consummation or termination of the transaction.

(b) <u>Record Keeping.</u> Every broker shall keep a record of funds deposited in his/her escrow accounts, which records shall clearly indicate the date and from whom the broker received the money, date deposited along with the source of the money and check number, date of withdrawal with the name of the person receiving such withdrawal, and other pertinent information concerning the transaction and shall clearly show for whose account the money is deposited and to whom the money belongs. Every broker shall also keep a copy of each check deposited into and withdrawn from the escrow account for a period of three years from the date of issuance. All such funds and records shall be subject to inspection by the Board or its agents.

(c) <u>Salespersons Prohibited from Holding Funds.</u> A real estate salesperson or broker engaged by another broker shall immediately turn over all deposit money or other money received to such employing broker. No salesperson shall at any time hold client funds.

(11) <u>Conflicts of Interests:</u> A broker or salesperson must act honestly and ethically and in the best interests of their client at all times.

(a) A broker or salesperson shall not buy, sell, rent, mortgage, or acquire any interest in, or represent a client in the buying, selling, renting or exchange of real property in which the broker or salesperson or his/her kin has a personal financial interest unless the broker or salesperson shall fully disclose in writing to all parties to the transaction the nature of his/her interest and unless the parties shall provide the broker or salesperson with written acknowledgment of such disclosure.

(b) A broker shall not take an option, either directly or indirectly, upon real property for the lease or sale of which the broker has been approached by the owner to act as a broker without first disclosing that such broker is now a prospective purchaser or lessor and no longer acting as a broker for the owner.

(c) A broker or salesperson shall not accept a "net" listing from an owner or landlord for the sale or rental of real property in which the commission is unspecified.

(d) <u>Conveying Offers.</u> All offers submitted to brokers or salespeople to purchase or rent real property that they have a right to sell or rent shall be conveyed forthwith to the owner of such real property.

(12) <u>Attorney Services.</u> No broker or salesperson shall advise against the use of an attorney in any real property transaction.

(13) <u>Agency Disclosure</u>. A real estate broker or salesperson shall provide to a prospective purchaser or seller of real estate a notice developed and approved by the board which clearly discloses the relationship of the broker or salesperson with the prospective purchaser or seller of the real estate.

The notice approved by the Board shall be provided to a prospective purchaser or seller at the time of the first personal meeting between the prospective purchaser or seller and the broker or salesperson for the purpose of discussing a specific property.

Where the broker or salesperson has obtained the informed consent of both the purchaser and seller to represent both of them such broker or salesperson must, at the time of obtaining the informed consent, provide written notice to the purchaser and seller of the consensual dual representation and otherwise comply with the following requirement noted herein.

(a) A broker or salesperson shall request a prospective purchaser or seller to sign and date such notice, provide the original to the prospective purchaser or seller and maintain a copy with their records for a period of three years from the date on the notice.

(b) If a prospective purchaser or seller declines to sign the notice the broker or salesperson shall make a notation indicating the date the notice was given to the prospective purchaser or seller, that the prospective purchaser or seller declined to sign it, and the reason therefor, if any, given by the prospective purchaser or seller. The broker shall maintain such notice for a period of three years from the date on the notice.

(c) Nothing herein shall require written notice to each prospective purchaser or seller who comes to an open house showing of real property provided, however, the broker or salesperson, by sign, poster, distributed listing literature or property description form conspicuously discloses the agency relationship. Where the listing literature or property description form is distributed at an open house the written disclosure of the agency relationship therein shall be more conspicuous than any other written terms.

(d) All such records and notices are subject to inspection by the Board or its agents.

(14) **Additional Grounds For Discipline**. No real estate broker or salesperson shall violate, or attempt to violate, directly or indirectly, or assist or abet the violation of, or conspire to violate any provision of the relevant licensing law, the regulations herein or order of the Board.

(a) no broker or salesperson shall practice while his/her ability to do so is impaired by drugs, alcohol or other reason.

(b) no broker or salesperson shall practice while his/her license is expired, revoked suspended or otherwise not valid.

(c) no broker or salesperson shall discriminate in the provision of services on the basis of age, marital status, gender, sexual preference, race, religion, socioeconomic status or disability.

(d) no broker or salesperson shall attempt to procure a license by false pretenses or in any way aid another in obtaining a license by false pretenses.

(e) a broker or salesperson shall only assume those duties and responsibilities for which he/she has adequate preparation and for which competency has been acquired and maintained.

(f) a broker or salesperson shall comply with all the laws of the Commonwealth, the United States and those of any other state in which he/she is licensed.

(g) a broker or salesperson shall report to the Board within thirty days his or her conviction of any crime including any misdemeanor or felony under the law of the Commonwealth, the United States or laws of another jurisdiction which if committed in Massachusetts would constitute a crime under Massachusetts law.

(h) a real estate broker and salesperson who fraudulently certifies to the Board completion of the educational curriculum described in 254 CMR 5.03 may, following a hearing, which hearing may be waived by such broker or salesperson, be subject to the suspension of their license until such time that the Board is satisfied that the educational curriculum has been completed.

(i) a broker or salesperson upon notice of suspension or revocation of his license shall deliver his/her license to the offices of the Board within seven days of the receipt of such notice.

254 CMR 4:00: **Real Estate School Authorization**.

(1) **Purpose**. In order to provide the real estate education that can qualify individuals for licensure as real estate brokers or salespersons or provide continuing education a real estate school must be authorized by the Board.

(2) **Applications.** Applications for authorization as a real estate school must be made on the form prescribed by the Board and accompanied by the required fee. The Board shall verify the locations suitability for occupancy.

(3) **Renewal.** School authorizations are valid for two years from the date of issuance and shall be renewed biennially.

(4) **Single Location Authorized**. Each location at which a school operates must be separately authorized (and the Board may set a limit on the number of separate locations for an authorized school).

(5) **Authorized Agents**. Each authorized school must designate one individual as an authorized agent. The authorized agent shall:

(a) maintain records documenting the attendance of individuals including the name of individuals, the dates on which the individuals attended the school and the date on which the individuals completed either the curriculum for licensure as a real estate broker or salesperson, the continuing education curriculum for licensed brokers and salespeople or the instructor curriculum. Each authorized school shall maintain the record of each individual for at least two years following the completion of the curriculum by such individual;

(b) ensure that only individuals who complete the 24 hours of education for salesperson's, 30 hours of education for brokers or 12 hours of continuing education for brokers and salesperson's are certified, in a form prescribed by the Board, as meeting the educational requirements for licensure or renewal of licensure;

(c) shall notify the Board of any change in the address or telephone number of the authorized school or any change of the authorized agent within seven days of such change.

(d) ensure that only qualified instructors are permitted to teach the curriculum that contributes toward certification for licensure or continuing education.

(6) **Rescinding of Authorization.**

The Board may suspend, revoke or refuse to renew the authorization of any school which fails to adhere to the rules and regulations of the Board including:

(a) failure to maintain records as required by 254 CMR 4.00(5)(a);

(b) failure to provide appropriate notice to the Board of any change of address, telephone number or of the authorized agent;

(c) failure to provide the Board or its agents with copies of or access to requested information;

(d) failure to use the exact name of the authorized school on any postings, advertisements, solicitations or any other medium of communication;

(e) failure to have an qualified instructor, in accordance with 254 CMR 4.00(7), in the classroom with the individuals taking the curriculum described in 254 4.00(5)(b) during the time that it is provided;

(f) obtaining a school authorization by false pretenses or fraudulent representation;

(g) discriminating against an individual based on age, marital status, gender, sexual preference, race, religion, socioeconomic status or disability;

(h) failing to provide an individual completing the curriculum for licensure as a broker or salesperson or for continuing education with appropriate certification of completion of such curriculum;

(i) providing certification of completion to an individual who has not completed such curriculum;

(j) combining any part of the broker, salesperson, instructor or continuing education curriculum into a single curriculum or offering.

(k) failure to offer the curriculum for licensure and renewal established by the Board.

(7) **Instructor Qualification.**

(a) **Requirements To Become An Instructor**. No person may act as an instructor of the salesperson or broker curriculum in any authorized real estate school unless such person verifies to the Board satisfaction of the requirements established in 254 CMR 4.00(7)(a)1. through 4.

(1) Instructors must hold a current brokers license issued by the Board.

(2) Instructors must have a minimum of two years work experience as a real estate broker involving at least 25 hours per week.

(3) Instructors must have co-taught or audited the curriculum in an authorized school before they may teach it.

(4) Instructors must have a minimum of 30 hours of instruction in an instructor training program which has been approved by the Board.

(b) **Issuance of Instructor Authorization**. The Board may issue authorization to act as an instructor to any person who has satisfied the requirements of 254 CMR 4.00(7)(a)1. through 4 or the equivalent in lieu thereof as determined by the Board.

(c) **Use of Specialists**. Instructors may employ specialists to teach particular portions of the salesperson or broker curriculum and such specialists need not obtain authorization from the Board. Specialists may not be employed to teach the entire curriculum.

254 CMR 5:00: Continuing Education.

(1) **Continuing Education Requirement**. Effective January 1, 1999 no license of a real estate broker or salesperson will be renewed unless they verify, in a form and manner determined by the Board, that they have completed the continuing education requirements established in M.G.L. c. 112, § 87XX 1/2.

(2) **Educational Curriculum**. The Board shall publish the curriculum which will form the basis of the continuing education requirement and may change such curriculum from time to time as necessary, consistent with M.G.L. c. 112, § 87XX 1/2.

(3) **Verification Of Compliance**. With each renewal of their license, a broker or salesperson must certify to the Board that they have completed the 12 hours of continuing education in the curriculum published by the Board pursuant to 254 CMR 5.02. Authorized schools shall maintain records for each individual broker or salesperson who has completed the continuing education curriculum for a period of at least three years following completion of the curriculum.

(4) **Inactive Status**. Licensed brokers and salespersons who fail to comply with the continuing education requirement shall have their license placed on an inactive status by the Board. Brokers and salespersons designated inactive are prohibited from practicing as such. An inactive broker may receive a referral fee from a licensed active real estate broker when making a referral of a person to such licensed active broker. Nothing herein shall authorize inactive real estate brokers and salespersons to engage in brokering as defined in M.G.L. c.112, § 87PP.

(5) **Recording Of Inactive License Status**. Licensees placed on an inactive status shall not be issued a license.

254 CMR 6:00: Promotional Sales of Out of State Real Property.

(1) **Prohibition On Broker Sales Activity**. No broker shall offer for sale in the Commonwealth an interest in real property which is located in a land development of another state unless the owner or developer of such land development registers such property with the Board.

(2) **Filing Requirement**. Prior to promoting for sale an interest in real property located in a land development of another jurisdiction the owner or developer of such real property shall register it with the Board on the form and paying the fee prescribed by the Board. Such registration shall be renewed annually.

(3) **Inspections**. The Board may inspect any out of state real property developments seeking registration or registered with it. The costs of any inspection shall be borne by the owner or developer. Following an inspection of an out of state real property development the Board shall issue a written report. Such report shall be kept on file with the Board during the time that the out of state real property development is currently registered with the Board and for one year following the termination or expiration of such registration. The owner or developer of such out of state real property shall also maintain such report in its files while such registration is current and for one year following the termination or expiration of such registration.

(4) **Advertising Notice of Registration**. Once the Board registers an out of state real property development the owner or developer of such development must note, in a form to be determined by the Board, the fact of such registration in all its subsequent advertisements in the Commonwealth.

(5) **Sales By Brokers**. No interest in any real property located in an out of state real property development shall be subject to any promotional advertisement, offering for sale or sold in the Commonwealth unless it is offered for sale and sold by a licensed Massachusetts broker. Promotional advertising as used herein means any advertising material offered through any means of communication in the Commonwealth.

(6) **Brokers Notice to Board**. A broker acting on behalf of an owner or developer of an out of state real property development shall notify the Board in writing of such status within seven days of accepting the client.

254 C.M.R. 7.00: Apartment Rentals.

(1) **Notice To Prospective Tenants**. Brokers and salespersons engaged in renting real property, whether by written agreement or not, shall provide each prospective tenant with a written notice which states whether the prospective tenant will pay any fee for such service, the amount of such fee, the manner and time in which it is to be paid and whether or not any fee or any portion thereof will be payable by the tenant if a tenancy is not created. This written notice must be given by the real estate broker or salesperson at the first personal meeting between the

broker or salesperson and a prospective tenant. It must be signed by the real estate broker or salesperson, contain the license number of such broker or salesperson, be signed by the prospective tenant and contain the date such notice was given by the broker or salesperson to the prospective tenant. Where a prospective tenant declines to sign such written notice the real estate broker or salesperson must note on such written notice the tenants name and the refusal to sign such notice.

(2) Record Maintenance And Inspection. A copy of the written notice referred to in 254 CMR. 7.00 shall be maintained by the real estate broker or salesperson for a period of three years from the date on which the notice was provided to the prospective tenant. Real estate brokers or salespersons shall furnish the notice to the board, its investigators or other agents upon request.

(a) Brokers shall maintain all rental listings and written documents that demonstrate the availability of an apartment at the time it is advertised for rental for a period of three years from the date on which such apartment is rented.

(b) Brokers shall maintain a copy of any check, money order and written cash receipt for any fees, deposits or payments made by a prospective tenant or actual tenant for a period of three years from the date of issuance. Brokers shall also maintain a copy of any check issued on an escrow account over which they have issuing authority for a period of three years from the date of issuance.

(c) Any advertisement concerning the availability of an apartment shall disclose in print no smaller than that for the apartment itself that "The apartment advertised may no longer be available for rental".

(3) Fees For Service. No real estate broker shall charge any fee to a prospective tenant unless a tenancy is created or in those cases where no tenancy in real property is created unless the prospective tenant has agreed in writing to pay such a fee.

CHCKLST\RESTATRE.DOC

REAL ESTATE BROKER BOND

POLICY NUMBER: _____

THIS ORIGINAL FORM MUST BE COMPLETED BY THE INSURANCE AGENT OR BOND COMPANY AND THE POWER OF ATTORNEY MUST BE ATTACHED

KNOW ALL PERSONS BY THESE PRESENTS:

That we, _____
(name exactly as it appears or will appear on the broker license)

of _____ Town of _____
(address as it appears or will appear on the broker license)

County of _____ State of _____

as Principal, and _____

a corporation organized under the laws of the State of _____
and duly authorized to transact business in the Commonwealth of Massachusetts, as Surety, are held and firmly bound unto the Commonwealth of Massachusetts, as Obligee, the sum of **FIVE THOUSAND AND 00/100 DOLLARS ($5,000.00)** for the payment of which sum the said principal and surety do jointly and severally bind themselves, their heirs, executors, administrators, successors and assigns, and each and every one of them firmly by these presents.

THE CONDITION OF THIS OBLIGATION IS SUCH THAT WHEREAS, the Principal has made application to the Board of Registration of Real Estate Brokers and Salesmen for a license to engage in the business of Real Estate Broker as defined in Chapter 112 of the General Laws as amended.

NOW, THEREFORE, if the said Board of Registration of Real Estate Brokers and Salesmen shall grant the application and issue the license above referred to and if the Principal shall faithfully account for all funds entrusted to him in his capacity of Real Estate Broker, then this obligation shall be null and void; otherwise to remain in full force and effect, subject however to the following conditions:

No. 1. This bond shall be continuous in form; the liability of the surety hereunder may however be terminated by giving thirty days written notice thereof, by registered or certified mail, to the Board of Registration of Real Estate Brokers and Salesmen in a form acceptable to such Board; and upon giving such notice, the Surety shall be discharged from all liability under this bond for any act or omission of the Principal occurring after the expiration of thirty days from the date of service of such notice.

No. 2. That any person aggrieved by an act of the Principal named in this bond in violation of the provisions of said Chapter 112 may proceed against the Principal or Surety herein, or both, to recover damages.

No. 3. That nothing contained herein shall be construed to impose upon the Surety any greater liability in the aggregate than the total amount of his bond.

IN WITNESS WHEREOF, the said Principal and Surety have signed and sealed this instrument this _____ day of
_____ 19____

Witness _____

     _____
     Principal

Witness _____

     By _____
     Attorney-in-Fact

NOTHING CONTAINED HEREIN SHALL BE CONSTRUED AS THE GRANTING OF A BROKER LICENSE OR AUTHORIZATION TO PRACTICE THE BUSINESS OF REAL ESTATE BROKER. THIS ORIGINAL BOND, ONCE COMPLETED, MUST BE SUBMITTED TO THE MASSACHUSETTS BOARD OF REGISTRATION OF REAL ESTATE BROKERS AND SALESMEN, 100 CAMBRIDGE STREET, ROOM 1313, BOSTON, MA 02202.

Massachusetts License Law 12-37

MASSACHUSETTS BOARD OF REGISTRATION OF REAL ESTATE BROKERS AND SALESPERSONS
MANDATORY AGENCY DISCLOSURE - AGENCY RELATIONSHIP

The purpose of this disclosure is to enable you to make informed choices before working with a real estate licensee. It must be provided at the first personal meeting that you have with an agent to discuss a specific property. THIS IS NOT A CONTRACT. It is a disclosure notice for your information. BE SURE TO READ THE DESCRIPTIONS OF THE DIFFERENT TYPES OF AGENCY REPRESENTATION ON THE OTHER SIDE OF THIS DISCLOSURE

CONSUMER INFORMATION

1. Whether you are the buyer or the seller you can choose to have the advice, assistance and representation of your own agent. Do not assume that a broker is acting on your behalf unless you have contracted with the broker to represent you.

2. All real estate licensees must, by law, present properties honestly and accurately

3. If you are a seller you may authorize you listing agent to cooperate with agents from other firms to help sell your property. These cooperating agents may be subagents who work for the seller or buyer's agents.

4. If you are the buyer you have the option of working with seller's or buyer's agents. This decision will depend on the types of services you want from the real estate agent. A buyer should tell sellers' agents, including subagents, only what he/she would tell the seller directly.

CONSUMER RESPONSIBILITY

The duties of a real estate licensee do not relieve the consumer of the responsibility to protect his/her own interests. Consumers with questions on whether and how real estate agents share fees should pose them to the agent. If you need advice for legal, tax, insurance or other matters it is your responsibility to consult a professional in those areas.

ACKNOWLEDGMENT

I have provided this disclosure form to _____
PRINT NAME OF CONSUMER

I will be assisting the above named consumer as a (check one)　☐ Sellers Agent　☐ Buyers Agent

_____　_____　_____
SIGNATURE OF REAL ESTATE AGENT　　　　　　　　LICENSE NUMBER　　　DATE - MONTH-DAY-YEAR

I have read this agency disclosure form IN ITS ENTIRETY ON BOTH SIDES. I understand that this form is for agency disclosure AND NOT A CONTRACT . It was provided to me by the agent named above.

CHECK HERE ☐ Buyer ☐ Seller

_____　_____
SIGNATURE OF CONSUMER　　　　　　　　　　　　DATE - MONTH-DAY-YEAR

As a consumer I recognize that I need not select any agency representation at this time. Therefore, I decline to sign this disclosure. Any additional reason for declining to sign:

_____
PRINT NAME OF CONSUMER AND REASON, IF ANY

Massachusetts License Law　12-38

TYPES OF AGENCY REPRESENTATION

SELLER'S AGENT

When a seller engages the services of a listing broker that seller becomes the broker's client. This means the broker, and its subagents, represent the seller. They owe the seller undivided loyalty, utmost care, disclosure, obedience to lawful instruction, confidentiality and accountability. They must put the seller's interest first and negotiate for the best price and terms for their client, the seller. (The seller may also authorize subagents to represent him/her in marketing its property to buyers)

BUYER'S AGENT

When a buyer engages the services of a broker then that buyer becomes the broker's client. This means the broker represents the buyer. The broker owes the buyer undivided loyalty, utmost care, disclosure, obedience to lawful instruction, confidentiality and accountability. The broker must put the buyer's interest first and negotiate for the best price and terms for their client, the buyer.(The buyer may also authorize subagents to represent him/her in locating property)

DISCLOSED DUAL AGENT

A broker can work for both the buyer and the seller on the same property provided such broker obtains the informed consent of both parties. The broker is then considered a disclosed dual agent. This broker owes the seller and the buyer a duty to deal with them fairly and honestly. In this type of agency relationship the broker does not represent either the seller or the buyer exclusively and they can not expect the brokers undivided loyalty. Also, undisclosed dual agency is illegal.

CHCKLST\DISCLOSE.DOC

Attorney

We must first receive a LETTER OF GOOD STANDING issued by the SJC along with a cover letter that includes the applicant's mailing address, birthday, and a non-refundable application fee of 20 dollars. Once these materials are received we will mail (do not pick up) the appropriate documents for your completion. The issue date is always on the first ant the 15 of each month provided the completed application is received prior to that date. Letters of Good Standing are valid for 90 days and must be valid at the issuance of the Massachusetts license.

Law School Student

Massachusetts law school students are eligible to take the Salesman examination *without* first taking the Real Estate Salesman course provided he/she has completed a course in property law at a Massachusetts Law School. A waiver (of the education) allowing the applicant to take the examination will be sent upon receipt of a certified transcript from the appropriate Law School and a written request for an educational waiver. This type of waiver is valid for two years and a new waiver can be issued with a new transcript should the 2 years expire.

Connecticut, Rhode Island, West Virginia, Nebraska, Iowa and Mississippi

Complete reciprocity for both Salesmen and Brokers from the first day of licensure. We will send an application upon receiving a CERTIFIED RECORD OF LICENSE HISTORY from the appropriate state's Real Estate, showing a current license, Commission along with the name, mailing address, birthday of the applicant, and a non-refundable application fee of 20 dollars for brokers and 12 dollars for salesmen. Certified Records are valid for 90 days and must be valid at the issuance of the Massachusetts license.

Oklahoma

Salesmen and Brokers that have been licensed for *two years* have complete reciprocity. We will send an application upon receiving a CERTIFIED RECORD OF LICENSE HISTORY from the Oklahoma Real Estate Commission, showing a current license, along with the name, mailing address, birthday of the applicant, and a non-refundable application fee of 20 dollars for brokers and 12 dollars for salesmen. Certified Records are valid for 90 days and must be valid at the issuance of the Massachusetts license.

Salesmen and Brokers less than two years - See "All Other States" below.

New York

Brokers only providing they have been licensed for *two years* have complete reciprocity. We will send an application upon receiving a CERTIFIED RECORD OF LICENSE HISTORY from the New York Real Estate Commission , showing a current license, along with the name, mailing address, birthday of the applicant, and a non-refundable application fee of 20 dollars. Certified Records are valid for 90 days and must be valid at the issuance of the Massachusetts license.

Brokers who have been licensed for Less than two years and Salesmen who have been licensed for any length of time - See "All Other States" below.

New Hampshire

Salesmen and Brokers may apply for a waiver that will allow the applicant to take only the State portion of the Massachusetts without the pre-license education. Waivers will be sent upon receipt of a CERTIFIED RECORD OF LICENSE HISTORY from the Real Estate Commission in New Hampshire, showing a current license, along with a written request for a waiver. Waivers are valid for two years. Certified Records are valid for 90 days and must be valid at the issuance of the waiver.

Maine

Brokers who have been licensed for three years may take the *State* portion of the Massachusetts examination. You must first submit to the Board a CERTIFIED RECORD OF LICENSE HISTORY from the Maine Real Estate Commission , showing a current license, along with a written request for an educational waiver. The waiver allows you to take only the state portion of the examination. Waivers are valid for two years . Certified Records are valid for 90 days and must be valid at the issuance of the waiver.

Brokers not licensed three years or salespeople; See "All Other States" below.

Vermont

No waivers or reciprocity.

All Other States

From the first day of licensure in the other state we will waive all educational and apprenticeship requirements and allow the candidate to take the entire Massachusetts examination at their level of licensure in the other state. The license in the other state must be current at the time the waiver is issued. A Candidate handbook that includes an education waiver will be sent upon receipt of a CERTIFIED RECORD OF LICENSE HISTORY from the appropriate state and a written request for an educational waiver. Waivers are valid for two years . Certified Records are valid for 90 days and must be valid at the issuance of the waiver.

LICENSE ISSUE DATES ARE THE FIRST AND FIFTEENTH OF EACH MONTH PROVIDED THE COMPLETED APPLICATION AND REQUISITE DOCUMENTS ARE RECEIVED PRIOR TO THAT DATE.

CHCKLST\RECINFO

LAPSED LICENSE POLICY

RELEVANT LICENSING LAW DOES PROVIDE A GRACE PERIOD FOR THE LATE RENEWAL OF A LICENSE. THE BOARD HAS CONSISTENTLY PERMITTED RENEWALS FOR UP TO TWO YEARS BEYOND EXPIRATION PROVIDED THE FOLLOWING PROCEDURES ARE FOLLOWED. BE ADVISED, HOWEVER, THAT THE PRACTICE OF REAL ESTATE WHILE ONE'S LICENSE IS EXPIRED IS NOT PERMITTED.

☞ A LICENSE THAT HAS BEEN EXPIRED FOR UP TO ONE YEAR AND NINE MONTHS MAY BE RENEWED BY SUBMITTING PAYMENT OF THE RENEWAL FEE AND A LATE FEE OF $25.00 TOGETHER WITH THE ORIGINAL RENEWAL FORM. IF YOU NO LONGER HAVE THE ORIGINAL RENEWAL FORM CONTACT THE BOARD FOR A DUPLICATE DO NOT ATTEMPT TO SUBMIT PAYMENT WITHOUT A FORM.

☞ A LICENSE THAT HAS BEEN EXPIRED FOR MORE THAN ONE YEAR AND NINE MONTHS BUT LESS THAN TWO YEARS WILL REQUIRE THE PAST DUE RENEWAL FEE AND LATE FEE BE PAID ALONG WITH THE PAYMENT FOR THE NEXT (CURRENT) RENEWAL CYCLE. YOU WILL FIRST NEED TO CONTACT THE BOARD FOR A NEW RENEWAL FORM (THE FORM ORIGINALLY SENT TO YOU FOR ONE CYCLE WILL NOT SUFFICE) THIS MUST BE **RECEIVED** NO LATER THAN TWO YEARS AND FIVE DAYS BEYOND EXPIRATION. IN THE CASE OF A BROKER THE BOND MUST BE CURRENT AND ON FILE WITH THE BOARD OR RENEWAL WILL NOT BE ALLOWED.

IF YOUR LICENSE HAS BEEN LAPSED FOR MORE THAN TWO YEARS (OR YOUR ATTEMPTED PAYMENT WAS NOT **RECEIVED** WITHIN TWO YEARS AND FIVE DAYS) YOUR LICENSE CAN NOT BE RENEWED. HOWEVER, INDIVIDUALS (NOT CORPORATIONS OR PARTNERSHIPS) MAY BE ELIGIBLE FOR ONE OF THE FOLLOWING WAIVERS.

☞ BROKERS AND SALESPERSONS LAPSED TWO TO FOUR YEARS ARE ELIGIBLE FOR AN EDUCATIONAL WAIVER THAT WILL ALLOW THE APPLICANT TO TAKE THE EXAMINATION AT THE PREVIOUS LEVEL OF LICENSING. THE TEST MUST BE PASSED AND THE NEW LICENSE PAID FOR PRIOR TO THE FOUR YEAR ANNIVERSARY DATE OF THE EXPIRED LICENSE.

☞ BROKERS LAPSED BETWEEN FOUR AND SIX YEARS ARE ELIGIBLE TO RETAKE THE BROKER COURSE AND BROKER EXAMINATION. AFTER THE APPLICANT COMPLETES THE BROKER COURSE WORK AT AN APPROVED SCHOOL THE EDUCATION CERTIFICATE ISSUED BY THE SCHOOL MUST BE SUBMITTED TO THE BOARD FOR ENDORSEMENT PRIOR TO MAKING A RESERVATION FOR THE EXAMINATION. THE COURSE MUST BE COMPLETED, THE TEST MUST BE PASSED AND THE NEW LICENSE MUST BE PAID FOR PRIOR TO THE SIX YEAR ANNIVERSARY DATE OF THE EXPIRED LICENSE.

☞ SALESPEOPLE LAPSED MORE THAN FOUR YEARS MUST BEGIN ANEW WITH THE SALES COURSE. THE EXPERIENCE UNDER THE PREVIOUS LICENSE CAN NOT BE USED TO SATISFY THE AFFILIATION PREREQUISITE TO QUALIFY FOR THE BROKER LICENSURE.

☞ BROKERS LAPSED MORE THAN SIX YEARS MUST BEGIN ANEW WITH THE SALESPERSON COURSE, EXAMINATION AND LICENSURE.

PLEASE BE ADVISED: IF YOU ATTEMPT PAYMENT BY PERSONAL CHECK AND THE BANK DOES NOT HONOR THE CHECK FOR ANY REASON THEN NO PAYMENT HAS BEEN MADE. THIS MAY BRING YOU OUTSIDE OF ANY GRACE PERIOD OR BOARD POLICY FOR RE-LICENSURE AS NOTED ABOVE. IT IS YOUR OBLIGATION TO ENSURE THAT A PERSONAL CHECK (IF USED) IS HONORED BY YOUR BANK. OTHER ACCEPTABLE FORMS OF PAYMENT ARE; MONEY ORDER; AND BANK OR CASHIER'S CHECK.

TO REQUEST A WAIVER SEND A WRITTEN REQUEST TO:

MASSACHUSETTS BOARD OF REAL ESTATE
100 CAMBRIDGE STREET - ROOM 1313
BOSTON, MA 02202

☞ **CORPORATIONS, LIMITED PARTNERSHIPS AND GENERAL PARTNERSHIPS** MUST RENEW WITHIN TWO YEARS OF EXPIRATION. IF RENEWAL IS NOT MADE WITHIN THE TWO YEARS MUST LICENSE THE CORPORATION ANEW.

CHCKLST\LAPSPOL

Massachusetts License Law   12-41

IN ORDER TO MAKE THE REQUESTED CHANGES YOU MUST PROVIDE THE BOARD WITH THE FOLLOWING DOCUMENTATION

NAME CHANGE

GENERAL PARTNERSHIP

YOU MUST SUBMIT A NOTARIZED COPY OF THE PARTNERSHIP AGREEMENT AND INCLUDE THE ADDENDUM THAT CHANGES THE NAME.

LIMITED PARTNERSHIP

YOU MUST SUBMIT A CERTIFICATION FROM THE MASSACHUSETTS SECRETARY OF STATE SHOWING THE NEW NAME

CORPORATION

YOU MUST SUBMIT A CERTIFICATION FROM THE MASSACHUSETTS SECRETARY OF STATE SHOWING THE NEW NAME

A REPLACEMENT WALL CERTIFICATE IS EIGHTEEN DOLLARS, CHECK OR MONEY ORDER, PAYABLE TO THE "COMM OF MA".

THE ABOVE CHANGES REQUIRE A NEW WALL CERTIFICATE, THE FEE IS EIGHTEEN DOLLARS. PAY BY CHECK OR MONEY ORDER MADE PAYABLE TO THE "COMM OF MA". IF YOU OPERATE UNDER A "D/B/A" YOU MUST SEND THE BOARD A CERTIFIED COPY OF THE D/B/A CERTIFICATE.

SOLE PROPRIETORSHIP

YOU MUST SUBMIT A CERTIFIED COPY OF THE D/B/A (DOING BUSINESS AS) CERTIFICATE ISSUED BY THE LOCAL CITY OR TOWN HALL. SOLE PROPRIETORSHIPS DO NOT RECEIVE A WALL CERTIFICATE.

CHANGE OF CORPORATE OFFICERS OR PARTNERS

CORPORATION: THE CHANGES IN CORPORATE OFFICERS MUST BE FILED WITH THE MASSACHUSETTS SECRETARY OF STATE. ONCE THE CHANGE HAS BEEN MADE YOU MUST SUBMIT TO THIS BOARD A CERTIFICATE OF CHANGE OF DIRECTORS OR OFFICERS, ORIGINAL OR CERTIFIED COPY.

LIMITED PARTNERSHIP: A CHANGE IN PARTNERS OF A LIMITED PARTNERSHIP MUST BE FILED WITH THE MASSACHUSETTS SECRETARY OF STATE. CERTIFICATION OF THE CHANGE OF PARTNERS BY THE SECRETARY OF STATE MUST BE SUBMITTED TO THIS BOARD.

GENERAL PARTNERSHIP: A CHANGE IN PARTNERS OF A GENERAL PARTNERSHIP REQUIRES A NEW NOTARIZED PARTNERSHIP AGREEMENT BE FILED WITH THIS BOARD.

DESIGNATING A NEW BROKER OF RECORD

CORPORATION: IF THE NEW BROKER OF RECORD IS ALREADY AN OFFICER OF THE CORPORATION YOU MUST SUBMIT A NOTARIZED COPY OF THE MINUTES OF THE MEETING THAT DESIGNATED THE NEW BROKER. IF THE NEW BROKER OF RECORD IS A NEW CORPORATE OFFICER THE MINUTES MUST ACCOMPANY A CHANGE IN OFFICERS (ABOVE).

LIMITED PARTNERSHIP: IF THE NEW BROKER OF RECORD IS ALREADY A PARTNER YOU NEED ONLY NOTIFY THE BOARD IN WRITING. OTHERWISE THE NOTICE MUST ACCOMPANY THE NEW PARTNER DOCUMENTATION (ABOVE).

GENERAL PARTNERSHIP: IF THE NEW BROKER OF RECORD IS ALREADY A PARTNER YOU NEED ONLY NOTIFY THE BOARD IN WRITING. OTHERWISE THE NOTICE MUST ACCOMPANY THE NEW PARTNERSHIP AGREEMENT (ABOVE).

DISSOLUTION AND/OR DEATH OR SEVERANCE OF BROKER

GENERAL AND LIMITED PARTNERSHIPS

- IF THE PARTNERSHIP DISSOLVES LICENSE ISSUED TO THE PARTNERSHIP IS NULL AND VOID AND THE BROKER OF RECORD MUST NOTIFY THE BOARD IN WRITING.

- IF THERE IS MORE THAN ONE REMAINING PARTNER BUT NONE ARE LICENSED REAL ESTATE BROKERS THEN THE PARTNERSHIP LICENSE IS NULL AND VOID AND THE PARTNERSHIP CAN NO LONGER PRACTICE REAL

ESTATE. HOWEVER, THE PARTNERSHIP MAY APPLY FOR A ONE YEAR NON-RENEWABLE TEMPORARY BROKER LICENSE SO THAT BUSINESS CAN BE CONCLUDED.

- IF THERE IS ONE REMAINING PARTNER WHO IS LICENSED AS A REAL ESTATE BROKER HE MUST ACT AS A SOLE PROPRIETORSHIP UNDER HIS INDIVIDUAL LICENSE.(SEE SOLE PROPRIETORSHIP)

- IF THERE IS ONE REMAINING PARTNER WHO IS NOT A LICENSED REAL ESTATE BROKER HE CANNOT ACT AS A BROKER EITHER INDIVIDUALLY OR UNDER THE VOIDED PARTNERSHIP LICENSE. HOWEVER, HE MAY APPLY FOR A ONE YEAR NON-RENEWABLE TEMPORARY BROKER LICENSE TO BE ISSUED TO THE PARTNERSHIP SO THAT BUSINESS MAY BE CONCLUDED*.

CORPORATIONS

- IF THE CORPORATION CEASES YOU MUST SEND A LETTER OF DISSOLUTION ISSUED BY THE SECRETARY OF STATE AT 617-727-2850

- IF THE ONLY CORPORATE OFFICER WHO IS A LICENSED MASSACHUSETTS BROKER LEAVES THE CORPORATION THEN THE CORPORATE BROKER LICENSE IS NULL AND VOID AND THE CORPORATION OR IT'S OFFICERS CANNOT PRACTICE REAL ESTATE. HOWEVER THE CORPORATION MAY APPLY FOR A ONE YEAR TEMPORARY NON-RENEWABLE BROKER LICENSE (ABOVE) SO THAT THE CORPORATION CAN CONDUCT BUSINESS WHILE A NEW BROKER OFFICER IS PROCURED. IN NO EVENT MAY THE CORPORATION CONTINUE TO PRACTICE REAL ESTATE BEYOND THE TERM OF THE TEMPORARY LICENSE*.

SOLE PROPRIETORSHIP

- IF YOU ARE THE SOLE OWNER OF YOUR BUSINESS AND YOU ARE A LICENSED REAL ESTATE BROKER YOU MAY OPERATE AS A SOLE PROPRIETOR

- IF YOU DO NOT OPERATE YOUR BUSINESS UNDER YOUR EXACT NAME YOU MUST FURNISH THIS BOARD WITH A CERTIFIED COPY OF THE D/B/A ISSUED BY THE CITY OR TOWN WHERE THE BUSINESS IS LOCATED.

CHANGING FROM A GENERAL PARTNERSHIP TO A SOLE PROPRIETORSHIP (INDIVIDUALLY OWNED BUSINESS)

THE BROKER PARTNER WHO IS NOW A SOLE OWNER MUST SEND A LETTER DISSOLVING THE PARTNERSHIP.

CHANGING FROM A LIMITED PARTNERSHIP OR CORPORATION TO A SOLE PROPRIETORSHIP (INDIVIDUALLY OWNED BUSINESS THAT IS NOT INCORPORATED)

THE BROKER OF RECORD MUST SEND A LETTER INDICATING THE CORPORATION IS NO LONGER OPERATING AND A LETTER OF DISSOLUTION ISSUED BY THE SECRETARY OF STATE MUST ACCOMPANY IT.

NEW WALL CERTIFICATE

A REPLACEMENT WALL CERTIFICATE IS EIGHTEEN DOLLARS, CHECK OR MONEY ORDER, PAYABLE TO THE "COMM OF MA".

WALL CERTIFICATES ARE NOT ISSUED TO SOLE PROPRIETORSHIPS.

BUSINESS NAME

IF A CORPORATION OR PARTNERSHIP OR INDIVIDUAL BROKER WISHES TO ACT UNDER A NAME DIFFERENT FROM HIS/HER OWN EXACT NAME OR THAT OF THE LICENSED CORPORATION OR PARTNERSHIP A CERTIFIED COPY OF THE D/B/A (DOING BUSINESS AS) CERTIFICATE MUST BE SUBMITTED TO THIS BOARD.

SEND DOCUMENTATION TO: MASSACHUSETTS BOARD OF REGISTRATION OF REAL ESTATE BROKERS AND SALESMEN, 100 CAMBRIDGE STREET, ROOM 1313, BOSTON, MASSACHUSETTS 02202, PHONE: (617) 727-2373

---

*ONE YEAR TEMPORARY LICENSES ARE ISSUED TO THE BUSINESS ENTITY NOT AN INDIVIDUAL. THE TEMPORARY LICENSES ARE NOT RENEWABLE. THE TERM OF THE TEMPORARY LICENSE IS CALCULATED FROM THE DATE OF SEVERANCE OF THE BROKER PARTNER OR BROKER OFFICER OR DATE OF DISSOLUTION OF THE PARTNERSHIP. IN THE CASE OF THE DISSOLUTION OF A CORPORATION NO TEMPORARY LICENSE WILL BE ISSUED.)
(APPLICAT\CORPREQ.DOC)

13 Review of Basics

Before we go into some of the detailed use of mathematics in real estate applications, it is a good idea to review the basic concepts of fractions, decimals, and percentages. These basics form the foundations for all of the math work that we will cover and an understanding is a must.

Note: Answers to all problems can be found in the Answer Key at the end of each chapter.

Fractions

A fraction is a mathematical expression that indicates a part of a whole.

TERMS:

Numerator and **Denominator**:

$$\frac{2}{3} = \frac{\text{the numerator}}{\text{the denominator}}$$

Proper fraction (less than one):

$$\frac{1}{4}$$

Improper fraction (more than one):

$$\frac{3}{2}$$

Mixed number (whole number plus a fraction):

$$1\frac{1}{2}$$

Addition of Fractions

1) Fractions must have the same or common denominator to be added.
2) Fractions should be converted to the lowest common denominator (LCD).
3) Numerators should be added and the denominator of the answer should be the same as the lowest common denominator.
4) Numbers should be converted to improper fractions before adding.
5) Answers should be converted from improper fractions to mixed numbers.
6) Reduce if necessary.

EXAMPLE:

$$\frac{1}{2} + \frac{1}{4}$$

Lowest common denominator = 4

$$\frac{1}{2} + \frac{1}{4} = \frac{2+1}{4} = \frac{3}{4}$$

PROBLEMS:

1) $\frac{1}{3} + \frac{3}{4} =$ 2) $\frac{2}{5} + \frac{3}{8} =$

3) $2\frac{1}{3} + \frac{1}{6} =$ 4) $3\frac{1}{4} + \frac{1}{8} =$

5) $1\frac{1}{3} + 2\frac{1}{4} =$

Subtraction of Fractions

The same basic rules for the addition of fractions apply in the subtraction of fractions.

1) Fractions must have a common denominator to be subtracted.
2) Fractions should be converted to the lowest common denominator.
3) The numerators should be subtracted and the denominator of the answer should be the same as the lowest common denominator.
4) Mixed numbers should be converted to improper fractions before subtracting.
5) Answer should be converted from an improper fraction to a mixed number.
6) Reduced answer if necessary.

EXAMPLE:

$$1\frac{2}{5} - \frac{3}{10} = \frac{7}{5} - \frac{3}{10} = \frac{14}{10} - \frac{3}{10} = \frac{11}{10} = 1\frac{1}{10}$$

PROBLEMS:

6) $\frac{2}{3} - \frac{1}{6} =$

7) $1\frac{1}{4} - \frac{3}{8} =$

8) $3\frac{1}{4} - 2\frac{3}{5} =$

9) $2\frac{1}{3}$

$-\frac{5}{4}$

10) $3\frac{1}{4} - 1\frac{1}{8} =$

Multiplication of Fractions

There are three ways to express multiplication of fractions:

$$\frac{1}{2} \times \frac{1}{3} = \frac{1}{2} \cdot \frac{1}{3} = \frac{1}{2}\left(\frac{1}{3}\right)$$

1) Change mixed numbers to improper fractions.
2) No need to convert to the lowest common denominator.
3) Multiply the numerator by the numerator.
4) Multiply the denominator by the denominator.
5) Reduce where possible.
6) Convert answer from an improper fraction to a mixed number.

EXAMPLE:

$$1\frac{1}{2} \times 2\frac{1}{4} = \frac{3}{2} \times \frac{9}{4} = \frac{3 \times 9}{2 \times 4} = \frac{27}{8} = 3\frac{3}{8}$$

PROBLEMS:

11) $\frac{1}{3} \times \frac{2}{5} =$ 12) $2\frac{1}{4} \times \frac{1}{3} =$

13) $3\frac{1}{5} \times \frac{3}{2} =$ 14) $1\frac{3}{4} \times 2\frac{1}{8} =$

15) $\frac{1}{4}\left(2\frac{1}{5}\right) =$

Division of Fractions

TERMS: Divisor into dividend equals quotient.

$$\text{divisor} \overline{)\,\text{dividend}}^{\text{quotient}} \qquad\qquad 4\overline{)\,12}^{\,3}$$

1) Change mixed numbers to improper fractions.
2) No need to convert to the lowest common denominator.
3) Invert the divisor.
4) Proceed as in multiplication.

EXAMPLE:

$$\frac{1}{2} \div \frac{1}{3} = \frac{1}{2} \times \frac{3}{1} = \frac{1 \times 3}{2 \times 1} = \frac{3}{2} = 1\frac{1}{2}$$

PROBLEMS:

16) $\frac{2}{3} \div \frac{4}{5} =$ 17) $1\frac{1}{4} \div \frac{1}{2} =$

18) $2\dfrac{1}{2} \div 1\dfrac{1}{5} =$

19) $1\dfrac{1}{4} \div 2\dfrac{1}{7} =$

20) $\dfrac{1\dfrac{1}{4}}{2\dfrac{1}{3}} =$

Decimals

A decimal is an expression that divides a whole into subdivisions of 10.

EXAMPLE:

$$\dfrac{1}{10} = .1 \qquad \dfrac{1}{10} \text{ of } \dfrac{1}{10} \text{ or } \dfrac{1}{100} = .01$$

Addition of Decimals

Line up the decimal points and add numbers with the decimal point in the answer directly below the decimal points in the problem.

EXAMPLE:

$1.38 + .2 + 12.6 =$

$$\begin{array}{r} 1.38 \\ .20 \\ +12.60 \\ \hline 14.18 \end{array}$$

Subtraction of Decimals

Line up the decimal points and subtract numbers with the decimal point in the answer directly below the decimal points in the problem.

EXAMPLE:

$1.24 - .1 =$

$$\begin{array}{r} 1.24 \\ - .10 \\ \hline 1.14 \end{array}$$

PROBLEMS:

21)   .24
    + .03
    _____

22)   1.14
    + 3.2
    _____

23)   16.08
    - 11.2
    _____

24)   7.06
      1.3
    + .002
    _____

25)   12.16
    - .304
    _____

26)   23.04 + .134 + 2.63 + .2 =

Multiplication of Decimals

Don't line up the decimal points. The number of decimal places in the answer must equal the sum of the decimal places in the products.

EXAMPLE:

$$\begin{array}{r} .23 \\ \times .4 \\ \hline .092 \end{array}$$

PROBLEMS:

27)   1.14
    × .3
    _____

28)   2.4
    × .12
    _____

29)   321.7
    × .03
    _____

30)   16.14
    × .2
    _____

31) 12.4 × .02 =

32) 1.6 (.04) =

33) 2.3 × .04 × 12.2 =

Division of Decimals

Before division can begin, the decimal point must be eliminated from the divisor. Move the decimal point to the right in the divisor as necessary. Move the decimal point to the right in the dividend the same number of spaces. Proceed with the division. A whole number (e.g., 23) has an assumed decimal point after it (e.g., 23.). The decimal point in the quotient is right above the decimal point in the dividend.

EXAMPLE:

$$.04 \overline{) 2.488} \quad = \quad .04 \overline{) 2.48.8} \quad \text{(62.2)}$$

PROBLEMS:

34) $.2 \overline{) .48}$ 35) $3.2 \overline{) 64}$ 36) $2. \overline{) 1.6}$

37) $.02 \overline{) 8}$ 38) $0.3 \overline{) .15}$

Percent

Percentage is a method of expressing a part of a whole where the whole is considered to be 100. If we considered a dozen donuts as the whole, or 100 percent, and you ate 6 of them, you would have eaten 6 of the 12, or 50 percent of the 100 percent.

When dealing with percents in real estate applications, you must be able to convert the percent to either a fraction of a decimal to proceed with the calculation. Therefore, we will look at how to convert from percents to fractions or decimals and back again.

Percent to Decimal

To convert a percent to a decimal, drop the percent sign and move the decimal two places to the left.

EXAMPLE:

$$25\% = .25_{\sim}\% = .25$$

PROBLEMS:

39) 50% =   40) 5% =

41) 125% =   42) 37.5% =

43) 15% =

Decimal to Percent

To convert a decimal to a percent, move the decimal point two places to the right and add the percent sign.

EXAMPLE:

$$.25 = .25_{\sim}. + \% = 25\%$$

PROBLEMS:

44) 50 =   45) .01 =

46) .625 =   47) 15.0 =

48) .8 =

Percent to Fraction

To convert a percent to a fraction, put the number over 100, drop the percent sign, and reduce the fraction.

EXAMPLE:

$$20\% = \frac{20}{100} = \frac{1}{5}$$

PROBLEMS:

49) 5% =   50) 40% =

51) 125% =   52) 12.5% =

53) $37\frac{1}{2}\%$ =

Fraction to Percent

To convert a fraction to a percent, multiply by 100 and add the percent sign.
If the fraction is a mixed number, convert to an improper fraction first.

EXAMPLE:

$$\frac{1}{5} = \frac{1}{5} \times \frac{100}{1} = \frac{100}{5} = 20 + \% = 20\%$$

PROBLEMS:

54) $\dfrac{1}{2} =$ 55) $\dfrac{1}{4} =$

56) $\dfrac{6}{5} =$ 57) $1\dfrac{3}{4} =$

58) $\dfrac{2}{3} =$

Decimal to Fraction

To convert a decimal to a fraction, remove the decimal point and put the number over 1 with as many zeros as there are decimal places.

EXAMPLE:

$$.25 = \frac{25}{100} = \frac{1}{4}$$

PROBLEMS:

59) $.23 =$ 60) $1.4 =$

61) $.7 =$ 62) $.150 =$

63) $24.5 =$

Fraction to Decimal

To convert a fraction to a decimal, divide the denominator into the numerator. If the number is a mixed number, convert it to an improper fraction first.

EXAMPLE:

$$1\frac{1}{4} = \frac{5}{4} = 4\overline{)\,5}^{1.25} = 1.25$$

PROBLEMS:

64) $\dfrac{1}{2}$ =

65) $\dfrac{3}{4}$ =

66) $1\dfrac{1}{5}$ =

67) $4\dfrac{1}{2}$ =

68) $2\dfrac{1}{3}$ =

Self-Quiz

You should use a separate piece of paper for the work on all math self-quizzes.

1) $\dfrac{1}{4} + \dfrac{2}{3} =$

2) $1\dfrac{1}{8} - \dfrac{3}{4} = \dfrac{3}{8}$

3) $2\dfrac{1}{3} \times 1\dfrac{1}{4} =$

4) $\dfrac{1}{5}\left(\dfrac{2}{3}\right)$

5) $2\dfrac{1}{4} \div 1\dfrac{1}{2} =$

6) $\dfrac{1\frac{1}{4}}{\frac{1}{8}} =$

7) $1.38 + 7.5 =$

8) $23.5 - .23 =$

9) $2.16 \times .3 =$

10) $25\,(1.6) =$

11) $4\,\overline{)\,2.88}$

12) $\dfrac{.12}{.3} =$

13) Convert 15% to a decimal

14) Convert 3.8 to a percent

15) Convert 110% to a fraction

16) Convert $1\dfrac{1}{4}$ to a percent

17) Convert $\dfrac{1}{3}$ to a percent

18) Convert $\dfrac{1}{8}$ to a decimal

19) Convert $2\dfrac{2}{5}$ to a decimal

20) Convert $\dfrac{1}{20}$ to a decimal

Answer Key

Problems

1) $1\frac{1}{12}$ 2) $\frac{31}{40}$ 3) $2\frac{1}{2}$ 4) $3\frac{3}{8}$ 5) $3\frac{7}{12}$

6) $\frac{1}{2}$ 7) $\frac{7}{8}$ 8) $\frac{13}{20}$ 9) $1\frac{1}{12}$ 10) $2\frac{1}{8}$

11) $\frac{2}{15}$ 12) $\frac{3}{4}$ 13) $4\frac{4}{5}$ 14) $3\frac{23}{32}$ 15) $\frac{11}{20}$

16) $\frac{5}{6}$ 17) $2\frac{1}{2}$ 18) $2\frac{1}{12}$ 19) $\frac{7}{12}$ 20) $\frac{15}{28}$

21) .27 22) 4.34 23) 4.88 24) 8.362 25) 11.856

26) 26.004 27) .342 28) .288 29) 9.651 30) 3.228

31) .248 32) .064 33) 1.1224 34) 2.4 35) 20

36) .8 37) 400 38) .5 39) .50 40) .05

41) 1.25 42) .375 43) .15 44) 5,000% 45) 1%

46) 62.5% 47) 1500% 48) 80% 49) $\frac{1}{20}$ 50) $\frac{2}{5}$

51) $1\frac{1}{4}$ 52) $\frac{1}{8}$ 53) $\frac{3}{8}$ 54) 50% 55) 25%

56) 120% 57) 175% 58) $66\frac{2}{3}\%$ 59) $\frac{23}{100}$ 60) $1\frac{2}{5}$

61) $\frac{7}{10}$ 62) $\frac{3}{20}$ 63) $24\frac{1}{2}$ 64) .5 65) .75

66) 1.2 67) 4.5 68) $2.33\frac{1}{3}$

Self-Quiz

1) $\dfrac{11}{12}$ 2) $\dfrac{3}{8}$ 3) $2\dfrac{11}{12}$ 4) $\dfrac{2}{15}$ 5) $1\dfrac{1}{2}$

6) 10 7) 8.88 8) 23.27 9) .648 10) 40

11) .72 12) .4 13) .15 14) 380% 15) $1\dfrac{1}{10}$

16) 125% 17) $33\dfrac{1}{3}\%$ 18) .125 19) 2.4 20) .05

14 Measurement

The real estate professional will deal with a variety of issues involving measurement of distance, area and volume. Some examples might include:

* How many square feet of land on this lot?
* How deep is this one-acre lot with 200 - foot frontage?
* How many cubic feet of loam should be ordered?
* Do you have any 2,000-square-foot ranches?

In order to be prepared to deal with these concepts, we need to look at some figures involving area and volume calculations.

Area

Area is expressed in **square measure,** that is, square inches, square feet, square yards, etc. In calculation area (or volume) we must multiply like units of measure. Feet must be multiplied by feet and not by inches or yards. If one dimensions is given in feet and the second in yards, one must be converted to the other so that we are dealing with "apples and apples."

If question is, "How many square feet are there?" it is a good idea to convert both distances to feet in the beginning so that the answer will come out in square feet. This will avoid having to convert from square yards to square feet at the end of the problem.

Rectangle

A rectangle is a four sided figure whose angles are all right angles (90°). Area of a rectangle equals length times width.

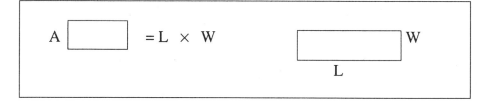

EXAMPLE: How many square feet of land in a lot 100 feet long and 80 feet wide?

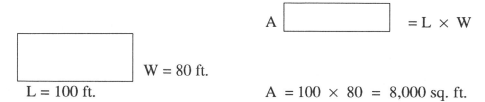

PROBLEMS:

1) What is area of a lot 120 feet long and 85 feet wide?

2) If a lot is 120 feet by 200 feet, what is the cost of the lot if a square foot costs $2.75?

Triangle

A triangle is any three-sided figure.

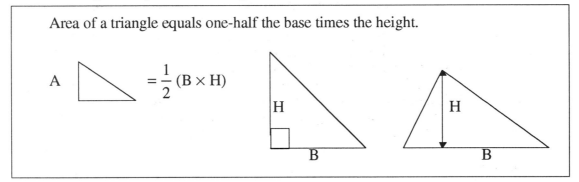

Area of a triangle equals one-half the base times the height.

$$A \quad = \frac{1}{2}(B \times H)$$

If the triangle is a right triangle (one angle equals 90°), the side of the triangle is also the height.

EXAMPLE: How many square feet of land in a triangular lot with two perpendicular sides of 80 feet and 100 feet (perpendicular means a 90° angle)?

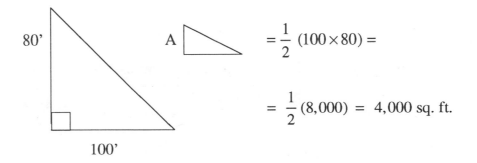

$$A \quad = \frac{1}{2}(100 \times 80) =$$

$$= \frac{1}{2}(8,000) = 4,000 \text{ sq. ft.}$$

EXAMPLE: What is the square footage to be painted on the peak of a house in the following figure?

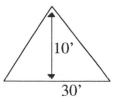

$A \triangle = \frac{1}{2}(30 \times 10) = \frac{1}{2}(300) = 150$ sq. ft.

PROBLEMS: 3)   What is area of a triangular lot where two sides are 150 feet and 200 feet, if the angle between the two sides is 90° ?

4)   What is the area of a triangular lot with a base of 200 feet and a height (or altitude) of 90 feet?

Trapezoid

A trapezoid is a four-sided figure where only two side are parallel.

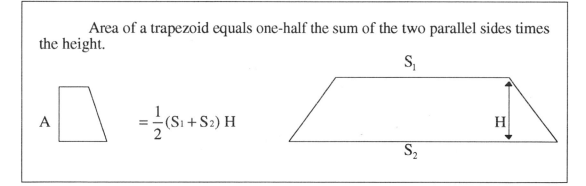

Area of a trapezoid equals one-half the sum of the two parallel sides times the height.

$A = \frac{1}{2}(S_1 + S_2) H$

EXAMPLE: What is the area of the following lot?

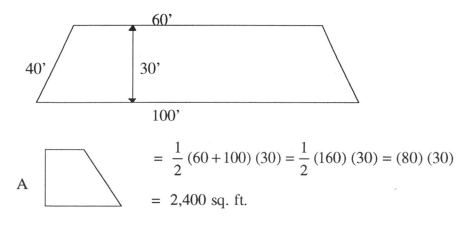

$= \frac{1}{2}(60 + 100)(30) = \frac{1}{2}(160)(30) = (80)(30)$

$= 2,400$ sq. ft.

EXAMPLE: What is the area of the following lot?

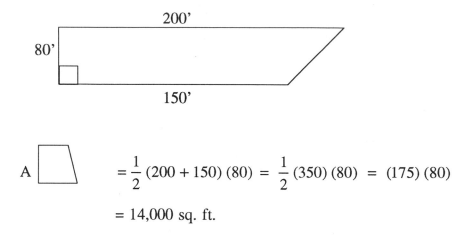

A 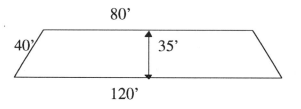 $= \dfrac{1}{2} (200 + 150) (80) = \dfrac{1}{2} (350) (80) = (175) (80)$

$= 14,000$ sq. ft.

PROBLEMS: 5)   What is the area of the following lot?

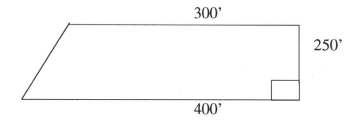

6)   How many acres in the following plot? Round off to the nearest acre. (1 Acre = 43,560 sq. ft. See section dealing with acreage calculations in this chapter.)

Circle

Area of a circle equals π times the radius squared.

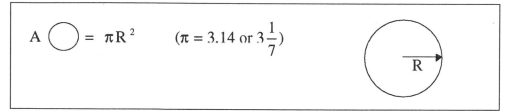

The radius of a circle is the distance from the center to the circumference.

The diameter of a circle is the line that passes through the center from one side of the circle to the other.

The radius is $\frac{1}{2}$ of the diameter.

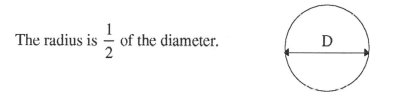

π is the number of times the diameter of any circle will fit around the circumference of the circle (3.14 or $3\frac{1}{7}$: either value of π may be used.)

EXAMPLE: What is the area of a circular lot whose radius is 70 feet?

$$A \bigcirc = \pi R^2 = \left(3\frac{1}{7}\right)\left(70^2\right) = \frac{22}{7} \times 4900 = 15,400 \text{ sq. ft.}$$

PROBLEMS: 7) What is the area of a circular lot whose radius is 28 feet?

8) What is the area of a circular swimming pool with a 40 foot diameter?

Acreage

An **acre** is a measurement that deals with area. The acre contains 43,560 square feet.

To convert square footage into acres, all that is necessary is to divide that subject land area by 43,560 square feet.

EXAMPLE: A lot contains 24,100 square feet. What is the acreage?

$$24,100 \div 43,560 = .55 \text{ (approximately)}$$

EXAMPLE: How many acres are in a lot that contains 96,423 sq. ft.?

$$96,423 \div 43,560 = 2.2 \text{ (approximately)}$$

To convert acres to square feet, multiply the acreage times 43,560 square feet.

EXAMPLE: How many square feet does a lot containing 1.75 acres contain?

$$43,560 \times 1.75 = 76,230 \text{ sq. ft.}$$

EXAMPLE: A lot contains one third of an acre. What is the square footage of the lot?

$$43,560 \times \frac{1}{3} = \frac{43,560}{3} = 14,520 \text{ sq. ft.}$$

NOTE: As with any math problem, the fraction or decimal equivalent may be used. The use of either will be dictated by what is asked for in the question, the type of problem being done, or ease and accuracy of the student.

Volume

In the area problems we have dealt with, we have had two dimensions and expressed the results in square measure (i.e., square inches, square feet, square yards, etc.). Now we will deal with three dimensions in calculating volume. Volume is expressed in cubic measure (e.g., inches times inches times inches equals cubic inches). As in the area problems, all measurements should be in the same unit (feet times feet times feet rather than inches times feet times feet).

Rectangular Volume

The volume of a rectangular figure such as a room is length
times width times height.

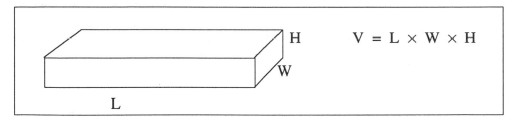

$$V = L \times W \times H$$

EXAMPLE: What is the volume of a room that is 10 feet wide by 15 feet long with an 8-foot ceiling?

$$V = L \times W \times H$$

$$= 15 \times 10 \times 8 = 1200 \text{ cu. ft.}$$

PROBLEMS: 9) How many cubic feet of water will a pool hold that is 15 feet wide, 30 feet long, and 7 feet deep?

10) How many cubic feet of loam are needed to cover a lawn 50 feet by 100 feet if the loam is to be 6 inches deep?

Triangular Volume

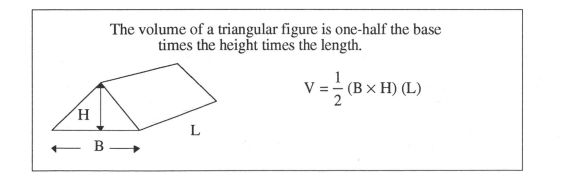

The volume of a triangular figure is one-half the base
times the height times the length.

$$V = \frac{1}{2}(B \times H)(L)$$

EXAMPLE: What is the volume of a tent with a base of 8 feet, a height of 6 feet, and a length of 10 feet?

$$V = \frac{1}{2}(B \times H)(L) = \frac{1}{2}(8 \times 6)(10) = \frac{1}{2}(48)(10)$$

$$= (24)(10) = 240 \text{ cu. ft.}$$

PROBLEMS: 11)   What is the volume in cubic feet of a tent with a base of 3 yards, a height of 9 feet, and a length of 12 feet?

12)   What is the volume of the same tent as that in Problem 11 expressed in cubic yards?

Cylinder

The volume of a cylinder is the area of the circular base (πR^2) times the height:

π times the radius squared times the height.

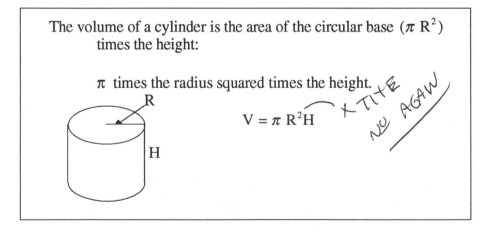

$$V = \pi R^2 H$$

EXAMPLE: What is the volume of a cylinder 6 feet high with a base whose radius is 7 feet?

$$V = \pi R^2 H = \frac{22}{7} \times 49 \times 6 = \frac{22}{1} \times 7 \times 6 = 154 \times 6 = 924 \text{ cu.ft.}$$

PROBLEMS:

13) How many cubic feet of wood in a tree that is 6 feet in diameter and 20 feet high?

14) How many cubic yards of grain can a silo hold that is 30 ft. in diameter at the base and 60 feet high?

Perimeter

The perimeter is the distance around the outside of a figure.

EXAMPLE:

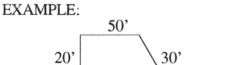

$P = 20 + 50 + 30 + 60 = 160$ ft.

EXAMPLE:

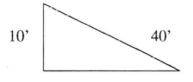

$P = 10 + 40 + 20 = 70$ ft.

EXAMPLE:

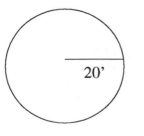

$P \bigcirc = \pi D$

$P = (3.14)(40) = 125.60$ ft.

Note: The perimeter of a circle is also known as the circumference.

Self-Quiz

1) How many square feet of wall-to wall carpet are needed for a room that is 12 feet long and 9 feet wide?
2) How many square yards of sod are needed on the lawn of a house that is 30 ft. by 45 feet, on a lot that is 90 feet by 150 feet?
3) How many square feet in a triangular lot that is 80 feet and 100 feet one two sides with a 90° angle between the two sides.
4) What is the area of the following lot?

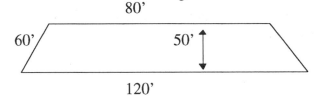

5) What is the area of a circular lot whose diameter is 200 feet? What is the acreage?
6) What is the volume of a room that is 12 feet wide, 18 feet long with a 9 foot ceiling?
7) What is the cost of a driveway that is 18 feet wide and 90 feet long, if the hot top is 6 inches thick and costs $2.10 per cubic foot and the contractor charges $15.00 per square yard of driveway surface to roll the driveway?
8) How many cubic yards of air in an attic that is 21 feet wide if the roof peak is 15 feet high and the house is 15 yards long?
9) What is the cost of a three-year lease on a building 200 feet by 475 feet if the lease cost is $9.00 per square foot per year?
10) What is the cost of a fence around a 100-foot-long and 90-foot-wide lot if the fence costs $16.00 per foot?

Answer Key

Problems

1) 10,200 sq. ft.
2) $66,000
3) 15,000 sq. ft.
4) 9,000 sq. ft.
5) 3,500 sq. ft.
6) 2 acres
7) 2,464 sq. ft. or 2,461.76 sq. ft.
8) 1257 1/7 sq. ft. or 1,256 sq. ft.
9) 3, 150 cu. ft.
10) 2,500 cu. ft.
11) 486 cu. ft.
12) 18 cu. yds.
13) 565.2 cu. ft., or $565\frac{5}{7}$ cu. ft.
14) 1,570 cu. yds. or $1,571\frac{3}{7}$ cu. yds.

Self-Quiz

1) 108 sq. ft.
2) 1,350 sq. yds.
3) 4,000 sq. ft.
4) 5,000 sq. ft.
5) 31,400 sq. ft.
   .72 acres (approx.)
6) 1,944 cu. ft
7) $4,401
8) 262.5 cu. yds.
9) $2,565,000
10) $6,080

15 Formulas

Much of the real estate math that will be encountered will involve math formulas of one type or another. Therefore, we will review some principles that will prepare the student to solve these types of math formulas.

To begin, let us use one fairly easy math example:

EXAMPLE: If a house sold for $210,00 and the real estate commission is 6% of the sell price, what was the amount of the commission?

FORMULA:

$$\text{Sell Price} \times \text{Rate} = \text{Commission}$$
$$\$210,000 \times .06 = ?$$
$$\$210,000 \times .06 = \$12,600$$

To solve this type of problem, we need to know two things before we can proceed to solve for the third. Most people do not have too much difficulty understanding the type of problem shown above, i.e., the sell price and rate are known and we must solve for the commission. The confusion begins to arise when the thing we do not know and must solve for is the sell price or the rate.

EXAMPLE: What did a house sell for if the REALTOR received a $6,600 commission and the commission rate was 6% of the sell price?

EXAMPLE: What was the rate of commission charged if a house sold for $210,000 and the broker received a $12,600 commission?

Instead of memorizing two new formulas,

$$\text{Sell Price} = \frac{\text{Commission}}{\text{Rate}} \quad \text{and} \quad \text{Rate} = \frac{\text{Commission}}{\text{Sell Price}}$$

there is a Formula Aid that can be used to help set up the problem and indicate what math step needs to be taken.

Start with the original formula:
Sell Price $\times$ Rate = Commission

If we show the Aid as:

AID $\quad \dfrac{C}{SP \times R}$

we can be given any two bits of information and tell what to do to get the third.

Let us take each of the three possible situations and see how the Aid would indicate what step to take.

SITUATION 1:   Sell Price = $210,000

Rate = .06   AID $\dfrac{C}{SP \times R}$

Commission = ?

If we cover the term we are solving for (commission), the aid will indicate what step to take with the other two.

AID $\boxed{\dfrac{}{SP \times R}}$ = $210,000 X .06 = $12,600

SITUATION 2:   Sell Price = $210,000

Rate = ?   AID $\dfrac{C}{SP \times R}$

Commission = $12,600

If we cover the term we are solving for (rate), the Aid will indicate what step to take with the other two.

AID $\boxed{\dfrac{C}{SP}}$ $=$ $\dfrac{\$12,600}{\$210,000}$ = .06 = 6%

SITUATION 3:   Sell Price = ?

Rate = .06   AID $\dfrac{C}{SP \times R}$

Commission = $12,600

If we cover the term we are solving for (sell price), the Aid will indicate what step to take with the other two.

AID $\boxed{\dfrac{C}{R}}$ $=$ $\dfrac{\$12,600}{.06}$ = $210,000

This approach can be taken with any formula in solving real estate math problems. The following table shows some of the more common formulas used in solving real estate math problems and the corresponding Aid for each formula.

Table of Formula Aids

Formula	Aid
Length × Width = Area $\qquad$ L × W = A	$\dfrac{A}{L \times W}$
Principal × Rate × Time = Interest $\qquad$ P × R × T = I	$\dfrac{I}{P \times R \times T}$
Base × Rate = Percentage $\qquad$ B × R = P	$\dfrac{P}{B \times R}$
*Sell Price × Rate = Commission $\qquad$ SP × R = C	$\dfrac{C}{SP \times R}$
*Amount × Rate = Interest $\qquad$ A × R = I	$\dfrac{I}{A \times R}$
*Appraised Value × Assessment Rate $\quad$ AppV × AssR = AssV = Assessed Value	$\dfrac{AssV}{AppV \times AssR}$
*Assessed Value × Tax Rate $\qquad$ AssV × TR = Tax = Annual Tax	$\dfrac{Tax}{AssV \times TR}$
*Cost × Depreciation Rate = Depreciation $\qquad$ C × R = D	$\dfrac{D}{C \times R}$
*Investment × Rate of Profit = Profit $\qquad$ I × R = P	$\dfrac{P}{I \times R}$
*Investment × Rate of Loss = Loss $\qquad$ I × R = L	$\dfrac{L}{I \times R}$
*Investment × Rate of Return = Net Income $\quad$ I × R = NI	$\dfrac{NI}{I \times R}$
*Value × Capitalization Rate = Net Income $\quad$ V × CR = NI	$\dfrac{NI}{V \times CR}$

Note: These formulas are variations of the basic formula: B × R = P.

Self-Quiz

PROBLEMS:

1) What is the area of a lot that is 100 feet long and 150 feet wide?

2) What is the width of a 10,000-square-foot lot that is 200 feet long?

3) If a parcel is 80 feet wide and has 9,600 square feet, what is the frontage?

Answer Key

1) 15,000 sq. ft.
2) 50 ft.
3) 120 ft.

16 Interest

As a part of providing mortgage guidance and counseling, the real estate broker and salesperson should be able to perform math calculations relating to interest.

The basic formula that will be used in solving interest problems is as follows:

Principal × Rate × Time = Interest

$$P \times R \times T = I$$

The following terms should be understood:

Principal - the amount borrowed or loaned (e.g., $1,000 loan)
Rate - the percent charged for use of the money (e.g., 8% or .08)
Time - duration (in years) of the loan (e.g., 1 year)
Interest - the charge for the use of the principal (e.g., $P \times R \times T$)

EXAMPLE:

$$P \times R \times T = I$$

$$\$1,000 \times .08 \times 1 = \$80.00$$

In dealing with interest math, let us first work with loans of one-year duration and then move on to the more complicated calculation for loans that are not one even year.

One-Year Loans

As we noted in the earlier chapter on formulas, the interest formula $P \times R \times T = I$ converts to the Formula Aid:

AID

$$\frac{I}{P \times R \times T}$$

This AID will be used for all interest calculations. In approaching any of the following problems, the student should:

1) List the parts to the formula - P,R,T, and I
2) Fill in the information available
3) Set up the formula using the AID
4) Solve the problem

Solve for Interest

EXAMPLE: What is the interest due on $5,000 borrowed at 8% for 1 year:

Principal = $5,000

Rate = .08

Time = 1

Interest = ?

AID $\boxed{\dfrac{I}{P \times R \times T}}$

The AID indicates:

$$P \times R \times T = 5,000 \times .08 \times 1 = \$400 \text{ in Interest}$$

PROBLEM: 1)   What interest will be due on $10,000 loan at 9% for 1 year?

Solve for Rate

EXAMPLE: What was the interest rate charged if a $12,000 loan yielded $720 in interest after one year?

Principal = $12,000

Rate = ?

Time = 1

Interest = $720

AID $\boxed{\dfrac{I}{P \times R \times T}}$

The AID indicates:

$$\frac{I}{P \times T} = \frac{720}{12,000 \times 1} = \frac{72}{12,000} = \frac{9}{150} = \frac{3}{50} = 50\overline{)3.00}^{.06} = 6\% \text{ Rate}$$

PROBLEM: 2) At the end of one year, a $5,000 bank account had earned $250. What rate of interest was the bank paying?

Solve for Principal

EXAMPLE: How much should be invested at 11% interest to earn $385 after 1 year?

Principal = ?

Rate = .11

Time = 1

Interest = $385

AID $\dfrac{I}{P \times R \times T}$ — DIVIDED BY LWE

The AID indicates:

$$\dfrac{I}{R \times T} = \dfrac{385}{.11 \times 1} = \dfrac{385}{.11} = .11\overline{)385.00} = \$3,500 \text{ Principal}$$

$$\begin{array}{r} 3500. \\ .11\overline{)385.00} \\ \underline{33} \\ 55 \\ \underline{55} \end{array}$$

PROBLEM: 3) What was the amount borrowed at 8% interest if $560 is due in interest after 1 year?

Solve For Rate

EXAMPLE: What interest rate was charged if an $18,000 loan returned $19,440 principal and interest after 1 year?

Principal = $18,000

Rate = ?

Time = 1

Interest = $1,440

AID $\dfrac{I}{P \times R \times T}$

The AID indicates:

$$\frac{I}{P \times T} = \frac{1,440}{18,000 \times 1} = \frac{1,440}{18,000} = \frac{36}{450} = \frac{18}{225} = 225\overline{)18.00}^{.08} = 8\% \text{ Rate}$$

PROBLEM: 4) If $4,000 put in the bank for 1 year grew to $4,280, what interest rate was paid?

Non-One-Year Loans

Now that we have dealt with interest problems where time was one year ($T = 1$), let us look at situations where time is either less than a year or more than a year and therefore becomes a factor in solving the problem. (Time must be shown as a part of a year - 6 months = 1/2 or .5).

Solve For Interest

EXAMPLE: What is the interest on $30,000 borrowed at 9% interest for 2 years?

Principal = $30,000

Rate = .09   AID $\boxed{\dfrac{I}{P \times R \times T}}$

Time = 2

Interest = ?

The AID indicates:

$$P \times R \times T = 30,000 \times .09 \times 2 = 2,700 \times 2 = \$5,400 \text{ Interest}$$

PROBLEM: 5) What interest will $2,000 earn if put in the bank for 3 years at 6% interest?

Solve For Rate

EXAMPLE: At what rate does $20,000 have to be in the bank to earn $800 in 6 months?

Principal = $20,000

Rate = ?

AID $\boxed{\dfrac{I}{P \times R \times T}}$

Time = .5
   (Show time as part of a year)
Interest = $800

The AID indicates:

$$\frac{I}{P \times T} = \frac{800}{20,000 \times .5} = \frac{800}{10,000} = .08 \text{ or } 8\% \text{ Rate}$$

PROBLEM: 6) A $4,000 loan cost $70 in interest after 3 months.
             What was the interest rate?

Solve For Principal

EXAMPLE: How much was borrowed if the interest at 8% came to $384 in 18 months?

Principal = ?

Rate = .08

AID $\boxed{\dfrac{I}{P \times R \times T}}$

Time = 1.5

Interest = $384

The AID indicates:

$$\frac{I}{R \times T} = \frac{384}{.08 \times 1.5} = \frac{384}{.12} = .12\overline{)384.00} = \$3,200 \text{ Principal}$$

$$
\begin{array}{r}
3200 \\
.12\overline{)384.00} \\
\underline{36} \\
24 \\
\underline{24} \\
\end{array}
$$

PROBLEM   7)   How much was put in the bank if after 2 months at $8\frac{1}{2}\%$ the interest amounted to $68?

Daily Interest Problems

Often money is not borrowed or loaned in neat time packages of years or even months. So we must deal with interest calculations for so many days. (For interest calculations, use 360 days in a year and 30 days in a month.)

The general approach for this type of problem is:
1)   Calculate the yearly interest by the methods used previously.
2)   Divide by 12 to get monthly interest.
3)   Divide by 30 to get daily interest.

Now we can multiply these amounts by the number of years, months, and days the money was borrowed for and add them together to get the total interest.

EXAMPLE: What is the interest on $2,000 borrowed at 8% for 5 days?

AID
$$\boxed{\frac{I}{P \times R \times T}}$$

Annual Interest = $2,000 X .08   = $160 / year
Monthly Interest = 160 ÷ 12   = $13.333 / mo.
Daily Interest = 13.33 ÷ 30   = $.444 / day
Interest for 5 days = $.444 X 5   = $2.22

Note: Math should be carried to three decimal places until the answer is reached, and then rounded off to two places.

PROBLEM: 8) What interest is due on $3,500 borrowed for 14 days at 9%?

EXAMPLE: What is the interest on $3,000 at 7% for 1 year, 8 months and 10 days?

AID $$\frac{I}{P \times R \times T}$$

Annual Interest =	$3,000 X .07	= 210 X 1	= $210.00
Monthly Interest =	210 ÷ 12	= 17.50 X 8	= $140.00
Daily Interest =	17.50 ÷ 30	= .583 X 10	= $5.83
Total Interest =			$355.83

PROBLEM   9)   What is the interest charge if $4,000 borrowed at 11% for 2 years, 3 months and 21 days?

EXAMPLE: What is the interest on $4,000 borrowed at 6% from February 15, 1995 to June 22, 1998?

Elapsed Time of Loan =	**Year**	**Month**	**Day**
	1998	6	22
-	1995	2	15
	3	4	7

= 3 years, 4 months, 7 days

AID $$\frac{I}{P \times R \times T}$$

Annual Interest =	$4,000 X .06	= $240 X 3	= $720.00
Monthly Interest =	240 ÷ 12	= 20.00 X 4	= $ 80.00
Daily Interest =	20.00 ÷ 30	= .667 X 7	= $ 4.67
Total Interest =			$804.67

PROBLEM: 10)   What is the interest on $8,000 borrowed at 12 % interest from April 10, 1995 to August 20, 1997?

EXAMPLE: What is the interest charge on $2,400 borrowed at 10% interest from October 20, 1996 to December 10, 1999?

		Borrowed one month

Elapsed Time of Loan =

	Year	**Month**	**Day**
	1999	~~12~~ 11	~~10~~ 40
-	1996	10	20
	3	1	20

= 3 years, 1 month, 20 days

AID $$\frac{I}{P \times R \times T}$$

Annual Interest =	$2,400 X .10	= $240 X 3	= $720.00
Monthly Interest =	240 ÷ 12	= 20.00 X 1	= $ 20.00
Daily Interest =	20.00 ÷ 30	= .667 X 20	= $ 13.34
Total Interest =			$753.34

PROBLEM: 11)   What is the interest on $3,300 borrowed at $8\frac{1}{2}$% from September 16, 1994 to June 12, 2000?

Amortization

Amortization can be defined as the systematic liquidation of a debt. As mentioned in Chapter 7 the direct reduction mortgage is by far the most common type of amortization method for residential real estate. This math chapter has used the simple interest method for calculations but, the direct reduction method is based on a compound interest formula. For our purposes we do not need to know the formula since there are tables, books, and some calculators that can be used to compute the monthly principal and interest payment (refer to the bottom of the last page of Chapter 7 for an abbreviated table).

In this section we will illustrate how the amount of interest versus principal changes in relation to the constant monthly payment using the simple interest formula. For our example let's assume we have entered into a loan agreement for $100,000.00 at 9% for 30 years. Using the table at the end of Chapter 7 we find at the intersecting point for 30 years and 9% the figure $8.05. This means for every $1,000.00 borrowed you will have to pay back $8.05 for the next 30 years. In this example we have borrowed $100,000.00 therefore, 100 multiplied by $8.05 per month gives us a constant monthly payment of $805.00 to repay the principal and interest on this note. Remember this payment remains the same for the whole 30 years or 360 months.

To compute the total interest to be paid over the term of the note just multiply the monthly payment by the number of months of the note and then subtract the original principal amount. In this example the total interest would be:

$$\$805 \times 360 \text{ mos.} = \$289,800 \text{ Total of monthly payments}$$
$$\underline{- 100,000} \text{ Original principal balance}$$
$$\$189,800 \text{ Total interest}$$

Most people are amazed with the amount of interest that is paid throughout the life of the typical direct reduction note.

It is also interesting to see how the interest and principal change in relation to the constant monthly payment. Using the figures from our example we can follow the payments for the first three months of this note using the simple interest formula:

1st Month: $\$100,000 \times .09 \times \dfrac{1}{12} = \$750$ Interest for first month

$805 Payment (P&I Constant) - $750 = $55 Towards principal

Therefore, the principal balance for month #2 is
$100,000 - $55 = $99,945

2nd Month: $\$99,945 \times .09 \times \dfrac{1}{12} = \$749.59$ Interest for second month

$805 Payment - $749.59 = $55.41 Towards principal

Principal balance for month #3 is
$99,945 - $55.41 = $99,889.59

3rd Month: $\$99,889.59 \times .09 \times \dfrac{1}{12} = \$749.17$ Interest for third month

$805 Payment - $749.17 = $55.83 Towards principal

Principal balance for month #4 is
$99,889.59 - $55.83 = $99,833.76

If you follow these steps for each monthly payment you'll notice that while the interest is decreasing in each payment the principal reduction is increasing. You will also note that for many years the amount of principal being reduced at the beginning of the note is somewhat insignificant in relation to the total principal.

The ability to be able to use some of these calculations will be helpful to you when advising your clients. As an example, a buyer may ask how much they could save on the preceding note if the term were for 20 instead of 30 years. Try it!

Self-Quiz

1) What interest would $30,000 loaned for 1 year at 8% yield?
2) If a bank loaned $25,000 for 1 year and received $2,250 in interest, what rate was charged?
3) How much would you invest for 1 year at 12 % to yield $2,400 interest?
4) What was the rate of interest if a $40,000 loan for 1 year return a total of $42,400 principal and interest?
5) If $8,000 is put in a bank for 3 years at 8%, what interest would it generate?
6) A $13,000 loan for 6 months at 7% would yield what interest?
7) What rate of interest would be charged for a $16,000 loan to produce $5,760 in interest after 4 years?
8) How much would be invested at 8% for 4 months to yield a $160 interest?
9) What is the interest on a $20,000 loan at 8% for 2 years, 3 months, 10 days?
10) What is the interest on a $7,000 loan at 10% from August 25, 1995 to March 16, 1998.

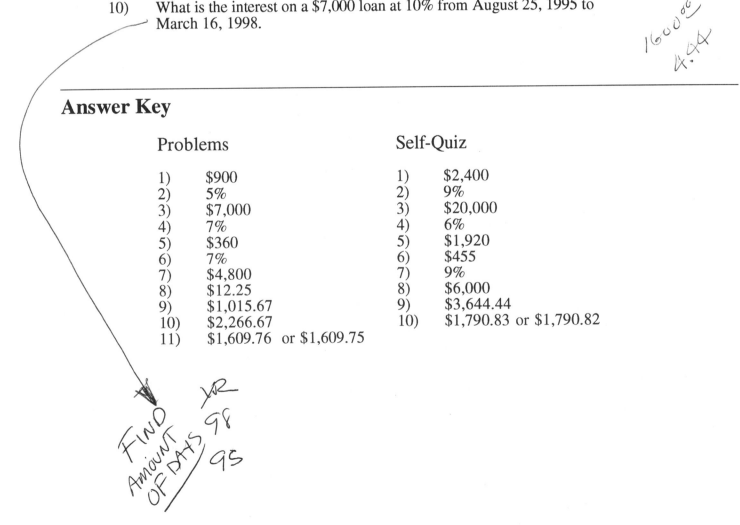

Answer Key

Problems		Self-Quiz	
1)	$900	1)	$2,400
2)	5%	2)	9%
3)	$7,000	3)	$20,000
4)	7%	4)	6%
5)	$360	5)	$1,920
6)	7%	6)	$455
7)	$4,800	7)	9%
8)	$12.25	8)	$6,000
9)	$1,015.67	9)	$3,644.44
10)	$2,266.67	10)	$1,790.83 or $1,790.82
11)	$1,609.76 or $1,609.75		

17 Profit and Loss

The approach to solving profit and loss math problems is very similar to solving the interest problems in the previous chapter. One thing that is new is ending up with less than we started, as in the case of a loss.

The basic formulas for calculating profit and loss problems are:

Profit

> Investment × Rate (of profit) = Profit
>
> I × R = P

Loss

> Investment × Rate (of loss) = Loss
>
> I × R = L

In dealing with either profit or loss calculations, the rates are expressed as a percentage of investment. Thus, if a man invests $4,000 and one year later his investment has grown $1,000 to $5,000, we would say that he has a 25% profit, not 20%. We compare the $1,000 to the original $4,000.

Now, let us deal with profit calculations first and then problems involving loss.

Profit Problems

The profit formula $I \times R = P$ converts to the AID:

AID

$$\frac{P}{I \times R}$$

We shall use this AID to indicate the appropriate math step to be taken.

Solve For Profit

EXAMPLE: If $20,000 is invested and returns a 10% profit, what is the amount of the profit?

Investment = $20,000

Rate = 10%

Profit = ?

AID $\dfrac{P}{I \times R}$

The Aid indicates:

$I \times R = \$20,000 \times .10 = \$2,000$ Profit

PROBLEMS: 1) If a $60,000 investment realizes a 15% profit after 3 years, what is the amount of the profit?

2) If a house is purchased for $180,000 and sold for a 25% profit, what did it sell for?

Solve For Rate

EXAMPLE: If a piece of property bought for $124,000 sold for a $15,500 profit, what was the rate of profit?

Investment = $124,000

Rate = ?

Profit = $15,500

AID $\dfrac{P}{I \times R}$

The Aid indicates: $\dfrac{P}{I} = \dfrac{15,500}{124,000} = \dfrac{1}{8} = 12.5\%$ Profit

PROBLEMS: 3)   Mrs. Jones paid $180,000 for her house. She sold it for a $60,000 profit. What was her rate of profit?

4)   Mr. Brown sold his building for $320,000. If he paid $200,000 for it what was his rate of profit?

Solve For Investment

EXAMPLE: A piece of land sold for an 8% profit that amounted to $12,800. What was the original investment?

Investment = ?

Rate = 8%   AID $\boxed{\dfrac{P}{I \times R}}$

Profit = $12,800

The Aid indicates:

$$\frac{P}{R} = \frac{12,800}{.08} = \$160,000 \text{ Investment}$$

PROBLEMS: 5)   XYZ Corporation sold a building for a 15% profit. The profit was $28,500. What did the building cost?

6)   Mr. White sold his building for $255,000, which amounted to a 20% profit. What did the building cost him?

Note: This type of problem will not fit the normal formula I × R = P. We don't know I or P. We need to use a new formula:

Investment × Rate of Sell Price = Sell Price.

See if you can develop the Aid using a Rate of S.P. of 120%.

Loss Problems

The treatment of loss problems and the loss formula is very similar to dealing with the profit problems.

The loss formula $I \times R = L$ converts to the formula AID:

AID $$\boxed{\dfrac{L}{I \times R}}$$

We shall use this AID to indicate the appropriate math step to be taken.

Solve For Loss

EXAMPLE: If $120,000 is invested and the investor has a 10% loss, what is the amount of the loss?

Investment = $120,000

Rate = 10%   AID

Loss = ?

The Aid indicates:

$I \times R = 120,000 \times .10 = \$12,000$ Loss

PROBLEMS: 7)   If an $180,000 investment shows a 15% loss after 2 years, what is the amount of the loss?

8)   A three-family house that was purchased for $220,000 had a fire. The owner was not insured. If he sold the house for a 60% loss, what did he sell it for?

Solve for Rate

EXAMPLE: If an acre of land purchased for $90,000 sold at an $18,000 loss, what was the rate of loss?

Investment = $90,000

Rate = ?   AID $\dfrac{L}{I \times R}$

Loss = 18,000

The Aid indicates:

$$\frac{L}{I} = \frac{18,000}{90,000} = 20\% \text{ Loss}$$

PROBLEMS: 9)   A group of investors purchased a building for $240,000 and sold it later for a $48,000 loss. What was the rate of loss?

10)   Jones sold his summer cottage for $80,000. If he paid $100,000 for it, what was his rate of loss?

Solve For Investment

EXAMPLE: A store sold for a loss of $19,200, which was a 12% loss. What was the original investment?

Investment = ?

Rate = 12%   AID $\dfrac{L}{I \times R}$

Loss = 19,200

The Aid indicates:

$$\frac{L}{R} = \frac{19,200}{.12} = \$160,000 \text{ Original Investment}$$

PROBLEMS: 11) A piece of property that was foreclosed sold at a 6% loss. If that loss amounted to $11,400, what did the owner originally pay for the property?

12) Two business partners sold their building for $198,000 which amounted to a 10% loss. What did the building cost them originally?

Note: This type of problem will not fit the normal formula I × R = L. We don't know I or L. We need to use a new formula:

Investment × Rate of Sell Price = Sell Price.

See if you can develop the AID using a Rate of S.P. of 90%.

Self-Quiz

1) A builder constructs a house for $130,000 and sells it at a 16% profit. What was his profit?
2) If a speculator sold an investment for $168,000 that had originally cost $140,000 what is the rate of profit?
3) Farmer Jones sold a parcel of property at 25% profit, which amounted to $48,000. What did the parcel cost him?
4) Property that was purchased for $180,000 later sold at a 15% loss. What was the selling price?
5) A hardware business sold for $120,000 five years after it had been purchased for $150,000. Was the result a profit or a loss and what was the rate?
6) A half-acre lot sold at a 2% loss, which amounted to $960. What did the owner pay for the lot originally?
7) Jones paid $160,000 for a piece of investment property and later sold it at 15% profit to a builder. Two years later the builder sold it at a 10% loss. How much did the builder sell it for?
8) A building cost $170,000 and the buyer made improvements of $15,000. After 3 years, it is sold for a 10% profit. What did it sell for?

9) Jones bought a condominium for $120,000 and sold it for a 10% loss to Smith, who later resold it for a 10% profit. What did Smith sell the condominium for?

10) A builder paid $80,000 for a two-acre lot and built a house that cost $120,000. If he wants to realize 15% on his total investment, what must he sell the house for?

Answer Key

Problems

1)	$9,000
2)	$225,000
3)	33 1/3%
4)	60%
5)	$190,000
6)	$212,500
7)	$27,000
8)	$88,000
9)	20%
10)	20%
11)	$190,000
12)	$220,000

Self-Quiz

1)	$20,800
2)	20%
3)	$192,000
4)	$153,000
5)	20% Loss
6)	$48,000
7)	$165,600
8)	$203,500
9)	$118,800
10)	$230,000

18 Return on Investment

When dealing with buyers and sellers in the commercial or income property segment of the real estate field, the broker or salesperson will find that one of the major factors is profitability. Where the residential home buyer is concerned with community, schools, neighborhood, room sizes, and number of baths, the commercial or income property buyer wants to know, "Will it be profitable?" Another way of putting the question is "What will I get back for what I have put in?" or " What will my return on investment be?" We need to look at some of the math steps involved in these types of calculations so we can be prepared to work with buyers and seller asking these questions.

The formula we shall use in solving return on investment problems (R.O.I.) is as follows:

$$\text{Investment} \times \text{Rate of Return} = \text{Net Income}$$
$$I \times R = N.I.$$

The following terms should be understood:

Investment - the amount of money the buyer puts into the transaction (if not otherwise stated, assume the purchase price equals investment).

Rate of return - comparison net income to investment expressed as an annual percentage.

Net income - income less expenses (expressed annually).

EXAMPLE: An apartment house that sold for $160,000 has an annual return on investment of 12%. What is the annual net income?

Investment = $160,000

Rate of Return = .12   AID

Net Income = ?

$$\frac{N.I.}{I \times R}$$

The AID indicates:

$$I \times R = \$160,000 \times .12 = \$19,200 \text{ Net Income}$$

PROBLEMS: 1)   What would the net income per year be on a business that cost $200,000 if the rate of return is 9% per year?

2) If a parcel of commercial property had an R.O.I rate of 11% and cost $240,000, what would the monthly net income be? (annual income divided by 12)

EXAMPLE: A four-family is listed at $375,000. If the net income is $22,500 per year what is the annual rate of return?

Investment = $150,000

Rate of Return = ? AID $$\boxed{\dfrac{N.I.}{I \times R}}$$

Net Income = $22,500

The AID indicates:

$$\frac{N.I.}{I} = \frac{22,500}{375,000} = 375,000\overline{)22,500}^{.06} = 6\% \text{ Return}$$

PROBLEMS: 3) A group of summer cottages is for sale for $190,000. The income after expenses (net income) is projected at $2,375 per month. What would be the annual rate of return on investment?

4) A three-family house has rents of $500 per month each, taxes of $2,400 per year, and other annual expenses of $1,600. If the property were purchased for $175,000, what would be the rate of return? (Net Income = Total Income - Expenses)

EXAMPLE: What should a buyer pay for an apartment building if he wants a 15% return on investment and the yearly net income is $45,000?

Investment = ?

Rate of Return = .15

Net Income = $45,000

AID $\boxed{\dfrac{\text{N.I.}}{\text{I} \times \text{R}}}$

The AID indicates:

$$\frac{\text{N.I.}}{\text{R}} = \frac{45,000}{.15} = .15\overline{)45,000.00} = \$300,000 \text{ Investment}$$

with quotient $300000.$

PROBLEMS: 5) If an investor wishes to realize 12% on his investment, what should he offer to pay for a business with an annual net income of $48,000?

6) What should a buyer pay for a four-unit apartment building with $550 per month rent from each apartment with yearly expenses of $10,000 if he wants his annual rate of return to be 10%?

EXAMPLE: A) What is the R.O.I. on an investment that is listed at $120,000 if the net income is $14,400 per year?

Investment = $120,000

Rate of Return = ?

Net Income = $14,400

AID $\boxed{\dfrac{\text{N.I.}}{\text{I} \times \text{R}}}$

The AID indicates:

$$\frac{\text{N.I.}}{\text{I}} = \frac{14,400}{120,000} = 120,000\overline{)14,400.00} = 12\% \text{ R.O.I.}$$

with quotient $.12$

B) Using the information from the previous example, What would the return on investment be if the buyer invested $90,000 and obtained bank financing of $30,000? Assume the financing decreased the net income by $1,800 per year for interest expense.

Investment = $90,000

Rate of Return = ?   AID

$$\boxed{\dfrac{\text{N.I.}}{\text{I} \times \text{R}}}$$

Net Income = $12,600
($14,400 - $1,800 Interest Expense)

The AID indicates:

$$\frac{\text{N.I.}}{\text{I}} = \frac{12,600}{90,000} = 90,000\overline{)12,600.00}^{.14} = 14\% \text{ R.O.I.}$$

Note: If the problem does not indicate amount financed, R.O.I. should be figured on total cost. Also note the increase in R.O.I. through the use of financing.

PROBLEMS: 7) Jones purchased a business for $200,000 with $50,000 cash and $150,000 bank financing. If annual gross income is $25,000 and annual expenses are $15,000:

A) What is the R.O.I. based on total cost?

B) What is the R.O.I. based on Jones's investment if the bank financing increases expenses by $6,000 per year?

8) A farmer has 10 acres of land that net him $600 per acre per year.

A) What should he pay to get a 5% return on total investment?

B) How much should he put down of his own money to realize a 20% return on his investment? The interest expense will amount to $150 per month for the portion financed.

EXAMPLE: An appraiser has been asked to establish the capitalization rate of a parcel that has a net income of $8,400. The property was purchased for $140,000 with $100,000 cash and $40,000 bank financing.
(See income approach in Appraisal chapter.)

Note: An appraiser is concerned with total cost or value and does not consider what portion is bank financed. He refers to the R.O.I. rate as a capitalization rate.

Investment = $140,000 (Market Value)

Rate of Return = ? (Capitalization Rate)   AID $\boxed{\dfrac{\text{N.I.}}{\text{I} \times \text{R}}}$

Net Income = $8,400

The AID indicates:

$$\frac{\text{N.I.}}{\text{I}} = \frac{8,400}{140,000} = 140,000\overline{\smash{)}8,400.00}^{.06} = 6\% \text{ Capitalization Rate}$$

PROBLEMS: 9) The net income of a parcel of commercial property is $24,000. If the capitalization rate is 6%, what is the market value of the property?

10) What is the value of $10,000 received as net annual income capitalized at 25%?

Self-Quiz

1) A business is listed for sale for $140,000. If the yearly R.O.I. is 8%, what is the annual net income?

2) What is the annual rate of return on an investment that cost $90,000 if the monthly net income is $450?

3) What was the purchase price of a building with a net income of $36,000 and a return on investment rate of 9%?

4) A farmer bought 80 acres of land at $500 per acre. He paid $10,000 in cash and financed the balance with a local bank. What is his return on his cash investment if the annual net income is $100 per acre?

5) An appraiser has been hired to estimate market value on a building that has a net annual income of $23,400. In his judgment, this type of property should have capitalization rate of 9%. What is the appraised market value?

6) A business has an 8% rate of return yearly and is for sale for $90,000. At this price, what would be the monthly net income?

7) A business sold for $220,000 and shows an 11% rate of return. If the taxes are $3,000 per year and other expenses are $7,000 per year, what is the annual gross income?

8) A five-unit apartment building is listed at $525,000. If the R.O.I. is 10% and the income from rents is $70,000 per year what are the annual expenses?   V x R = NET

9) A six-unit apartment building has monthly rents of $600 each. The annual expenses are insurance $1,400, taxes $4,200, utilities $3,600, and the other expenses $2,800. What should an investor pay for the property to realize a 6% R.O.I.?

10) An investment has a capitalization rate of 15% and produces $9,600 net income per year, what would an appraiser estimate as market value?

Answer Key

Problems		Self-Quiz	
1)	$18,000	1)	$11,200
2)	$2,200	2)	6%
3)	15%	3)	$400,000
4)	8%	4)	80%
5)	$400,000	5)	$260,000
6)	$164,000	6)	$600
7)	a) 5% b) 8%	7)	$34,200
8)	a) $120,000 b) $21,000	8)	$17,500
9)	$400,000	9)	$520,000
10)	$40,000	10)	$64,000

Handwritten: 7200 / 12,000 / 43,200 / 31,200

19 Taxation

The various levels of government, federal, state, county, city, or town finance their activities through taxes. This may include a wide variety of taxes such as income tax, meals tax, sales tax, gasoline tax, liquor tax, etc. The tax we are most concerned with in dealing with real estate issues is the property tax.

The cities or towns use a tax on real estate as a major source of funds to finance the operations of their local government, such as schools, police and fire protection, public works, and city administration.

Those in the real estate profession need an understanding of how taxes are determined to provide guidance to both buyers and seller in making real estate decisions.

There are two formulas we need to use in working with property tax math:

$$\text{Appraised Value} \times \text{Assessment Rate} = \text{Assessed Value}$$

$$\text{Assessed Value} \times \text{Tax Rate} = \text{Annual Tax}$$

In working with these formulas, the following terms should be understood:
1) **Appraised value** - the market value of property (what it would sell for).
2) **Assessment rate** - the percent of the appraised value (market value) that will be taxed.
3) **Assessed value** - the value that is assigned as a base for determining taxes.
4) **Tax rate** - the amount that will be charged per $1,000 of assessed value as taxes (some states use a mill rate, per $1 of assessed value).
5) **Taxes** - the amount due the city or town (usually expressed on a yearly basis).

Now let us look at the two formulas, one at a time.

Solve for Assessed Value

$$\text{Appraised Value} \times \text{Assessment Rate} = \text{Assessed Value}$$

EXAMPLE: A house is appraised for $250,000. If the assessment rate is 60% of market value, what is the assessed value?

Appraised Value = $250,000

Assessment Rate = .60   AID $\dfrac{\text{Ass.V}}{\text{App.V} \times \text{Ass.R}}$

Assessed Value = ?

The AID indicates:

App.V × Ass.R = 250,000 × .60 = $150,000 Assessed Value

PROBLEM: 1)   A house is appraised at $190,000 market value. If the assessment rate is 80%, what is the assessed value?

Solve for Appraised Value

EXAMPLE: If the assessed value of a piece of property is $56,000 and the assessment rate is 35% of market value, what is the appraised value (market value)?

Appraised Value = ?

Assessment Rate = .63   AID $\dfrac{\text{Ass.V}}{\text{App.V} \times \text{Ass.R}}$

Assessed Value = $56,000

The AID indicates:

$$\frac{\text{Ass.V}}{\text{Ass.R}} = \frac{56,000}{.35} = 56,000.00 \div .35 = 160,000 \text{ Appraised Value}$$

PROBLEM: 2)   If property is assessed at $188,000, what is the appraised value if the assessment rate is 80%?

EXAMPLE: If property is appraised at $196,000 and assessed at $137,200, what is the assessment rate?

Appraised Value = $196,000

Assessment Rate = ?

Assessed Value = $137,200

AID $\dfrac{\text{Ass.V}}{\text{App.V} \times \text{Ass.R}}$

The AID indicates:

$$\frac{\text{Ass.V}}{\text{App.V}} = \frac{137,200}{196,000} = 137,200 \div 196,000 = 70\% \text{ Assessment Rate}$$

PROBLEM: 3) If property is assessed at $187,200 and has a market value of $208,000, what is the assessment rate?

Solve for Annual Tax

Now let us look at the second property tax formula.

Assessed Value × Tax Rate = Annual Tax

EXAMPLE: If a house is assessed at $120,000 and the tax rate is $20 per $1,000, what are the annual taxes?

Assessed Value = $120,000

Tax Rate = $20 / $1,000

Annual Tax = ?

AID $\dfrac{\text{Ann.Tax}}{\text{Ass.V} \times \text{TaxR}}$

The AID indicates:

$$\text{Ass.V} \times \text{TaxR} = \$120,000 \times \frac{\$20}{\$1,000} = 120 \times 20 = \$2,400 \text{ Annual Rate}$$

PROBLEM: 4) If the tax rate is $18 per $1,000 for a house that is assessed at $160,000, what are the monthly taxes?
(Calculate annual tax and divide by 12.)

Solve For Assessed Value

EXAMPLE: What is the assessed value of a home paying $2,700 in yearly taxes if the tax rate is $15 per $1,000?

Assessed Value = ?

Tax Rate = $15 / $1,000   AID $\dfrac{\text{Ann.Tax}}{\text{Ass.V} \times \text{TaxR}}$

Annual Tax = $2,700

The AID indicates:

$$\frac{\text{AnnTax}}{\text{TaxR}} = \frac{2,700}{15} = 2,700 \div 15 = \$180,000 \text{ Assessed Value}$$

PROBLEM: 5) What is the assessed value of a parcel of property if the tax rate is $21 per $1,000 and the yearly taxes are $3,570?

Solve For Tax Rate

EXAMPLE: If a house that pays $1,920 per year in taxes is assessed for $64,000, what is the tax rate?

Assessed Value = $64,000

Tax Rate = ?   AID $\dfrac{\text{Ann.Tax}}{\text{Ass.V} \times \text{TaxR}}$

Annual Tax = $1,920

The AID indicates:

$$\frac{\text{AnnTax}}{\text{Ass.V}} = \frac{1,920}{64} = 1,920 \div 64 = \$30 \text{ per } \$1,000 \text{ Tax Rate}$$

PROBLEM: 6) A house is assessed for $80,000 and pays $200 per month in taxes, what is the tax rate?

In some cases the problem may require the use of both formulas.

EXAMPLE: If the appraised value of property is $100,000 with an assessment rate of 60% and a tax rate of $40 per $1,000, what are the monthly taxes?

Appraised Value = $100,000

Assessment Rate = .60   AID
$$\frac{Ass.V}{App.V \times Ass.R}$$
Assessed Value = ?

The AID indicates:

App. V × Ass.R = 100,000 × .60 = $60,000 Assessed Value

Now that we know the assessed value, we can use the second formula.

Assessed Value = $60,000

Tax Rate = $40 / $1,000   AID
$$\frac{Ann.Tax}{Ass.V \times TaxR}$$
Annual Tax = ?

The AID indicates:

Ass. V × Tax R = 60 × 10 = $2,400 Annual Tax

The annual tax is $2,400 but the problem asked for monthly taxes, therefore:

$$\frac{2,400}{12} = \$200 \text{ Monthly Tax}$$

In case it isn't apparent which formula you should use, merely list both sets of required factors and formula aids. If you have two terms for a formula, solve for the third.

FORMULA 1

Appraised Value

Assessment Rate AID $\dfrac{\text{Ass.V}}{\text{App.V} \times \text{Ass.R}}$

Assessed Value

Formula 2

Assessed Value

Tax Rate AID $\dfrac{\text{Ann.Tax}}{\text{Ass.V} \times \text{TaxR}}$

Annual Tax

Note: The Assessed Value appears in both formulas. It is necessary to solve one formula to get the assessed value to use in the second formula.

PROBLEM: 7) The market value of a piece of property has been appraised at $130,000. The assessment rate in the town is 60%. If the annual taxes are $2,730, what is the tax rate per $1,000?

8) What is the appraised value of a property in a city that carries a $24.00 per thousand of assessed value for a tax rate and an 80% assessment rate if the taxes are $280.00 per month?

Mill Rate

So far, we have dealt with tax rates that were expressed as dollars per $1,000 of assessed value.

Instead of expressing the tax rate as dollars per $1,000, some locations use dollars per $100, dollars per $10, or dollars per $1 of assessed valuation. When this is done, the tax is still the same but the manner of expressing the rate is slightly different.

The following table will illustrate:

Assessment	Tax Rate	Calculation	Annual Tax
$80,000	$25/$1,000	$80 \times 25 =$	$2,000
$80,000	$2.50/$100	$800 \times \$2.50 =$	$2,000
$80,000	$.25/$10	$8,000 \times .25 =$	$2,000
$80,000	.025/$1	$80,000 \times .025 =$	$2,000

When the tax rate is expressed as, .025 per $1, this is referred to as the **mill rate** and can be called 25 mills.

The student should understand the relationship shown in the above table. Then, no matter how the tax rate is given, it can be converted to the method most familiar.

EXAMPLE: What are the annual taxes if the assessment is $50,000 and the tax rate is 42 mills?

42 Mills = .042/$1 of Assessment

= $42/$1,000 of Assessment

PROBLEM: 9)   If the assessed value is $165,000 and the annual taxes are $2,640.

A)   What is the tax rate per thousand?

B)   What is the mill rate?

C)   What is the tax rate per $100 of assessed value?

Self-Quiz

1) Property is appraised at $112,000 and the assessment rate is 90% of market value. What is the assessed value?
2) What is market value of land that has an assessed value of $49,200 if the assessment rate is 60%?
3) If property with an assessed value of $141,000 has an appraised value of $188,000, what is the assessment rate?
4) Jones bought a piece of property that is assessed for $112,000. If the tax rate is $26.40 per $1,000, what are his yearly taxes? What are his monthly taxes?
5) What is the assessed value of property if the monthly taxes are $220 and the tax rate is $30 per $1,000?
6) If the tax rate is $30 per $1,000, what is the assessed value on a building that pays $2,700 in annual taxes?
7) What is the tax rate per $1,000 for a parcel assessed for $110,000 that pays $6,050 per year in taxes?
8) Smith sold Brown a two-family house with an appraised value of $130,000. The assessment rate is 70% and the tax rate is $21 per $1,000. What are the annual taxes?
9) The yearly taxes on Jones's property are $1,872. If the taxes based on a tax rate of $26 per $1,000 of assessed valuation and the assessed value is set at 60% of appraised value, what is the appraised value?
10) The market value of a piece of property is $80,000 and the assessed value is based on 75% of the market value. If the taxes are $200 per month, what is the tax rate per $1,000?

Answer Key

Problems		Self-Quiz	
1)	$152,000	1)	$100,800
2)	$235,000	2)	$82,000
3)	90%	3)	75%
4)	$240	4)	$2,956.80
5)	$170,000		$246.40
6)	$30/$1,000	5)	$88,000
7)	$35/$1,000	6)	$90,000
8)	$175,000	7)	$55.00
9)	$16/$1,000, .016/$1(16 mills), $1.60/$100	8)	$1,911
		9)	$120,000
		10)	$40.00

20 Proration and Settlement

The math calculations necessary to determine the dollar amounts on the settlement statement prepared at closing may be of several different types. An item may affect buyer or seller, or both. It may be an adjustment where it is stated (e.g., the buyer owes the seller $100 for a refrigerator), or there may be some calculation needed to determine the dollar amount (e.g., the tax stamps due at $2.28/$500 of selling price times the actual sell price).

One additional type of adjustment is called proration. You prorate something when expenses or income must be divided between buyer and seller as of the date of passing (e.g., property tax, insurance, or rents).

In this chapter, we shall look at the math necessary to calculate each one of these types. When deciding whether an amount should be a debit or a credit on the settlement statement, it may be helpful to remember **debit** or **credit** as **from** or **to** the party affected. An amount paid to the seller would be a credit to the seller. Four separate steps should be used:

1) Calculate the amount of money involved.
2) Who is affected...buyer, seller or both?
3) Is the money coming from or to him?
4) Make entry on the settlement statement.

EXAMPLE 1: The buyer owes $750 for the title examination fee.
1) Calculate the amount involved - $750.00
2) Who is affected - Buyer
3) Is the money coming from or to him - From.
4) Make the entry - $750.00 from (debit) the buyer.

Note: See the settlement statement after Example 3 for the solution.

EXAMPLE 2: The seller owes $820.80 in excise tax stamps.
1) Calculate the amount involved - $820.80
2) Who is affected - Seller.
3) Is the money coming from or to him - From.
4) Make the entry - $820.80 from (debit) the Seller.

Note: See the settlement statement after Example 3 for the solution.

EXAMPLE 3: The buyer owes the Seller $60.00 for fuel oil left in the tank.
1) Calculate the amount involved - $60.00
2) Who is affected - Buyer and Seller.
3) Is the money coming from or to him - From (debit) the buyer to (credit) the seller.
4) Make the entry - $60.00 from (debit) buyer and $60 to (credit) seller.

Note: See the settlement statement after Example 3 for the solution.

	Buyer		Seller	
	Debit (from)	Credit (to)	Debit (from)	Credit (to)
Example 1: Title Examination Fee	$750.00			
Example 2: Tax Stamps			$820.80	
Example 3: Fuel Adjustment	$60.00			$60.00

PROBLEM: 1) Take the following adjustments and enter them on the settlement statement.
  A) Buyer owes fee for recording new deed and mortgage $50.00.
  B) Seller owes fee for discharging old mortgage $20.00.
  C) Buyer owes seller $120 for refrigerator.

	Buyer		Seller	
	Debit (from)	Credit (to)	Debit (from)	Credit (to)
A)				
B)				
C)				

Proration

Some of the adjustments at settlement involve calculating expenses that one party owes the other as of the day of settlement. These adjustments are called prorations. The proration may be to the advantage of either buyer or seller depending on the circumstances. The most common items that may require prorating are taxes and rents.

Taxes

EXAMPLE: Jones is buying a house from White and settlement is taking place on January 15. The taxes were paid by White to the city for the year ending in December.

Note: In calculating prorations, the seller is responsible for expenses up to and including the day of settlement.

The annual taxes are $2,880.

1)   Calculate the amount involved - number of days × daily rate

(15 × $8 = $120.)

Number of days - seller is responsible up to and including passing date
= 15 days.

Daily rate - $2,880 divided by 360 days = $8/day
or $2,880 divided by 12 months = $240
$240/month divided by 30 days/month = $8/day.

2)   Who is affected - buyer and seller.
3)   The money coming from or to - From the seller to the buyer.
4)   The entry - $120 from (debit) the seller and $120 to (credit) the buyer.

	Buyer		Seller	
	Debit (from)	Credit (to)	Debit (from)	Credit (to)
Property tax adjustment		$120.00	$120.00	

PROBLEM: 2)   A buys a house from B on November 15. The seller had already paid the taxes through the end of the year. This means that 1-1/2 months of property tax should be adjusted. If the annual taxes are $1200, what is the settlement statement entry?

	Buyer		Seller	
	Debit (from)	Credit (to)	Debit (from)	Credit (to)

Rents

When the property being sold is income property, there is almost always a rent adjustment to be made. It is highly unlikely that all tenants have paid their rents up to the exact day of settlement, no more or no less. The adjustment must be figured for each apartment separately as they may each differ in amount of rent, date rent is paid, and whether or not the rent is overpaid or underpaid as of the settlement date.

EXAMPLE: A two-family is being sold with settlement to take place on November 20. The first floor tenant pays $540 per month and has paid through November. The second-floor tenant pays $480 per month and has paid through October. He has not paid his November rent yet. Assume the buyer will be collecting the November rent from the second floor tenant. What is the rent adjustment due at settlement?

Rental Unit 1:

1)   Calculate the amount involved - number of days × daily rate

= 10 days × $18.00 = $180.00

2)   Who is affected - buyer and seller.
3)   The money coming from or to - from the buyer to the seller.
4)   The entry (wait until Unit 2 is figured).

Rental Unit 2:

1)   Calculate the amount involved - number of days × daily rate

= 20 days × $16.00 = $320.00

2)   Who is affected - buyer and seller.
3)   The money coming from or to- from the buyer to the seller.
(When the tenant does not pay his rent, the full month will be received by the buyer; therefore the buyer pays the seller now).
4)   The entry (wait until Unit 1 and 2 are combined):

Rental Unit 1 - Seller owes Buyer $180.00
Rental Unit 2 - Buyer owes Seller $320.00
Net Effect - Buyer owes Seller $140.00

The entry therefore is $140.00 from (debit) buyer and $140 to (credit) Seller.

| | Buyer | | Seller | |
	Debit (from)	Credit (to)	Debit (from)	Credit (to)
Rent adjustment	$140.00			$140.00

PROBLEM: 3)   A two-family house is being sold with settlement to take place on June 6. The buyer will occupy the first floor which is now vacant. The second-floor tenant pays $570 per month and has paid through June. The seller is holding a $570 security deposit which should be turned over to the buyer at passing. What should the adjustment be?

| | Buyer | | Seller | |
	Debit (from)	Credit (to)	Debit (from)	Credit (to)

Proration Self-Quiz

What should the settlement adjustment be for the following problems? Use the settlement statement worksheet on the following page to show the answers. The solution is at the end of the chapter.

1) The buyer owes the bank a $200 mortgage application fee.
2) The seller owes the bank attorney $50 for preparing the deed.
3) There is a $20 fee for recording a second mortgage.
4) The broker's fee is 6% of the $93,000 sell price.
5) The pay-off figure on the existing mortgage is $14,350.
6) The dining room set is being sold for $200.
7) The bank is granting a $64,000 first mortgage.
8) The annual taxes are $1,200 and were paid through June. The passing is at the end of September.
9) A garage on the property is rented at $40 per month and the tenant has prepaid through the calendar year. The closing is set for October 31st.
10) A three-family house has tenants who pay rent as follows:

Tenant 1 - $690.00 per month.
Tenant 2 - $690.00 per month.
Tenant 3 - $600 per month.

They all pay their rent on the first of each month. The settlement date is September 20. Tenant 1 and 2 have paid through September. Tenant 3 has not paid September rent as yet. Assume the new owner will collect any late rental payments.

Proration Worksheet

Settlement Date:	Buyer's Statement		Seller's Statement	
	Debit (from)	Credit (to)	Debit (from)	Credit (to)

Proration Answer Key

Settlement Date:	Buyer's Statement		Seller's Statement	
	Debit (from)	Credit (to)	Debit (from)	Credit (to)
Problem 1 A) Recording fee	$50.00	$	$	$
B) Discharge fee			20.00	
C) Purchase refrigerator	120.00			120.00
Problem 2 Property tax adjustment	150.00			150.00
Problem 3 Rental adjustment		1,026.00	1,026.00	
SELF-QUIZ				
1) Mortgage application fee	200.00			
2) Deed preparation			50.00	
3) Recording fee (2nd mortgage)	20.00			
4) Broker's fee			5,580.00	
5) Mortgage pay off			14,350.00	
6) Dining-room set	200.00			200.00
7) First mortgage		64,000.00		
8) Property tax proration		300.00	300.00	
9) Rent proration		80.00	80.00	
10) Rent proration		60.00	60.00	

Settlement

In the day-to-day practice of real estate, brokers and salespeople will be listing property and preparing purchase and sale agreements. As part of this activity, it is necessary to develop the ability to prepare the initial forms, as well as the ability to interpret them once they have been formalized. In Real Estate chapters five and eight, you will find a treatment of contracts and listing agreements respectively. In this section we will concern ourselves with a settlement statement.

Real estate professionals also need to be capable of advising both buyers and sellers as to what their respective expenses are at the passing of papers. Who pays for what? Therefore, a knowledge of settlement statement preparation and analysis is especially helpful for both brokers and salespeople.

Local REALTOR ® boards and individual real estate offices will recommend the use of specific forms. The closing is also covered by RESPA (Real Estate Settlement Procedures Act) which requires that most new first mortgages conform to certain requirements and specific forms. In this chapter we use a simplified form for the settlement statement for illustrative purposes. Although the RESPA form serves the same purpose as our form does here, it is much more complicated.

The following is a problem in which you can practice the skill necessary to complete a settlement statement. The settlement statement is actually a list of the individual prorations, adjustments, and other costs incurred by either party that we have just learned. To complete the settlement between buyer and seller, all that needs to be done is to total the columns and find the difference between debits and credits on each side of the statement.

On the buyer's side of the statement there will be more debits (amounts coming from) than credits (amounts going to the buyer). Therefore, the difference represents the amount the buyer has to show up with in order to pass papers. The seller's side will usually have more credits than debits. The difference between these two columns represents the amount of funds to be received in excess of payments and other expenses which is called the **seller's proceeds**.

Settlement Problem

From the following hypothetical situation, sort out the figures needed to complete a settlement statement and fill out the blank statement sheet that follows:

You are a salesperson for XYZ Realty and on January 6 you listed a house at 17 Main Street in the city of Downtown, Massachusetts. The listing price was $260,000 and you are to receive a 6 percent commission on the selling price.

The house and property is assessed for $220,000 and the town has a tax rate of $15 per thousand of assessed valuation. The seller also owes the town a $2,600 sewer assessment charge for the new city sewerage system installed in the street last summer which would have to be paid at the closing.

On February 2 you show the house to a young couple who really like the area and want to make an offer. The prospective buyers offer $248,000 for the house and $1,000 for the refrigerator, stove, washer and dryer. The seller does not accept this offer but counteroffers with $256,000 plus $1,000 for the appliances. The buyers feel this is still a bit high and makes another offer $252,000 which is to **include** all appliances.

The owners of the property accept the $252,000 offer and agree to let the appliances stay as part of the purchase price. The buyers, shown to be strong, are putting a down payment of 30 percent of the purchase price on the property and intend to finance the rest at current rates for thirty years. The buyers also submitted a $15,000 deposit to be held in escrow until passing of papers.

At the March 15 closing, the sellers are required to pay off their existing mortgage. The bank has calculated this figure to be $80,000. Real estate taxes have been paid through the last calendar year. Tax stamps are $2.28 per $500 of selling price.

Other expenses include: title examination and attorney fees for the paperwork and recording of documents ($800), deed preparation ($75), one point to be paid by buyer on the amount financed. The bank also required the buyer to pay $150 for a plot plan and $200 for the appraisal report, a $20 fee for the discharge of the old mortgage, and $120 adjustment for heating fuel remaining in the tank.

Prepare as much of the settlement statement as possible before looking at the solution.

SELLER

252,000
15,120
1,149.12 — TAX STAMPS

BUYER

252,000
75,600 DOWN PAYMENT
15,000 ESCROW

Settlement Worksheet

Settlement Date:	Buyer's Statement		Seller's Statement	
	Debit (from)	Credit (to)	Debit (from)	Credit (to)

Settlement

Settlement Date:	Buyer's Statement		Seller's Statement	
	Debit (from)	Credit (to)	Debit (from)	Credit (to)
Selling Price	$252,000.00	$	$	$252,000.00
Deposited in Escrow		15,000.00		
New 1st Mortgage		176,400.00		
Old 1st Mortgage			80,000.00	
Tax Stamps			1,149.12	
Broker			15,120.00	
Sewer Assessment			2,600.00	
Real estate Tax		687.50	687.50	
Attorney	800.00			
Deed Preparation			75.00	
Points	1,764.00			
Plot Plan	150.00			
Appraisal	200.00			
Mortgage Discharge			20.00	
Fuel	120.00			120.00
	255,034.00	192,087.50	99,651.62	252,120.00
Due from Buyer		62,946.50		
Due to Seller			152,468.38	
Totals	255,034.00	255,034.00	252,120.00	252,120.00

21 Commissions

The approach to solving commission problems is basically the same as the other Base × Rate = Percentage problems that we have done in other chapters. The two new concepts we will consider are 1) commission split between offices or between individuals within the same office, and 2) calculating sell price when a seller wants to clear a certain net figure after commission.

The formula we will use in solving commission problems is:

$$\text{Sell Price} \times \text{Commission Rate} = \text{Commission}$$
$$SP \times R = C$$

The following terms should be understood:

Sell price - the dollar value a buyer pays for property.

Commission rate - the broker's fee expressed as a percent of the sell price.

Commission - the broker's fee in dollars.

EXAMPLE: A condo sells for $108,000 and the broker's commission is 6%. What is the amount of the commission?

Sell Price = $108,000

Rate = .06

Commission = ?

AID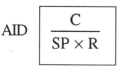

The AID indicates:

$SP \times R = \$108,000 \times .06 = \$6,480$ Commission

PROBLEM: 1) What would the commission be on a lot of land that sold for $127,000 if the real estate fee is 7%?

EXAMPLE: What did a house sell for if the real estate fee was 6% and the commission amounted to $17,100?

Sell Price = ?

Rate = .06   AID

Commission = $17,100

$$\boxed{\dfrac{C}{SP \times R}}$$

The AID indicates:

$$\frac{C}{R} = \frac{17,100}{.06} = 285,000 \text{ Sell Price}$$

PROBLEM: 2)   If the rate of commission is 7% and the broker's fee was $12,950, what did the property sell for?

EXAMPLE: If a parcel of property sold for $110,000 and the commission was $5,500, what percentage was the commission of the sell price?

Sell Price = $110,000

Rate = ?   AID

Commission = $5,500

$$\boxed{\dfrac{C}{SP \times R}}$$

The AID indicates:

$$\frac{C}{SP} = \frac{5,500}{110,000} = 5\% \text{ Commision Rate}$$

PROBLEM: 3)   An apartment building sold for $360,000. If the broker received $23,400, What was his rate of commission?

EXAMPLE: Two real estate offices co-broked on a 50-50 split on a house that sold for $240,000. If the fee was 6%, what did each agency receive?

Sell Price = $240,000

Rate = .06   AID $$\frac{C}{SP \times R}$$

Commission = ?

The AID indicates:

SP × Rate = $240,000 × .06 = $14,400 Total Commission

Each agency received 50% of the fee. Therefore, they each received

$$\frac{14,400}{2} = \$7,200 \text{ each}$$

PROBLEM: 4)   A home sold through the Multiple Listing Service (M.L.S.) for $310,000 and a 7% broker's fee. If the fee arrangement was 60-40, with 60% going to the selling office, how much did the listing office receive?

EXAMPLE: A seller wants to net $180,000 after a real estate commission of 7%. What should the property be advertised at (to the nearest dollar)?

This problem is a little different. In the formula SP × R = C, we only know R = 7%. However, if

    SP × 7% = Commission
we know
    SP × 93% = Net to Seller

Then we have a new formula, SP × Net Rate = Net Amount.

AID $$\frac{Net}{SP \times Net\ R}$$

The AID indicates:

$$\frac{180,000}{.93} = 193,548 \text{ Sell Price}$$

PROBLEM: 5)   What should a house sell for to net a seller $104,000 after a 6% commission (to the next higher $500 figure)?

Self-Quiz

1)   A building was sold for $210,000. If the broker's fee was 6% of sell price, what was the amount of the commission?

2)   Jones Realty charged 7% commission on a $194,000 sale, how much did the seller receive?

3)   What was the sell price of a condo if the agent charged 6% and received $7,800?

4)   If a real estate office charges 8% commission rate and received $13,200 for selling a piece of property, what was the sell price?

5)   A landowner wishes to sell some woodland he owns. What should the property be listed at if he wishes to net $108,000 after the broker's fee of 10%?

6)   Two offices co-broked on a 50-50 basis in selling a home for $335,000. The commission was 6%. The listing salesperson received 20% of the commission received by his office. What did he receive as a listing fee?

7)   A house sold for a 6% commission rate. The listing and selling broker split the commission equally and each received $5,940. What was the selling price of the house?

8)   A condominium sold for $140,000. The broker received 6% on first $100,000 and 4% for everything above $100,000. What was the total commission?

9)   A listing fee of 10% of the total commission was paid to salesperson A. The selling salesperson and the broker who owned the agency divided the commission on a 50-50 basis after deducting the listing fee. If the house sold for $180,000 and the rate was 6%, what did the selling salesperson receive?

10)   A listing fee of 10% of the total commission was paid to salesperson A. The selling salesperson and the broker who owned the agency divided the commission on a 50-50 basis. The listing fee is deducted from the selling salesperson's share. If the house sold for $180,000 and the rate was 6%, what did the selling salesperson receive?

Answer Key

Problems		Self-Quiz	
1)	$8,890	1)	$12,600
2)	$185,000	2)	$180,420
3)	6.5%	3)	$130,000
4)	$8,680	4)	$165,000
5)	$111,000	5)	$120,000
		6)	$2,010
		7)	$198,000
		8)	$7,600
		9)	$4,860
		10)	$4,320

22 Depreciation

Before we approach depreciation math problems and how to solve them, we should discuss some of the basic concepts of what depreciation is and how it affects those in the real estate field.

Depreciation is a reduction (decrease) in value. If you bought a car last year for $11,000 and today it is worth $9,000, your car would have depreciated by $2,000.

Appreciation is an increase in value. If you bought an antique clock last year for $1,000 and this year it is worth $1,500, your clock would have appreciated $500.

In dealing with real estate issues, the IRS does not allow the land itself to depreciate. Only the buildings or other improvements depreciate. Many of the issues involving depreciation will be influenced by the Internal Revenue Service regulations and what the government will allow for tax purposes. This affects how an accountant will keep financial records.

For example, an investment that costs $75,000 five years ago may now be worth $125,000 in market value. However, tax laws may allow us to depreciate the building in our records by $3,750 per year times five years or $18,750 from our original $75,000 cost. Therefore, our building would show on our accounting books as being worth $56,250 even though it would sell for $125,000 at current market value.

Depreciation concerns itself with reduction in value from original cost and not with current value.

The following terms should be understood:

Depreciation - a reduction (decrease) in value.

Appreciation - an increase in value.

Useful life - the number of years an asset will last before needing replacement.

Accrued depreciation - total depreciation to date (yearly depreciation times number of years)

Book value - value remaining after depreciation (original cost minus accrued depreciation)

EXAMPLE: A building cost $120,000 and has a useful life of 20 years.

Original Cost = $120,000
Useful Life = 20 years
Depreciation = $6,000/year ($120,000 divided by 20 years)

After one year, what is the accrued depreciation and book value?

Original Cost   = $120,000
Depreciation   = - $6,000
Book Value   = $114,000

Type of Depreciation

What we have just illustrated is called straight line depreciation. All that means is that we depreciate the same amount each year over the useful life of the item. In this case, we depreciated $6,000 each year over the 20-year useful life of the building.

There are other depreciation methods that allow different amounts of depreciation each year over the useful life. We do not need to get into those types for our purposes. Straight line depreciation will be used.

The formula we shall use in solving depreciation problems is as follows:

$$\text{Cost} \times \text{Depreciation Rate} = \text{Depreciation}$$
$$C \times DR = D$$

Note: Depreciation rate will be the yearly rate times the number of years.

EXAMPLE: A machine cost $10,000 and has a useful life of 5 years. What is the accrued depreciation after 2 years?

Cost = $10,000
Depreciation Rate = 40% (5 years =100%, 1 year = 20% × 2 years = 40%)
Depreciation = ?

$$AID \quad \boxed{\dfrac{D}{C \times DR}}$$

The AID indicates:

$$C \times DR = \$10,000 \times .40 = \$4,000 \text{ Accrued Depreciation}$$

PROBLEMS: 1)   A building cost $100,000 and has a useful life of 10 years. What is the depreciation after 3 years? What is the remaining book value?

2)   A company car cost $9,000 and has a useful life of 3 years. What is the annual depreciation, annual depreciation rate and accrued depreciation after 2 years?

EXAMPLE: A machine cost $8,000 and has a useful life of 4 years. If it has depreciated $6,000, what rate has it depreciated? What is the annual rate of depreciation?

Cost = $8,000

Depreciation Rate = ?　　　　AID $\dfrac{D}{C \times DR}$

Depreciation = $6,000

The AID indicates:

$$\frac{D}{C} = \frac{6,000}{8,000} = 75\% \text{ Depreciation Rate}$$

If 4 years of useful life = 100% depreciation, one year = 25% Annual Depreciation.

PROBLEMS: 3) A building cost $140,000 and has a useful life of 20 years. What is the depreciation per year in dollars and percent?

4) A machine cost $15,000 and has a book value of $10,000. What is the depreciation in percent? (Note: Cost - Depreciation = Book Value)

EXAMPLE: If a building has depreciated $16,000, which amounts to 20%, what was the original cost?

Cost = ?

Depreciation Rate = 20%　　　　AID $\dfrac{D}{C \times DR}$

Depreciation = $16,000

The AID indicates:

$$\frac{D}{DR} = \frac{16,000}{.20} = \$80,000 \text{ Original Cost}$$

PROBLEMS: 5) A building depreciates at 6% per year or $4,200 per year. What was the original cost?

6) If a machine depreciates at 5% per year, after how many years will the book value be 30% of original cost?

EXAMPLE: If land appreciates 10% per year, how much does an acre appreciate in 4 years if it cost $60,000

$$\boxed{\begin{array}{c} \text{Cost} \times \text{Appreciation Rate} = \text{Appreciation} \\ C \times AR = A \end{array}}$$

Cost = $60,000

Appreciation Rate = 40%   AID $\boxed{\dfrac{A}{C \times AR}}$

   (10% per year × 4 years)

Appreciation = ?

The AID indicates:

$C \times AR = \$60,000 \times .4 = \$24,000$ Appreciation

PROBLEMS: 7) A lot that cost $75,000 when bought 2 years ago has appreciated 15%. What is it worth today?

8) If a lot that cost $90,000 has appreciated $18,000 after 2 years, what is the annual appreciation (in percent)?

EXAMPLE: Jones bought a parcel for $80,000. The building was worth $60,000 and the land worth $20,000. If the building depreciated at 5% per year and the land appreciated at 10% per year, what was the parcel worth after 3 years?

Building: AID

$$\frac{D}{C \times DR}$$

The AID indicates: $C \times DR = \$60,000 \times .15$

$.05 \times 3$ years $= \$9,000$ Depreciation

Land: AID

$$\frac{A}{C \times AR}$$

The AID indicates: $C \times AR = \$20,000 \times .30$

$.10 \times 3$ years $= \$6,000$ Appreciation

	Original Cost	Dep./Apprec.	New Value
Building	$60,000	- $9,000	= $51,000
Land	$20,000	+ $6,000	= $26,000
			$77,000 Total Value

PROBLEMS: 9)   Smith paid $72,000 for a building valued at $60,000 on a lot worth $12,000. If the land appreciated 7% per year and the building had a useful life of 10 years, what was the value of the parcel after 2 years?

10)   A parcel sold for $108,000. The lot was worth $18,000. If the land did not appreciate at all and the building had a useful life of 20 years, what is the value of the parcel after 5 years?

Self-Quiz

1) A machine cost $18,000 and has a useful life of 10 years.
   What is the annual depreciation?
2) In the previous problem, what would be the book value after 6 years?
3) A building cost $100,000 and has a book value of $60,000.
   What is the depreciation in percent?
4) What was the original cost of a parcel that has depreciated 20% and is now worth $64,000?
5) Brown paid $200,000 for an apartment complex. Of the $200,000 the land was valued at $60,000. If the land appreciated 5% per year and the building has a useful life of 20 years, what was the value of the parcel after 10 years?

Situation: An asset cost $120,000 and has a useful life of 25 years.

6) What is the depreciation rate per year?
7) What is the depreciation per year?
8) What is the total percent depreciation after 3 years?
9) What is the accrued depreciation after 3 years?
10) What is the book value after 3 years?

Answer Key

Problems		Self-Quiz	
1)	$30,000, 70,000	1)	$1,800
2)	$3,000; 33 1/3%, $6,000	2)	$7,200
3)	$7,000; 5%	3)	40%
4)	33 1/3%	4)	$80,000
5)	$70,000	5)	$160,000
6)	14 years	6)	4%
7)	$86,250	7)	$4,800
8)	10%	8)	12%
9)	$61,680	9)	$14,400
10)	$85,500	10)	$105,600

Glossary

Abstract of Title A summary of the history of ownership of a parcel of property including each consecutive conveyance, liens, other encumbrances and the current status of each.

Abutter One whose land adjoins another parcel of property (including a road or another private parcel).

Acceptance The agreement of one party to a set of terms offered by a second party.

Accountability One of the duties of an agent under the law of agency that deals with the handling of escrow funds.

Accretion The gradual increase to land on a shore or riverbank by natural forces.

Accrued Items that have been accumulated over time. Such as depreciation or taxes.

Accrued Depreciation Total depreciation to date (yearly depreciation x number of years).

Acknowledgment Process where an authorized officer (usually a Notary Public) witnesses a signature and attests that the signer has stated that the signing is his/her "free act and deed" - intended to protect against duress.

Acre An area measurement equal to 43,560 square feet.

Actual Eviction Legal process where the landlord forces the tenant to vacate the premises (as opposed to constructive eviction).

Adverse Possession The process of gaining title to real property by open, continuous and notorious occupancy (for twenty years in Massachusetts); known as "Squatter's Rights". Similar to establishing an easement by prescription.

Ad Valorem Tax A tax based "according to valuation". Property taxes are based on the value of the property being taxed.

Agency The relationship between one person (Principal) and another (Agent) who is authorized to act in the first person's behalf.

Agency Disclosure The Massachusetts regulation (254 C.M.R. 2.05) that regulates the real estate broker sales person in informing and obtaining consent as to the agency representation to be utilized.

Agent One who is authorized to act for another; who is called the principal.

Air Rights The rights to the space above a piece of property.

Alienation Clause The clause in a mortgage that the balance becomes due in full if the property is sold or otherwise transfers ownership (such as foreclosure) also known as a Due-on-Sale clause.

Amortization The process of repaying a loan by making systematic payments of principal and interest over time until the balance is zero.

Anticipation The appraisal principal that value increases or decreases based on the future benefit or detriment that may be received.

Appraisal An estimate of value.

Appraisal Institute National association of real estate appraiser's who are governed by a code of ethics and control the awarding of various appraisal designations as Senior Residential Appraiser (SRA) and Member Appraisal Institute (MAI).

Appraised Value An estimate of what a parcel of property will sell for . An estimate of market value.

Appreciation An increase in value (opposite of depreciation).

Assemblage The process of combining two or more lots to make the resulting parcel more valuable. The increase in value is known as plottage.

Assessed Value Value which the city or town places on property as a base for determining taxes (appraised value times assessment rate).

Assessment Official value a city or town places on property to determine taxes (same as assessed value).

Assessment Rate The percent of the Assessed Value that will be taxed.

Assignment The transfer of rights and interests in property from one person to another. Example: assignment of a purchase and sale agreement or a mortgage.

Attorney at Law   A law professional who has taken and passed the bar exam.

Attorney in Fact One who is authorized to act for another. In real estate transactions this is done through a power of attorney. Does not need to be an attorney at law.

Avulsion The loss of land due to a sudden or violent act of nature.

Balloon Mortgage   A mortgage where one final payment, larger than any preceding payment, pays off the debt.

Bargain and Sale Deed Grantor affirms they hold title and grant whatever interest they have with no warranties. Often used by fiduciaries such as estate executors or officers of the court.

Base Line An imaginary line running east to west used by surveyors in the government (rectangular) survey method of property description.

Bilateral Contract A contract where one party agrees to do something in return for the second party's promise to also do something.

Bill of Sale A written contract between two parties for the sale of personal property.

Blanket Mortgage A mortgage secured by two or more parcels of property.

Blockbusting The practice of attempting to influence one to sell or rent with threats that persons of a particular protected class are entering the neighborhood.

Board of Appeals Local city or town committee that rules on matters of zoning variances.

Book Deeds and other documents relating to property transfer are recorded at the County Registry of Deeds in Massachusetts and become a specific page in a specific book in the record system. A deed has a specific book and page reference.

Book Value Value remaining after depreciation. Original cost less accrued depreciation.

Broker An individual who for consideration sells, rents, exchanges or negotiates options of real property.

Building Code A set of rules established by state or municipal government to regulate standards in the construction trades.

"Bundle of Rights" A concept used to describe all of the rights that an owner has in the property owned.

Buyer's Agent A real estate broker who represents the buyer not the seller and therefore has a fiduciary responsibility to the buyer.

ByLaws As relates to condominiums; the specific procedures for managing and regulating a condominium. Recorded with the Master Deed per M.G.L. c.183A.

Capitalization Rate (Cap Rate) Comparison of value to net income, used by an appraiser in estimating value of income property (net income divided by value).

Capital Reserve A reserve fund set up by a condominium management association to collect monies from unit owners on a regular basis to finance future capital improvements. Not to be confused with operating reserve.

Care That part of the law of agency that requires that the agent use his/her expertise in the principal's best interest.

Caveat Emptor A principal in law that means "let the buyer beware".

Certified Appraiser Professional appraisal designation under the Financial Institution's Reform, Recovery and Enforcement Act (FIRREA) requiring a specific amount of classroom hours of training, field experience and passing of state examinations.

Certificate of Reasonable Value A document issued by the Veterans' Administration which is based on an appraisal and is intended to insure the veteran that the price being paid for a piece of property is reasonable.

Certificate of Title Document issued by the land court under the "Torrens System" to verify the court decision and the property owner's title.

Chain of Title The history of ownership of each owner as grantor and grantee used in a title search for a parcel of real property.

Change One of the economic variables to value in real estate appraisal that recognizes that things are in a state of flux and do not remain constant.

Chattel An article of tangible personal property.

Chattel Personal A chattel (item of personal property) that is movable. Example: Furniture - a table.

Chattel Real A chattel (item of personal property) that is associated with a piece of real estate. Example: A lease.

Client The one who has hired an agent to perform a service for a fee.

Codicil A supplement or addition to a will.

Commercial Easement in Gross An easement in gross that is of a business or commercial nature; not personal. Example: Utility line.

Co-mingling of Funds To combine deposit funds received as an agent with broker's business or personal funds.

Common Areas In a condominium; all areas not owned as individual units and therefore for the use and ownership of all owners and tenants.

Common Driveway A type of easement where each of two abutters have the right to cross over the property of the other to gain access to their property (usually a garage).

Comparable A recently sold or currently for sale parcel of real estate that is similar to the subject property being appraised. Used as an indicator of value in a market comparison appraisal approach.

Comparative Market Analysis (CMA) An opinion of value derived by a market analysis by a licensed salesperson or broker.

Competency The state of having legal contractual capacity.

Competent Party One who has the legal capacity to enter into a contract.

Concurrent Estate Ownership by two or more persons at the same time. Example: Joint tenancy, tenancy by the entirety, tenancy in common.

Condemnation The administration or judicial procedure used when taking land by local, state or federal government for the public good called eminent domain.

Condemnee The property owner having title taken by eminent domain.

Condemnor The agency taking title to property by eminent domain.

Condominium An estate in real property in a multiple unit residential or commercial building consisting of the interest in an individual unit plus an undivided interest along with other unit owners in the common areas.

Condominium Budget The annual forecast of monies necessary to finance the Condominium Common Expenses.

Condominium Fee That part of the condominium budget for which the unit owner is responsible (% of common ownership x condo budget = condo fee. Usually computed for monthly payments).

Condominium Square Footage The number of square feet of space within an individual condominium unit.

Condominium Trust/Association The Management group of unit owners elected by the unit owners to manage the condominium's business as required by M.G.L. c.183A.

Condo "Super Lien" April 1993 change to Massachusetts General Law c.183 that allows the condominium association to collect up to 6 months due condo fees if available upon foreclosure; after taxes due, but before mortgage liens.

Confidentiality That part of the responsibility of loyalty in agency law that deals with matters of disclosure. The broker must disclose material facts about the property but not personal facts about the principal that may not be in the principal's interest.

Conformity The principle which holds that a house will hold its value better in an area of like type houses.

Consent One agreeing to terms of a contract does so without duress. Demonstrated by a Notary Public taking parties acknowledgment that this is their free act and deed.

Conservator An individual appointed by the court to act as a guardian.

Consideration Something given in exchange for something from another. Can be an article or a promise to do something. In real estate it is usually money exchanged for property as in a deed or money in exchange for a promise to perform as in a Purchase and Sale Agreement.

Constructive Eviction Action by landlord that makes it impossible to remain and therefore effectively terminates the tenancy. (As opposed to actual eviction).

Construction Mortgage A mortgage designed to finance the building of a new house or other building.

Contract A legally enforceable agreement between competent parties to perform a certain act for consideration.

Contract for Deed See Installment Contract.

Contribution The appraisal principle that deals with the amount of increase in value to a piece of property caused by improvements to the property (may be more or less than the cost of the improvement).

Conventional Mortgage A mortgage that is not insured (FHA Loan) or guaranteed (V.A. Loan) by the federal government. Includes loans backed by Private Mortgage Companies (PMI).

Cooperative Ownership A form of ownership where stock purchased in a corporation, partnership or trust entitles the owner to occupancy of one particular unit.

Corporeal Interest in property that is tangible such as buildings or trees as opposed to intangible such as an easement or a lease.

Cost Approach Method of real estate appraisal that estimates value by calculating replacement or reproduction cost.

Counter Offer The one receiving an offer (offeree) responds by offering a new set of terms as a new offer. The original offeree then becomes the new offeror.

Covenant Against Encumbrances Promises made by the grantor in a warranty deed that the property is free of all encumbrances not stated in the deed.

Covenant of Further Assurance Promises made by the grantor in a warranty deed that they will take any future action necessary to correct any title defects.

Covenant of Quiet Enjoyment Promises made by the grantor in a warranty deed that the grantee will hold the property free from the claims of third parties.

Covenant of Right to Convey Promises made by the grantor in a warranty deed that they have the right to convey title.

Covenants of Seisen Promises made by the grantor in a warranty deed that they are in possession and hold title.

Covenant of Warranty Promises made by the grantor in a warranty deed that they will defend against any claim against the title by a third party.

Cul-de-sac A road with an entry at one end and a circular turn around area at the other end.

Curtesy The right of the husband to a share of his wife's estate at the time of her death. (In Massachusetts, curtesy rights are one-third of the wife's estate at the time of her death).

Customer The third party in law of agency between a principal and an agent for whom some service is performed. When a seller (principal) hires a broker (agent) to sell a house; the buyer is the customer.

Decreasing Return Concept in appraisal that holds some improvements to real estate increase value by less than the amount invested.

Deed Written instrument that transfers ownership of real property from one party to another.

Deed Restrictions Provisions in a deed that limits the future use of the property.

Deed in Trust Deed used when a grantor (trustor) transfers title to a trust controlled by a trustee for the benefit of a beneficiary.

Defeasance Clause A clause used in a lease or a mortgage to cancel a certain right when a specific condition has been met.(Ex. to cancel the granting clause to the bank when the mortgage has been fully paid.)

Deficiency The amount of a debt not covered when the security for a loan is not sufficient. At the time of a foreclosure the debt not covered is a deficiency.

Delivery The legal act of transferring property. Must include the grantor's intent to transfer.

Demand One of the elements of value in appraisal. The amount of goods that the market will buy at a certain price. Associated with supply.

Demand Letter Under M.G.L. c. 93A Consumer Protection Law, the letter sent to the individual against whom the action is to be taken. Begins a 30 day response cycle that precedes any further legal action.

Demand Mortgage Mortgage where the lender (mortgagee) has the right to call the note due at any time.

Demise Conveyance of an interest in real estate for a specific period of time as in rent or lease.

Depreciation A reduction in value due to any cause. In appraisal of real estate it includes physical deterioration, functional obsolescence and economic obsolescence.

Descent Acquisition of an estate by means of inheritance. (Without a will)

Devise Transfer of property by means of a will. The owner (divisor) transfers to the recipient (divisee).

Devisee The person who receives the benefits of a will.

Devisor The person whose property is distributed under the terms of a will.

Direct Reduction Mortgage A mortgage where the monthly payment remains the same. The amount that goes towards interest decreases and the amount that goes towards principal increases over the life of the mortgage.

Disclosed Dual Agent An agent of both parties to a transaction who represents each one and has informed each of this relationship.

Disclosure One of the duties of agency (also known as duty of notice) that requires an agent to keep his/her principal informed of any matter that is in the principal's interest.

Disclosure Statement Notification from a lender to a borrower of financing terms and charges of a loan. Required by the Federal Truth-In-lending Law.

Divisee The recipient of real property by means of a will.

Divisor The donor of real property by means of a will.

Dockominium Condominium concept applied to boat docks.

Dominant Estate An estate that derives benefit from another estate (Servient Estate) as in an easement.

Dower The right of the wife to a share of her husband's estate at the time of his death. (In Massachusetts dower rights are one-third of the husband's estate at the time of death).

Dual Agency Agency where the real estate broker or sales person represents both the buyer and the seller. The law requires this dual agency to include informed consent and to be in writing.

Dual Agent An agent of both parties to a transaction who represents each one.

Due-On-Sale Clause Mortgage clause that requires the mortgage balance to be paid in full when property is sold.

Duress Force applied to make someone act against his/her will.

Easement An interest that one party (Dominant Estate) has to use the property of another (Servient Estate) as in a Right of Way.

Easement Appurtenant The right one property owner (Dominant Estate) has in the property of another (Servient Estate). Passes forward with the land. Ex. A common driveway or the right of Lot A property owner to cross Lot B to access a lake.

Easement by Necessity Easement created by the courts and required by need. Must have common grantor for dominant and servient estates. Example: Right of way to road when property is land-locked.

Easement by Prescription Easement created by open notorious and continuous use (20 years in Massachusetts) similar to acquiring title by adverse possession.

Easement in Gross An easement that does not pass with the land and has no dominant estate. Example: Utility easement.

Economic Forces Those activities in and around a community that involve business and economic development. Used as a principle in appraisal.

Economic Obsolescence Loss of value due a number of forces outside the property owners control including economic, environmental and social change. A principle used in appraisal.

Elderly Individuals 62 years of age or older - used in condominium conversion law in Massachusetts to set special condo conversion protection.

Emblements Growing crops that are produced annually through labor and industry. Considered personal property even before harvest. Also known as Fructus Industriales.

Eminent Domain The right of the government (Federal, State or Municipal) to take title to private property for the common good; through a process known as condemnation.

Encroachment When the property of one party intrudes on the property of another, i.e.,: a roof or deck overhanging the lot line.

Encumbrance Anything that lessens the value of a parcel of property; including liens and any encroachment.

Equitable Title Interest held by the buyer when a purchase and sale contract has been signed but prior to transfer of a deed when legal title is obtained.

Equity The value an owner has in property in excess of any mortgages or other liens.

Erosion The gradual decrease to land on a shore or riverbank by natural forces.

Estoppel A legal doctrine whereby a person is not allowed to deny a previous statement or act when an innocent party has relied on that statement or act. i.e., Incorrect mortgage balance given by a bank.

Estoppel Agent An agency that exists when a third party has reason to believe that an agency exists even though a formal principal - agent relationship has not been established.

Escalation Clause Stipulation in a contract that allows payments to increase based on certain conditions. Example: increase in interest rate in the event of late payment or default.

Escalated Lease Lease where the payments vary up or down with certain conditions such as a change in expenses (taxes, insurance, utilities) or late payments.

Escheat Process by which property reverts to the state when no will or heirs exist or when the property is abandoned.

Escrow Process where money and/or documents are held by a third party for two parties in a transaction.

Escrow Agent A neutral third party in a transaction who holds documents or monies until certain acts are completed by the individuals involved in a contract.

Estate The legal interest and rights that a party has in real property.

Estate for Term (Also known as estate for years) Tenancy for a specific period of time. Can be less than a year.

Estoppel Concept where a party cannot exercise rights contrary to a previous representation. Example: A town water bill relied on by a new owner could be challenged by estoppel when a new higher bill is charged.

Et Al "And others".

Et Ux "And wife".

Exchange A transaction whereby part of the consideration includes properties of "like kind" and/or use. Capital gains tax deferment may be obtained using an exchange if the transaction conforms to all requirement in IRS code 1031.

Excise Stamps Massachusetts tax stamps due when a deed is recorded at the Registry of Deeds at $2.28/$500 of selling price.

Exclusive Agency Owner gives one broker the right to sell a parcel of property but retains the right to sell himself without paying a commission.

Exclusive Office Listing The same as "exclusive agency".

Exclusive Right to Sell Owner gives one broker the right to sell a parcel of property and agrees to pay a commission when sold by anyone including the owner.

Executrix A female appointed by an individual to carry out the directions in their will.

Executor A male appointed by an individual to carry out the directions in their will.

Executor's Deed Deed used by the executor to an estate to sell property held by the estate.

Executed Contract A contract where all parties have fulfilled all terms.

Execution The signing and delivery of a document.

Executory Contract A contract that has not had the terms completed by one or both of the parties.

Express Contract A contract where the intent of the parties is clearly stated. May be verbal or written.

Express Agency An agency relationship created by mutual consent between a principal and agent. May be either oral or written.

Federal Civil Rights Act - 1866 The first of three major pieces of legislation that affects fair housing and prohibits any discrimination, including housing, when that discrimination is based on race.

Federal Discount Rate The interest rate the Federal Reserve Bank charges it's member banks.

Federal Fair Housing Act - 1968 (Title VIII) Federal law know as Title VIII that addresses discrimination in matters of housing including, protected classes, prohibited practices, new construction, financing, providing brokerage services and appraisal reports.

F.H.A. Mortgage A mortgage where the Federal Housing Administration (FHA) insures the bank against loss.

Fee Simple See Fee Simple Absolute

Fee Simple Absolute The highest form of estate - the holder possesses all of the rights possible - limited only by government rights and the rights of others. Also known as fee or fee simple.

Fee Simple on Condition Subsequent A condition in an estate where the duration cannot be determined from language in the deed but depends on the grantor's choice to end the estate. Not automatic - requires action by the grantor.

Fee Simple Defeasible A fee simple estate subject to a specific condition. There are two types, Fee Simple Determinable and Fee Upon Condition Subsequent.

Fee Simple Determinable An Estate in which the holders a fee simple title that ends upon the happening of a specific condition that can be determined from the deed and automatically ends when that specific condition takes place.

Fee Upon Condition Subsequent An estate in which the holder has a fee simple title that ends upon the occurrence of a certain condition. The original grantor must take action to regain title - not automatic.

Fiduciary One who is in a position of trust and confidence.

Financial Institution's, Reform, Recovery and Enforcement Act (FIRREA) Federal legislation setting minimum standards each state must establish to regulate the real estate appraisal profession.

First Right of Refusal See Right of First Refusal.

Fixture An article of personal property that has become real property by being attached to the realty .

Flat Lease (see Gross Lease).

Foreclosure The forced sale of a piece of real property by the lien holder when the terms of the contract have not been met.

Freehold Estate An estate for an indefinite period of time (as compared to a Non-Freehold or Lease Estate).

Fructus Industriales see emblements

Functional Obsolescence A loss in value due to outdated qualities caused by age or poor design. May be curable such as outdated electric wiring or incurable such as low ceiling height.

General Agent (Universal Agent) One who represents a principal within a single broad area. Ex: Property Manager for an apartment building.

General Power of Attorney One who is authorized to act for another in all matters (A/K/A a universal power of Attorney).

General Warranty Deed Same as warranty deed.

Government Survey Method of land description using a grid of imaginary East-West lines called base lines and North-South lines called meridians. This grid results in 6 mile by 6 mile townships that are further broken down into sections.

Graduated Lease A lease where the amount of rent increases over the term of the lease.

Grantee One who is receiving title to real property from a grantor.

Grantee/Grantor Indexes Public record books maintained at the county registry of deeds that lists the grantors and grantees of property transfers along with the book and page number of the associated real estate documents.

Grantor One who is giving title to real property to a grantee.

Ground Lease A lease for the land alone. Separates the ownership of the land and the buildings When the lessee constructs a building, it remains the lessee's property. Usually long term net leases. Also known as a "land lease".

Gross Income Total revenue from rents or other sources (prior to any deduction for any expenses).

Gross Lease A lease where the tenant (lessee) pays a fixed rental amount and the landlord (lessor) pays all expenses (also known as a Flat Lease).

Gross Rent Multiplier A ratio of Market Value compared to Gross Rent . Used by an appraiser to estimate value when the gross rent and the gross rent multiplier are known.

Habendum Clause That section of a deed beginning with "to have and to hold" which follows the granting clause and defines the extent of ownership the grantor is conveying such as Fee Simple or Life Estate.

Handicapped Person entitled to housing accommodations due to physical handicap under Massachusetts General Law c.22. Used in condominium conversion law in Massachusetts to set special condo conversion protection.

Heterogeneity Physical characteristic of being unique. Used in reference to real property. There is no exact duplicate (also known as non-homogeneity).

Highest and Best Use An appraisal concept that identifies the use of a parcel of property that produces the highest net return and therefore the highest value.

Holdover Tenant A person who remains after a tenancy has ended. See tenant at sufferance.

Home Equity Loan A loan secured by the equity in a piece of property. May be in addition to an existing first mortgage and usually set up as a line of credit.

Homestead Land that is owned and used as the family home. Many states allow protection from creditors for a homestead.

Implied Agency An agency that results by deduction or inference as opposed to an expressed (verbal or written) relationship.

Implied Contract A contract where the agreement of the parties is demonstrated by their acts and conduct and not by their words or written agreements.

Impound Account A trust account established to collect funds for the future needs of a parcel of real estate. Banks often establish impound accounts for taxes and insurance fees.

Impound Payment A periodic payment into an Impound Account

Improvements Additions to real property that are intended to increase value (more than maintenance or repair).

Imputed Notice Knowledge by an agent that is binding on the principal due to the principal- agent relationship even though the principal does not have first hand knowledge. Ex. Notice under a purchase and sale agreement requirement.

Income Approach Appraisal Technique that uses the amount of net income property will produce over its useful life to determine value. The net income (gross income less expenses) is divided by a capitalization rate determined by experience to determine value.

Incorporeal Intangible or non-possessory rights in real estate. No physical substance. Ex: right of way.

Increasing Return Concept in appraisal that holds some improvements to real estate increase value by more than the amount invested.

Independent Contractor One who is employed to perform an act but is not controlled as to how they accomplish the objective. An independent contractor is not an employee and as such in real estate brokerage the principal (broker) does not have to withhold taxes and social security.

Index Lease A lease that provides for an adjustment in rent based on changes to some index such as the consumer price index.

Installment Contract Contract for real estate where the buyer occupies the property during a period while making payments and receives a deed when all payments are complete.

Intangible Having no physical or material being. Example: Right of way.

Intestate Property owner dies without a will or with a will that is defective. Property changes ownership through the state laws of descent.

Involuntary Alienation Transfer of ownership against the owners will as in a foreclosure.

Joint Tenancy A type of concurrent estate (two or more persons) with co-owners having equal rights. Upon the death of one party interest passes to the surviving party (Right of Survivorship).

Judicial Deed Deed issued by a court appointed official.

Junior Mortgage Any mortgage that takes second priority to another lien on the property.

Laches Doctrine that action was not taken in a reasonable period of time. Similar to statute of limitations where time is specified.

Land Contract See Installment Contract.

Land Court Certificate Document issued by the land court as a result of a court decision under the Torrens System.

Law of Agency See Agency.

Lead Paint Notification Form Massachusetts lead paint law (M.G.L. c.111) requires the real estate broker or salesperson to notify a prospective purchaser of residential real estate of the dangers of lead paint and to obtain their signature on a form documenting this action.

Lease An agreement (written or verbal) between an owner (Lessor) and a tenant (Lessee) to grant the exclusive right of occupancy to real property for a specific period of time.

Lease Option A clause in a lease that gives the tenant the right to buy the property under certain conditions.

Lease Purchase A transfer of ownership that begins as a lease that ends with the purchase of the property by the lessee.

Leased Fee Estate The estate or rights the lessor has leased to the lessee.

Legal Description Description of property sufficient to identify what is being conveyed. Three types are:
1. Metes and Bounds, 2. Lot and Block, 3. Government Survey

Legality Quality of being within the law. A contract with an illegal element is void.

Legal Title Interest obtained by the grantee when the deed is signed and delivered (compared to equitable title).

Lessee The Tenant in a Landlord (Lessor) and Tenant (Lessee) relationship.

Lessor The Landlord in a Landlord (Lessor) and Tenant (Lessee) relationship.

Letter of Compliance Under the Massachusetts lead paint law (M.G.L. c.111) the letter issued to a residential property owner indicating the property met the requirements of the law.

Letter of Interim Control Under the Massachusetts lead paint law (M.G.L. c.111) a letter allowing a property owner one year to fully meet the requirements of the law after major hazards, such as peeling and chipping paint, have been taken care of.

License A use of property permitted by an owner for a specific purpose. Revocable at any time. May be verbal. Also a certification by the state to sell real estate.

Lien A right or interest that one party has in the property of another as security for a debt. (A financial encumbrance; a mortgage).

Life Estate An interest in real or personal property that is limited to the life of the owner or some other specified individual.

Lis Penden Latin meaning "Action Pending". Recorded legal document that gives notice that legal action is in process that may effect the subject property.

Listing Agreement An agreement between a seller and a broker to act as an agent for the sale of real property. May be written or verbal.

Littoral Rights Rights of land owners abutting oceans of standing bodies of water (Riparian Rights deal with rivers and streams - flowing bodies of water).

Location Economic characteristic of real property that indicates that value is affected by what exact site real property occupies including abutters, neighborhood and zoning.

Long Term Investment Economic characteristic of real property that indicates real property will last along time, more than a mortgage, often more than a lifetime as opposed to a short time - stocks, bonds etc.

Lot and Block Method of land description that refers to a specific lot within a grouping of lots on a block on a map or plat that has been recorded at the Registry.

Low or Moderate Income Total prior twelve month income of all unit occupants is less than 80% of area median income as set forth by HUD. Used in condominium conversion law in Massachusetts to set special condo conversion protection.

Loyalty That part of the law of agency that requires that the agent must act in the best interest of the principal (even when that is not in the best interest of the agent).

Market Approach Appraisal technique that compares the subject property to similar properties that have sold recently to establish value.

Market Value The most probable price property will bring assuming a knowledgeable seller and buyer and a fair and open market and a reasonable time to market.

Massachusetts Association of Real Estate Appraisers State association of real estate appraisers that sets standards, regulates membership and issues professional designations of accomplishment.

Massachusetts Commission Against Discrimination (M.C.A.D.) The state agency responsible for the administration of Massachusetts Fair Housing Law. This includes receiving any complaints in the state regarding fair housing.

Massachusetts Fair Housing (M.G.L. c. 151B) Massachusetts state law that addresses discrimination in matters of housing. Covers similar areas as Federal Title VIII but goes much further in who is protected under the law. More protected classes.

Master Deed The deed recorded when a condominium development is created as required by M.G.L. c. 183A.

Master Insurance Policy Insurance policy covering the overall condominium structure and common area. Names all unit owners and lenders as loss payees. Must be updated to reflect new owner and loss payee when individual unit changes ownership.

Member Appraisal Institute (MAI) Professional designation issued to real estate appraisers by the Appraisal Institute indicating competence in appraisal of all types of real estate.

Meridian An imaginary line running North and South used by surveyors in the Government (rectangular) survey method of property description.

Metes and Bounds Method of Land Description that "walks" the perimeter of the property and describes the distances, compass points and boundaries. Most common method of land description in Massachusetts.

M.G.I.C. Mortgage Guaranty Insurance Corporation , one of a number of Private Mortgage Insurance (PMI) Companies that privately insure a portion of a mortgage risk when a lending institution is not willing to assume it (typical with down payments of less than 20%).

M.G.L. c.183A Massachusetts General Law that regulates the formation, conversion and management of condominiums, both commercial and residential

Mill Rate Tax rate expressed as tax per $1.00 of assessed value (a mill is one-tenth of one cent).

Mineral Rights Subsurface rights to real property. May be granted separately from surface rights as in rights to oil, gas, minerals etc.

Mortgage A conditional conveyance of property as security for a loan. (Mortgage Deed).

Mortgage Buydown The lender will allow the borrower to pay one or more points at closing in return for a lower initial interest rate for one or more years. The borrower may then qualify for a larger mortgage loan.

Mortgage Deed Conditional conveyance of the property to the bank subject to the borrowers right of redemption. Referred to as the "mortgage".

Mortgage Note The written promise to pay money borrowed against real property as security.

Mortgagee Party lending money with property as security. (Ex: a bank).

Mortgagor Party borrowing money with property as security (buyer or borrower).

Multiple Listing A listing placed in a Multiple Listing Service (MLS) where member brokers agree to share listing with one another.

Negative Amortization A mortgage where the monthly payment agreed to does not cover the interest charged. The difference is then added to the principle balance.

Net Income Gross Income (total revenue) less expenses.

Net Lease A lease where the lessee (tenant) pays a fixed rent plus other expenses. (Also known as triple net when tenant pays taxes, insurance and other operating expenses).

Net Listing A listing where the seller is to receive a certain amount and the broker retains anything above that amount as a fee. Illegal in Massachusetts.

Non-Freehold Estate An estate for a definite period of time; a lease. (As compared to a Freehold Estate as in a deeded transfer of title).

Notice - Duty of notice See disclosure (duty of disclosure).

Novation A new obligation is substituted for an old obligation (A bank accepting a new note with a new mortgagor for an old note would do so by novation.)

Obedience That part of the law of agency that requires that the agent follow the principal's direction. (Requirement to violate the law is excluded).

Offer A promise by one party to act in a specified manner providing a second party acts in the manner requested.

Offeree Party receiving an offer from another party (buyer or seller).

Offeror Party extending an offer to another party (buyer or seller).

Open-End Mortgage A loan that is expandable by increments but with a total that does not exceed original limits. The total secured by one mortgage.

Open Listing A type of listing where two or more brokers are given a listing. The selling broker receives the total commission. The seller retains the right to sell.

Operating Reserve Reserve fund commonly established when new condominiums were formed (new or conversion). Typically two or three month's condo fee and used to provide initial operating capital for maintenance and repairs. Often combined with normal operating funds once project is fully sold and unit owners have taken over management. Not to be confused with capital reserve.

Opinion of Value An estimate of property value by a real estate broker or salesperson, does not require appraisers' license.

Option An agreement to keep an offer to purchase or to sell open for some period of time. The party agreeing to the option terms (usually the seller) is bound by the option but not the party making the option offer (usually the buyer).

Option Listing A listing to sell property where the broker retains the right to purchase the property.

Overimprovement An improvement that based on cost exceeds the highest and best use. Example: A $400,000 house built in a $200,000 neighborhood or a $50,000 kitchen that increases value by $30,000.

Package Mortgage A Mortgage loan that finances personal property such as furniture as well as real estate.

Page When used in reference to recording deeds, refers to the number assigned to a deed or other document within a specific book (as in book xxxx page xx) to specify location at the Registry of Deeds.

Percentage Lease A lease where the amount of rent for a period of time is based on a percentage of sales for that period.

Percent of Common Ownership In a condominium; the ratio of unit square footage to total of all unit square footage expressed as a percent. Used to determine unit owner's portion of total condominium budget.

Periodic Tenancy Same as tenancy from period to period.

Personal Property All property that is not real property. (An article that is moveable and not attached to the realty) Also called personalty.

Personal Easement in Gross An easement in gross that is of a personal nature and not commercial. Ex. Charlie has the right to cross Mary's property for access.

Personalty See Personal Property.

Physical Deterioration A reduction in property value due to a negative change in physical conditions. May be curable or incurable. Could be caused by physical elements such as weather or by normal usage.

Plat A map or plan of subdivided land showing individual lots and their boundaries and dimensions.

Plot Plan A map of an individual lot showing dimensions of the lot and the layout of any buildings or other improvements on the lot. Used by a bank and/or appraiser to verify that there is no encroachment or zoning violations such as set back violations.

Plottage See Assemblage.

Point A onetime charge for loaning money equal to one percent of the amount borrowed.

Point of Beginning(POB) The starting point in the Metes and Bounds method of property description.

Police Power The right of the government to enforce laws , statutes and regulations for the public welfare. Includes building codes and zoning ordinances.

Possession Rights The rights to occupy real property. Often granted separately from other rights as in the case of a lease.

Power of Attorney A written document authorizing one person to act for another to whatever extent specified.

Prescription Method of establishing an easement by open continuous and notorious use. In Massachusetts the time of usage is 20 years minimum. (Similar to acquiring title by adverse possession).

Pre-Qualification Process whereby a loan originator reviews a buyers' financial status to determine in advance the amount of mortgage that will be approved.

Primary Mortgage Market The market where banks or other lenders loan money directly to borrowers. (Those mortgages then may or may not be sold to other investors through the secondary mortgage market).

Prime Rate The rate that banks charge their best customers with the highest credit rating on unsecured and short term loans.

Principal
1) One of the main parties in a transaction (as in Seller and Buyer).
2) In an agency relationship, one who engages another (the agent) to act in his/her behalf.
3) In financial matter, the amount of debt owed, which added to interest constitutes the amount paid.

Probate Court That part of the court system that deals with wills and inheritance.

Procuring Cause The effort that brings about the desired result. In real estate the broker in an open listing that brings about the ready, willing and able buyer is the procuring cause and is entitled to the commission.

Progression An appraisal principle dealing with conformity that holds that property is increased in value when located near other property that is of higher value. Example: A house surrounded by more expensive homes.

Property The rights and interests (known as the Bundle of Rights) that an individual has in a thing that is owned. May be real or personal.

Protected Class A group of people under fair housing legislation that have been identified as receiving protection under the law. Usually because they have specifically experienced discrimination.

Puffing Exaggerated representations.

Purchase and Sale Agreement A written contract for the sale of real property between two parties, Seller and Buyer.

Purchase Money Mortgage A mortgage given by the buyer to the seller as part of the consideration in buying real property.

Quitclaim Deed A deed where the grantor (seller) transfers whatever interest he/she has in real property without any warranties. The Quitclaim Deed is the most common form of Deed in Massachusetts, however the Massachusetts Quitclaim Deed does contain some limited warranties.

Range Line An imaginary line running north and south in the government survey method of land description parallel to major north-south lines called meridians.

Range Strip A strip of land between two north-south range lines measuring 6 miles wide and used in the government survey method of land description.

Rate of Return Comparison of the net income to total investment for a parcel of income property expressed as an annual percentage.

Real Estate Land and whatever is attached to the land. Also known as Real Property or Realty.

Real Property See Real Estate

REALTOR® A registered trademark that may be used only by a licensed broker or salesman who is a member of the state and local real estate board chartered by the National Association of Realtors

Realty See Real Estate.

Reconciliation That part of the appraisal process where the appraiser compares the most appropriate appraisal method with the other methods used.

Recording Process of entering into public record the deed and other documents associated with the transfer of real property (the deed is so recorded at the Registry of Deeds and receives a book and page number where the deed has been filed).

Redlining The practice of a lending institution identifying a certain geographic area to receive different lending practices than other geographic areas. Identified with discrimination because this is often done in minority neighborhoods.

Registered Land Property, that under the Torrents System, has been to land court, received a judgment and now has a Certificate of Title documenting the land court decision.

Registry of Deeds County agency that records, files and controls deeds, liens and other paperwork relating to title of real property (known in some states as Recorder's Office or Bureau of Conveyance).

Regression An appraisal principle dealing with conformity that holds that property is decreased in value when located near other property of lesser value. Example: A house surrounded by less expensive homes.

Regulation Z See truth in lending.

Remainder Estate A type of estate held as a future interest by the one who will receive title at the end of a life estate (upon death of holder of a life estate, the remainder estate becomes a fee simple estate).

Remainderman The party holding a future interest as the third party to a life estate.

Rent The fixed, periodic payment by the lessee to the lessor for the use of the leased property.

Replacement Cost The cost at current prices to replace a structure with the same materials. Often used as the same as reproduction cost which requires similar design and materials but not the same.

Reproduction Cost Same as replacement cost but for a similar, not an exact duplication of a structure.

Residual That which is left over. In foreclosure, those monies in excess of outstanding debt and other costs.

Restrictive Covenant A private restriction in a deed that limits future use and rights. Not tied to zoning. Example: lot size, type of architecture; runs with the land.

Reverse Annuity Mortgage (RAM) Mortgage structured to reverse the standard payment to allow the bank to pay the borrower a fixed amount each month. Designed primarily for the elderly.

Reversionary Estate The estate left with the grantor when the estate being transferred is less than the estate previously received.

Reversionary Rights The rights remaining with the grantor when less than fee simple is transferred to a grantee. ex., life estate.

Right of First Refusal Right to have the first chance to purchase or lease a piece of property. May or may not specify additional terms such as price.

Right of Possession The right of the lessee to occupy the leased property.

Right of Recission The right of a borrower to cancel a financing agreement within three days after receiving a disclosure statement from a lender.

Right of Survivorship The right in Joint Tenancy (and Tenancy by the Entirety) for title to pass to the surviving joint tenant(s) upon the death of one of the owners.

Right -of-Way The right of one to pass over the property of another (a form of easement).

Riparian Rights The rights associated with property that abuts a flowing body of water such as a river or stream. Similar rights associated with the ocean, lake or other standing body of water are called Littoral Rights.

Rules and Regulations When associated with condominiums, refers to some guidelines to daily activities that help in harmonious condominium living. Ex: Parking Regulations and fines, use of tennis courts, swimming pools or other common areas, use of for sale signs, use of Habachis on decks etc. Usually not recorded at the Registry of Deeds.

Sale and Leaseback Property owner sells a piece of property and as part of the same transaction leases it back and keeps the right to occupy. Often used for accounting and tax purposes.

Sandwich Lease A lease where a tenant in lessor-lessee relationship leases to a third party.

Scarcity An appraisal principle that a reduction in the availability or supply of a good will increases its value.

Secondary Mortgage Market The market that purchases existing mortgages that were originally established in the primary mortgage market. Some government involvement in this market includes the Federal National Mortgage Association (FNMA), the Government National Mortgage Association (GNMA), and the Federal Home Loan Mortgage Corporation (FHLMC).

Section In the government survey method of land description, east-west township lines meet north-south range lines in a 6 mile by 6 mile township which is further subdivided into 36 one mile by one mile parcels called sections.

Security Deposit A payment by a tenant to a landlord to be held as assurance against default or damage to the property by the tenant.

Seller's Agent A real estate broker who represents the seller, not the buyer and therefore has a fiduciary responsibility to the seller.

Senior Residential Appraiser (SRA) Professional appraisal designation awarded by the Appraisal Institute indicating competence in appraisal of one to four family residences.

Servient Estate Property over which another piece of property (Dominant Estate) has a right of way.

Shared Equity Mortgage A mortgage where the borrower and lender agree to share in the increase in value of the property securing a loan.

Sheriffs Deed Deed used when property is sold by a sheriff by court order.

Single Agent One who represents one principal (Buyer or Seller) but not both.

Situs Refers to characteristic of location. See location.

6 (d) Certificate Document called for in Massachusetts General Law c.183 section 6 (d) issued by the condominium management association documenting the status of any condo fees or special assessment or other charges due by the unit owner. Must be present at transfer of ownership.

Smoke Detector A piece of equipment that sounds an alarm when the presence of smoke is detected. Can be battery powered or "hard wired" to the main source of electricity.

Special Agent (Limited Agent) One who is authorized to perform one specific task.

Special Power of Attorney One who is authorized to act for another in a limited range of matters.

Special Warranty Deed Deed that guarantees title to the grantee against any defects in title occurring during the grantors period of ownership but not before.

Specific Performance A remedy at law where the court will force a party to fulfill his/her part of a contract.

Square Foot Approach Appraisal technique of estimating cost by multiplying total square footage of times a constant of cost per square footage. Example: 2,000 sq. ft. X $100/sq. ft . = $200,000 estimated value.

Squatter's Rights See adverse possession.

Statute of Frauds State law that requires certain documents to be in writing to be enforceable.

Statute of Limitations The time limit within which legal action must be taken to be enforceable. Example: In Massachusetts the statute of limitations on Prescription and Adverse Possession is 20 years.

Steering The attempt to influence buyers by showing members of a protected class property in neighborhoods made up predominately of the same protected class while not showing properties in other neighborhoods.

Step-Up Lease Same as graduated lease.

Straight Lease See Gross Lease

Sub-Agent One acting as an agent for someone who is already acting as an agent for a principal. In a co-broke situation where both brokers are sellers agents, the listing broker is the agent of the seller principal and the selling agent is the sub agent.

Sublessee A tenant who has leased property from a tenant or lessee who then becomes the "sublessor".

Sublessor See sublessee.

Sublet A lease given by a lessee for a part of the premises or part of the time where the lessee retains some interest . Transfer of the total lease is an assignment.

Substitution Appraisal principle that holds a property's value is determined by the cost to substitute a comparable piece of property through purchase or construction.

Subsurface Rights Rights to real property that are beneath the surface including mineral rights, water rights and easements such as underground utilities.

Suit for Damages One of the legal remedies in the case of a contract default or nonperformance. Suit to recover compensation for financial losses suffered due to the contract non-performance.

"Super Lien" Provision of MGL c. 183 that gives a condominium association priority in collecting up to six months condo fees before mortgage obligations.

Supply and Demand Economic Principle used in property appraisal that holds value is influenced by the amount of property for sale (supply) and the number of potential buyers (demand).

Surface Rights Rights to real property on the surface of the property . (Not including rights above (air rights) or rights below, (mineral and other sub-surface rights).

Tangible Having physical or material being such as height, width, mass, weight. (As opposed to intangible such as an easement).

Tax Deed Deed used to convey property taken by the government for non-payment of taxes.

Tax Rate The rate set by the city or town which multiplied by property's assessed value will yield the property's annual tax.

Taxation The right of the government to levy charges on a piece of property. One of the government limits to rights of ownership.

Tax Stamps See Excise Stamps.

Tenancy at Sufferance A form of tenancy when the tenant remains after the legal tenancy is over.

Tenancy at Will A form of tenancy with no specific duration that can be terminated at any time by either party. Can be written or verbal. In Massachusetts either party must give 30 day minimum notice as of the rent due date.

Tenancy by the Entirety A type of joint tenancy restricted to husbands and wives. Provides for right of survivorship.

Tenancy for Years A form of tenancy that is less than freehold and has a set term with a specific end date. Can be for less than a year.

Tenancy from Period to Period A form of tenancy that is less than freehold and has no specific end date. Renews at the end of each period until one of the parties takes action to end the tenancy.

Tenancy in Common A type of concurrent estate (two or more persons) where co-owners each have an undivided interest in the property. No right of survivorship.

Tenancy in Partnership Ownership by a partnership as an entity and subject to the terms of the partnership, regards rights of the partners.

Tenant The party to whom real property is rented (lessee).

Term The length of time or duration of a lease.

Testate An individual who dies with a will dies testate; without a will intestate.

Testator One who dies testate - with a will.

Time Share A form of ownership that allows multiple owners of a piece of property each with an undivided interest for a fixed or variable time of a year. Ex. Ownership of week 36.

Title Reference A filing system at the County Registry of Deeds that records a document, such as a deed, in a specific book and on a specific page in that Book. Example: Book XXXX Pg. XX.

Title Search Process of reviewing public records at the Registry of Deeds to determine the state of ownership of a piece of real property.

Torrens System A system of registering title to real property (used in Massachusetts and other states), to verify ownership or title. Results in a Certificate of Title.

Township A division of property under the Government (Rectangular) Survey method of land description ,six miles by six miles, containing 36 sections, each one mile by one mile.

Township Line An imaginary line running east-west in the government survey method of land description parallel to major east-west lines called base lines.

Township Strip Strip of land between two east-west township lines measuring 6 miles and used in the government survey method of land description.

Trade Fixture A fixture attached to real property as a part of a tenant's trade or business. Can be removed by the tenant at the end of the lease.

Transferability The ability to transfer the legal bundle of rights without undue restrictions.

Triple Damages The Massachusetts Consumer Protection Law (M.G.L. c.93A) allows penalties of three times the actual damages in certain instances.

Triple Net Lease Lease where tenant pays rent plus taxes, insurance and other maintenance expenses. Technically redundant as net lease means the same but emphasizes the tenants payment of rent plus all expenses.

Tristram's Landing Massachusetts legal case that defined "procuring cause" in matters of real estate brokerage.

Trustor The grantor who conveys title to establish a trust.

Trustee The party in charge of administrating a trust after it has been established.

Trustees Deed Deed used to convey title from the trust by the trustee to a new grantee.

Truth in Lending A federal law known as Regulation Z that regulates loans by professional lenders to private individuals.

"Underwood" Case A Massachusetts court case "Underwood vs. Risman" which substantially altered the interpretation of lead paint and agency law. Major impact to the real estate profession.

Undisclosed Dual Agent Agency where the real estate broker or salesperson represents both the buyer and the seller but has not disclosed this to both parties. Illegal in Massachusetts.

Unilateral Contract A contract where one party makes a promise to perform without a second party promise to perform. Example: Reward for lost property.

Unit Deed A deed transferring title of an individual condominium unit from one party to another.

Unit-In-Place Appraisal method of estimating replacement cost by individual components of a piece of property and adding them together to arrive at estimated cost. Example: Carpentry + Electric + Plumbing + Carpeting etc. = Total Cost.

Unit Square Footage The number of square feet of area within an individual condominium unit.

Universal Agent (General Agent) one who is authorized to act for a principal in all matters pertaining to one general area. Example: Property Agent.

Useful Life The number of years a thing will last before needing replacement.

Usury Charging an unlawfully high rate of interest.

Utility Appraisal concept that relates to property's usefulness as a measure of value.

V.A. Mortgage A mortgage loan to an eligible veteran that is guaranteed by the Veteran's Administration (V.A.).

Valid Having legal, binding force.

Value What something is worth. The power of a good or service to command other goods in exchange.

Variable Rate Mortgage A mortgage where the interest rate changes over time based on some agreed upon index. Also known as an Adjustable Rate Mortgage (ARM)

Variance Permission to build, convert or otherwise use a parcel of property in violation of the zoning ordinances.

Vendee The buyer of real estate. The buyer under an installment contract.

Vendor The seller of real estate. The seller under an installment contract.

Void Having no binding legal force.

Voidable Having binding force but able to be broken by one of the parties.

Voluntary Alienation Transfer of title with the owners consent as in transfer by deed.

Warranty Deed Form of deed where the grantor makes certain warrants or guarantees to the grantee. The grantor will defend the title against all claims including those against prior owners (not commonly found in Massachusetts).

Waste Improper use or abuse of property by one in possession; such as a tenant.

Water Rights The rights a property owner has in regards to water within or abutting property owned. Includes sub-surface water and surface water . Rights in flowing bodies of water are riparian while rights to standing bodies of waters are littoral.

Will A written instrument disposing of property after an individuals death (testator).

Wraparound Mortgage Financing where a new mortgage is placed in a junior position to an existing mortgage; the new mortgage includes the existing first mortgage which is not paid off plus any new funds loaned.

Zoning An exercise of police power whereby a city or town limits property rights by determining what can be built within certain sections of a municipality.

Index

Americans With Disabilities Act (ADA), 11-9
A.R.M., 7-9
Abstract of title, 6-8
Acceptance, 5-3, 5-5, 6-6
Accretion, 6-16
Accrued depreciation, 22-1
Acknowledgment, 6-6
Acreage, 14-6
Actual eviction, 4-5
Ad valorem taxation, 1-7
Adverse possession, 6-15
Agency disclosure form, 8-12, 12-38
Agency disclosure law, 8-8
Agency disclosure, 8-8
Agent, 8-1
Air rights, 1-1
Alienation clause, 7-8
Amortization table, 7-16
Amortization, 7-7, 16-8
Anticipation, 9-6
Appraisal institute, 9-2
Appraisal process, 9-7
Appraisal, 9-1
Appraised value, 19-1
Appreciation, 22-1
Approaches to value, 9-8
Area, 14-1
Asbestos, 10-8
Assemblage, 9-6
Assessed value, 9-3, 19-1
Assessment rate, 19-1
Assignee, 5-8
Assignment, 4-7, 5-8
Assignor, 5-8
Assumption, 7-10
Attorney in fact, 6-6, 8-4
Avulsion, 6-16
Balloon mortgage, 7-9
Bank approval cycle, 7-3
Bargain and sale deed, 6-4
Base line, 6-11
Basic math review, 13-1
Bilateral contract, 5-2
Bill of sale, 5-7
Blanket mortgage, 7-8
Blockbusting, 11-1
Board of appeals, 1-7
Book value, 22-1
Book, 6-2
Broker, 8-1

Building code, 1-7
Bundle of rights, 1-6
Buyer agency agreement, 5-1
Buyer agent, 8-2
Buyer's agent, 8-2
Buyer's broker, 8-2
Bylaws, 3-4
Capital gains, 8-15
Capital reserve, 3-8
Capitalization rate, 9-10
Caveat emptor, 5-8, 10-1
Certificate of title, 6-8
Certified appraiser, 9-2
Ch. 93A (consumer protection), 5-8, 10-1
Chain of title, 6-7
Change, 9-6
Chattel personal, 1-2
Chattel real, 1-2
Chattel, 1-2
Civil Rights Act of 1866, 11-1
Client, 8-2
CMA, 9-10
Co-mingling of funds, 8-7
Codicil, 6-16
Commercial banks, 7-5
Commercial easement in gross, 2-4
Commission rate, 21-1
Commission, 21-1
Commissions negotiable, 8-12
Common areas, 3-3
Common driveway, 2-4
Comparable, 9-9
Comparative market analysis, 9-10
Competency, 5-4
Concurrent estate, 2-2
Condemnation, 1-7, 6-15, 9-3
Condemnee, 6-15
Condemnor, 6-15
Condo "super lien", 3-8
Condo association, 3-5
Condo budget, 3-5
Condo fee, 3-4
Condo trust, 3-5
Condominium conversion
        provisions, 3-7
Condominium conversion, 3-6
Condominium financing, 3-6
Condominium, 3-2
Confidentiality, 8-7
Conformity, 9-6
Consent, 5-4
Consideration, 5-3, 5-6, 6-5
Construction mortgage, 7-7
Constructive eviction, 4-5